"There is no client as scary as an innocent man."

J. Michael Haller, Criminal Defense Attorney, Los Angeles, 1962."

— Michael Connelly, *The Lincoln Lawyer*

TESTIMONIALS

...Mr. Vetro cared very deeply about the well-being of his students and the Hampton Bays community. He demonstrated a compassion and commitment to the student's development of good character and their education...a dedicated professional who wanted the best for all students and staff...He always conducted himself in a professional manner and was available and accessible for anyone who needed to speak to him. I credit a great deal...to Mr. Vetro. It was his keen insight and belief in the good of children that made a big difference in developing a high level, effective program...I believe in and trust his good character.

- **Dan Tomaszewski, Longwood High School BOE President/Hampton Bays Alternative Program Principal**

...The most important word I can think of to describe Frank is "Friend". I cannot begin to describe to you the amount of times Frank's generosity has moved me. A young middle school football player who could not afford cleats, he reached into his own pocket time and time again...Quietly to preserve the student's dignity, he never did it for credit but because "it was for the kids". He has had a profound impact on the lives of many students. Frank's diligence, dedication, and sensitivity have helped countless students during difficult periods in their lives. He has helped keep youngsters in school, provided families with community contacts to help them deal with a variety of problems, and worked tirelessly to be there in times of need. I have been fortunate to have such a wonderful, caring friend and colleague...

- **Marc Meyer, Hampton Bays Elementary School Principal**

It takes a very skilled individual to discipline students and still engender their trust and respect...that has been his reputation.

- **Joanne Loewenthal, Hampton Bays Superintendent (New York Times)**

The students are concerned for him.

- **Joanne Loewenthal, Hampton Bays Superintendent (Southampton Press)**

...A professional administrator who cared a great deal for the students and faculty members under his supervision. He worked hard to establish a collegial relationship that demonstrated care and empathy while holding staff members accountable in order to improve the quality of their performance. Students constantly developed meaningful relationships with Mr. Vetro based on his interactions with them. He disciplined them with respect, and often attended many extra-curricular events...Mr. Vetro went out of his way to establish positive relationships with parents and community members in order to gain their support for the improvement of the school system. He supported almost every fund raising event and participated in many others to attract support from students and parents...Mr. Vetro cares a great deal about the students and adults in his charge and strives to make a positive difference in them. There is no doubt in my mind that Frank is a great role model for his students. He roots for the underdog and creates an environment where all students are valued. By talking to parents and students, you will understand the magnitude of the impact he has made in the lives of so many.

- **Nicholas Dyno, Former Principal of Hampton Bays Secondary School/Assistant Superintendent in Southampton UFSD**

...A leader whose first priority is always the students in his building. He spends a great deal of time supporting the school. He attends the majority of sporting events and all after-school activities. The students and staff hold Mr. Vetro in high regard. Mr. Vetro relates exceptionally well to his colleagues, staff, and the students. He has a friendly personality and is a delight to work with.

- **Denise Romano, Hampton Bays Academic Dean of Students**

...demonstrates organizational skills, academic preparedness, solid decision making ability, leadership, but most of all respect and a desire for all students to succeed. His open door policy to the students, faculty and community members of Hampton Bays has created a new, energized academic climate in the high school....Mr. Vetro is a man of high character, strong morals, with a heart of gold...His commitment to Hampton Bays High School, faculty, students, and all community members is unparalleled...During my teaching and administrative career spanning 35 years...I have known few administrators who have displayed the qualities that Mr. Vetro possesses...It is a pleasure to call him a friend.

- **Daniel Nolan, Acting Assistant Principal in Hampton Bays UFSD/retired High School Principal-Miller Place and Port Jefferson UFSD**

...a terrific, intuitive young man whose honesty, ambition, and charm have touched me.

- **Nan O'Connor Roys, Former Assistant Superintendent of Middle Country Central School District.**

Dear Frank, I love you and I'm praying for all of this to be resolved so you'll be back with us. The kids spoke highly of you on Channel 12 and I heard they had signs supporting you. If I can do anything for you, let me know.

- **Marie Mulcahy, Hampton Bays BOE member**

Dear Frank, thanks for everything you do. Your personality makes work a pleasure.

- **Jennifer Boyer, Hampton Bays BOE member**

...You really are missed around here...People like you are just a presence that's missed when they aren't around...I am thinking about you. Take care of yourself...

- **Denise Romano, Hampton Bays Academic Dean of Students**

Dear Frank- Just wanted you to know that I am thinking of you…please let me know if there's anything I can do or if you just want to talk.

- **Donna Moss, Consultant at Hampton Bays UFSD**

I had the pleasure of first meeting Frank Vetro when he was thirteen years old…It was Frank's hard work, patience, mental attitude, and superior self-discipline that set him apart from the rest. Frank gave 100% of himself…and always displayed a willingness to help others who struggled…Frank is a loyal individual who is always willing to give back…He has continued to help students, adults, families, colleagues, and the entire educational community…He is one of the most likeable people I know…to know Frank is to know an individual who is impeccably honest, respected by all members of society, displays tremendous self-discipline, and is motivated to be a worthy citizen…

- **Xristos Gaglias, Master Instructor-Dae Han Taekwondo School**

…There is no doubt that his strength of character would speak volumes about the type of person that he is…He is one of those rare individuals who treats everyone as an equal…He listens and speaks to every individual with the same level of interest, concern, and respect…He approaches his job with an unadulterated, unpretentious, "roll up your sleeves and get dirty" kind of attitude. He gives the impression to students and teachers alike that he is another soldier in the trenches. He is as true and honest a person as you will meet; he does not put on airs, he does not try to be something that he isn't. He does not try to impress; he does not have to because who he is, is impressive enough. There is nothing Mr. Vetro does that does not seem genuine- because if he doesn't believe in something, he doesn't bother.

Ingrained in his approach to administration and education, is a genuine concern for and sincere interest in the lives of his students. He attends an assortment of extra-curricular activities, including; athletic events, concerts, musicals, art shows, field trips, dances and fund raisers. He does not speak to students; he speaks with them, allowing their voices and interests to be the focal point of conversations. He naturally integrates the understanding of concerned big brother into his stern administrative style. He disseminates discipline with a tough love approach; leaving no doubt in the minds of his students that he is there for them, doing what he can to help them reach their fullest potential.

Though there are many examples of the compassion that Mr. Vetro brings to his role as building principal, there is one example in particular that illuminates the concern he has for his students. There is a sophomore in Hampton Bays... a struggling student, and what some may consider a lost soul. Her father was killed in a car accident when she was three and she has lacked a positive male influence in her life since then. Mr. Vetro has made sure that she knows he cares. He attends her games, checks up on her in class, spends time after school playing paper football games and talking to her about what is going on in her life, he even shares peanut butter and jelly sandwiches with her at lunch. Mr. Vetro has taken time to make this student feel like she matters, he has provided a positive male role model that has been missing since her father passed away. He gets nothing out of this relationship but that is Mr. Vetro, he is not a "what have you done for me lately", type of guy. He is a "what can I do for you today" kind of guy.

...to see him in action, as an administrator, educator, mentor, role model, big brother, or friend is to know that he is a gentleman who respects people, no matter their status. It is to know that he is a kind, compassionate human being. It is to know that he is someone who takes his role as mentor and shaper of young minds seriously. If the majority of the people in this world treated each other with the respect Frank Vetro shows for others both professionally and personally the world would be a much more civilized place.

- **Virginia McGovern, Hampton Bays community member/teacher assistant at Southampton School District**

…Frank has earned the respect and trust of our faculty, staff, students, and parents. He has embraced the importance of being a leader. He is the first administrator at school and last to leave…He attends sporting events, concerts, art shows and fundraisers. He interacts with the students and is often times the only adult who speaks to the students about *their* interests…I worked very closely with Frank. He was very supportive…Frank never faltered, worked 24/7 to achieve his goal…The pressure was on, but he never wavered. Despite circumstances he was professional, dedicated, respectful, and always very considerate of my needs and my welfare. Frank is a fine young man whom I admire…He is kind, considerate and thoughtful. I am very proud of him and would be honored to call him my son.

- **Patricia McGovern, Hampton Bays Computer Teaching Assistant/community member**

Dear Frank…it takes a special kind of person to earn the respect of all these different types of students. You not only earned their respect but you also gained their trust…It takes a similar strength of character to be able to unite a faculty as diverse as the one in Hampton Bays. All of us, from the old fashioned ones, to the jocks, to the intellectuals, to the free spirits can see the integrity and dedication with which you do your job. If there is one thing we can all agree on it is that you genuinely love what you do and truly care about the kids…The building surely is not the same without you. We all support you and keep you in our thoughts.

- **Sara Holden, Hampton Bays English Teacher**

Dear Frank- I want to thank you for all you've done…You've helped me out a lot as an administrator and a friend. You are great at what you do…You are an excellent administrator and even yet, a better friend!

- **Tara Bowden, Hampton Bays Special Education Teacher**

Mr. Vetro…Hampton Bays H.S. is a better place with you here!

- **Val Stype, Hampton Bays Social Studies Teacher**

Dear Mr. Vetro- I would like to take the opportunity to thank you for all of your efforts and time spent with my children as well as all of the students in Hampton Bays. Your timely advice, continued support, and fair dealing with students is greatly appreciated...we recognize all the good you accomplished. We wish you continued success and will miss you should you not return. Please maintain your spirit and remember that your ability to relate to the children is a gift to be cherished and continued.

- **Irma Herzog, Hampton Bays Community Member**

...He has been the most sincere, loyal, and honest friend as well as colleague. Frank has always been a man of his word and students and teachers alike look to Frank for advice and guidance...He is an integral figure in my development as a person...Frank was inspiring because he was always so diligent and efficient. His professionalism was his outstanding trait. I always respected the way he presented himself at school...I respected his level headed approach to all situations and how admired he was by all of our fellow teachers. Frank Vetro is a man who is dedicated to serving the community and children. He is an excellent friend and role model to those who know him, and that is a long list of people.

- **Gilda Schultz, Newfield High School Math Teacher**

...A man of integrity and is extremely dedicated to his job. His quick ascent through the administrative ranks to become high school principal is indicative of his dependability and ability to deal with staff and public alike. Frank is an affable individual who can often be seen at school functions displaying a genuine interest in the well-being of students and staff....I have been a teacher in Hampton Bays for 29 years and can state without reservation that he is one of the finest administrators I've had the pleasure of working with.

- **James Arnone, Hampton Bays Elementary Teacher**

Frank is a diligent administrator...a global thinker; he sees the whole picture and does not make rash decisions. His attention to detail and tireless work ethic has earned the respect of this tightly knit community. Perhaps the most glowing tribute to Frank is his dedication to our students...This is a man who cares and that feeling is reciprocated.

- **Pat McCormack, Hampton Bays Elementary School Teacher/President Hampton Bays Teachers Association**

...You don't realize how much you care about a person until they are taken away from you...You mean a lot to a lot of people - and this whole incident has made that clear...you have friends who truly care about you- and will be here for you no matter what. None of us can imagine what you are going through...we want you to know you do not have to go through it alone. I know you are an intensely private person - but...you have fans on the sideline cheering you on- we are here to shoulder the pain any way that we can. Like Dyno said to me yesterday "If anybody can land on their feet, it's Frankie"- we all believe that...take care of yourself and know that you are in all of our hearts and minds. The Baymen can't wait to get their skipper back- so hurry home.

- **Virginia McGovern, Hampton Bays community member/teacher assistant at Southampton School District**

...Professional and sincere...I have nothing but positive praise for him. My wife and I have welcomed him into our home on many occasions and will continue to do so. He has spent time with my family and I consider him to be a friend and a valuable asset to our district.

- **Richard Berglin, Hampton Bays Elementary School Teacher and community member**

Just a quick note to let you know…there are so many of us behind you, hopefully that will give you strength. We believe in you so stay strong, be positive, and know that we care.

- **Jim and Sue Finnelly, Kim and Dave Steers, Hampton Bays community members**

Dear Frank…We have missed you. Can't wait for you to come back to the building. As you may have guessed, there is a real lack of leadership…

- **Roe Rea, Hampton Bays Business Teacher**

Dear Frank, it is very important to know that at no time did we (myself or mom and dad) think that any of this could be true! On the contrary we are outraged and upset to know that in this day and age anybody can say anything about anyone and be "believed". It's a total croc of crap as far as we are concerned…You have our support!

- **Lisa Marte, Hampton Bays Teacher**

Our dealings have been both professional and positive.

- **Carly Spezzacatena and Monica Lohr, Hampton Bays Parent Teacher Association Co-Presidents (Southampton Press)**

…I hope you know how much I believe in you as a principal… I have spent the day thinking of you and wishing there was some way to let you know that many people are there for you.

- **Roger Armstrong, Hampton Bays Social Studies Teacher/Union Representative**

…We are behind you. The kids at school want you back…they are saying wonderful things about you. Hang in there, remember we love you and we want you back. You are in my prayers and the prayers of many people.

- **Patricia McGovern, Hampton Bays Computer Teaching Assistant/community member**

…a quick note to let you know that I and my family are thinking about you. We support you…and are behind you 100% and our thoughts and prayers are with you…We miss you.

- **Lisa Marte, Hampton Bays Teacher**

Frank, hope you are hanging in there. This whole thing smells of a set up…You have only done good things for the students and staff here and we miss having you around. Take care, my prayers are with you.

- **Rich Iannelli, Hampton Bays Science Teacher**

Frank: I want to let you know how much you are missed here. A number of faculty and staff are asking about you and offering support…kids are wearing "Free Vetro" and "Bring Vetro back" t-shirts. Parents are asking me if there is anything they can do on your behalf. They support you and…appreciate all that you have done for their children. In all of my years I have never seen a showing of such support for a principal. Stay strong and positive. We are behind you.

- **Grace McGuire, Hampton Bays Principal Secretary**

Hi Frank, I just wanted to let you know that I was thinking of you and keeping you in my prayers. I have a great deal of respect for you and so do your workers and co-workers and students. I consider you a good administrator and enjoy working with you. I hope you are doing ok! I just wanted to tell you how much we all care about you.

- **Loretta Cahill, Hampton Bays Personnel Secretary**

Frank...Just a note to let you know that I hope this nightmare is resolved soon and you can get your life back to normal. Please let me know if there is anything I can do.

- **John McGeehan, Hampton Bays Social Studies Teacher**

I just wanted you know that I am behind you 100%...the staff and kids are really behind you and nobody believes the charges. If there's anything I can do to help, please don't hesitate to tell me. Hang in...John.

- **John Goodman, Hampton Bays Special Education Teacher**

...I wish you great luck and always enjoyed working with you. You have always been helpful and cooperative and a true professional.

- **Anna Rojas, Hampton Bays Principal Secretary**

Many people were talking about you today and many people asking about you too...all good. Everyone misses you here, it's very weird...miss you.

- **Tara Bowden, Hampton Bays Special Education Teacher**

I know him...I have had dealings with him regarding my sons, and I have known him to be a decent man...

- **Ms. Vlahadamis, Hampton Bays community member (Press of Manorville)**

I'd like to let you know how you've effected my life. You were patient with an adolescent that felt rushed, compassionate to a teen who felt abused, intuitive to a young mind that was distressed. YOU proved to me that being a strong male role model was achievable without the need to possess someone or manipulate them. I was a confused youngster with no guidance to speak of further than that of the examples set forth for me from nightly TV programming. You supported my eccentricities, sought out there value, and convinced me and other teachers that that wasn't a trait that made me an outsider. I was truly moved by your presence in my life during your tenure and the challenges you face daily, as I a father, a student, and now a man, view you not only as a mentor but a hero.

- **Adam Polins, Hampton Bays Student**

Only people who know nothing of your character and who like to get caught up in hype would judge you based on ridiculous allegations. So many people have had the privilege of working with you or having you as a teacher or principal.

- **Shannon Loetscher, Hampton Bays Student**

I want you to know I wouldn't have my diploma without your help let alone one of the top English 12 regent's scores in the school if it weren't for you.

- **Shannon Loetscher- Hampton Bays Student**

I've never had a better principal.

- **Edison Blakaj, Hampton Bays Student (New York Times)**

I miss you a lot and wish you were still our principal here. Hope everything works out for you…

- **Genna Kovar, Hampton Bays Student**

…I think I turned out ok, would certainly say that you had quite an influence. You were very good to not just me but everyone, I'll do whatever I can to help you.

- **Anthony Andrews, Hampton Bays Student**

Mr. Vetro…To me you were the only principal that was actually a principal. I haven't met a guy like you during my whole high school years or even the 5 years of college. You're a good man…just hang in there. If you need anything or there is anything I can help with just let me know.

- **Edin Blakaj, Hampton Bays Student**

Thank you for everything. You always tried to keep me on the straight and narrow and give me good advice. I wouldn't have been able to graduate high school if it wasn't for you. Students would be lost without educators like you standing up and pulling for them. I will always be grateful for having you as my principal and for the understanding and compassionate person that you are. Thank you for always sticking up for me and fighting for me. My family and I will always remember how you had my back!

- **Lauryn Armusewics, Hampton Bays Student**

From my perspective he was a good man.

- **Matt Weeks, Hampton Bays Student (Newsday)**

…I was a junior in your sophomore class at Floyd in 96-97. I left Floyd before the school year finished to move to Colorado. Anyway, I heard about what happened and for what it's worth- just wanted to wish you the best of luck…I always thought you were an outstanding teacher.

- **Joy Zuckerman, William Floyd High School Student**

…He was loved by all his students…his passion for teaching was so strong you couldn't help but want to learn…Mr. Vetro always wanted his students to succeed and would go out of his way to ensure they did. He was a positive role model and I am thankful I got to have him as a teacher.

- **Danielle Luc, Newfield High School Student**

Mr. Vetro maintained the authority of a teacher but had the presence of a friend. He was a young teacher when I was in his class. I'd guess he was in his 20's and the short age gap made it easier to get along. He was never in a rush. He always made time to explain things and even if you found yourself in trouble, he'd spin your punishment into a joke. You almost wanted to thank him for detention. He's a man I respect and hold in high regard.

The lessons I've taken away from him were never written in his lesson plan. He exemplified what it is to stand alone and be a person that others want to be. He didn't have to try. It was a personality trait that he had on his own and one that I have tried to achieve. I can only hope other students were able to see beyond the words written on the blackboard and appreciate the true life lessons that he shared in his actions and stories.

- **Bobby Gordon, Newfield High School Student**

Words cannot describe how much respect I have for this man. I can't imagine having to endure what he's been through. His drive and motivation to stand up for himself is unlike any other. He's a tremendous role model for all of us.

- **Samantha Krantz, Hampton Bays Student**

.

Standing on Principal

A Devoted Educator's Fight
against a Corrupt System

Frank J. Vetro

2nd edition

ISBN 13: 978194250014-8
ISBN 10: 194250014-8

Book cover credit Gina Esposito

For Rocco and Josephine Vetro, whose lives were spent so their children could have the opportunities they never had.

Contents

Part III: AND I WAS LEFT FOR DEAD

Acknowledgment

To family and friends mentioned throughout my story—I'd be nowhere without you. Thanks to my sister-in-law Tiffiny. To my nieces and nephew—the only time I was able to be stress free was when I was with Gabriella, Sophia, Rocco, Andrea, and Vittoria (the Secret Project Gang). To my former and current students—your loyalty has been life-saving.

To Eric and Linda Koppelman of iRADIOUSA, Ozzie Jusino and Joleen Cross—my new found friends who joined the cause. To Charles Gerace—you ignored the stigma and believed in me. To Linda Dickerson, Debbie Fryer-Carpluk, Kelly Noel, Matt Palmero and Kelly Olsen,— you listened when I needed an ear. To Joseph and Joanne Canfora of Century 21 Selmar Realty—for all of your support. To Charles Salzberg—you were never too busy to assist a novice. To Sophia— thanks again for always asking and helping. To Lara of Sayville Hot Yoga, Frank Fardella, Rafael Itara, Lindsay Grace, Martin Koppelman, Dakota Carney, Ron Pennisi, Mike Fak, Bill and Tara Coleman, Lori Scarpinella, Aunt Rose, Uncle Nick, Uncle Domenick, and Aunt Agata.

To those who offered information and those who were willing to be witnesses on my behalf but did not want to be mentioned—thank you. The amount of letters, cards, e-mails, phone calls, and words of encouragement I received make it impossible to list all the people who touched my heart. Please know that your thoughts will stay with me forever. For the vast majority, that's all you could do.

To the rest who claimed to be my friend—whose personal lives I've helped and whose careers I've helped advance; to those who said they were busy or in a tough spot, and drifted away; to the small percentage who could have done something to prevent this tragedy but turned a blind eye—to the cheap-shot artists who judged me, kicked me while I was down, and suppressed the truth: you get one chance in life to prove you're a friend. Know that I would've never done that to you. Know that your actions only pushed me harder. Know that if you ever need help, I will be there for you.

Author's Note

I want to thank you for taking time out of your life to read my story. My name is Frank Vetro, and I was the principal of Hampton Bays Secondary School until my life was dramatically altered. At the age of thirty-four authoring a book was the last thing on my things-to-do list. Events beyond my control have been the catalyst for what you are about to read. You will find that I made some errors in judgment that perhaps you may not have made. With all due respect, I believe you will also see glimpses of my character that you would find admirable and worthy of emulating. Please do not mistake anything you read as proof of my being on a self-indulgent ego trip. I made mistakes, of course, and have my share of low moments. I admit to my foibles and am never too proud to ask for forgiveness. However, the person described to the world in February 2006 is a fictitious character created by individuals driven to destroy me.

The people, places, and events mentioned are based on personal knowledge and evidence gathered through witness interrogation, social media networks, depositions, interrogatories, and other legal discovery. Some of it was gathered covertly. Keep in mind, the analyses and conclusions are generally a layman's opinion. For the most part this was written in real time, as a collection of raw thoughts. From time to time I jump back to help you gain perspective into my character and mind-set, as I was publicly guised as a person I would never be. At other times I delve deeper to connect my tragedy to global themes.

Please forgive any lack of creativity or proper syntax; I'm not a writer and had no aspirations of creating a literary work of genius. My intent was to inform, spur change, and prevent future injustices. Writing this book was a poultice to my psyche as I sat idly by watching a system destroy everything I worked so hard to obtain. It has kept my passion for fairness alive when I witnessed a world that wished to reject me from that standard. It's a story of failures and triumphs, disappointments and successes. It's my story and it will scare the hell out of everyone.

Prologue

Thursday November 28, 2013. It's a cold Thanksgiving morning. I just finished the annual 5k turkey trot. Before I head to my sister's for a feast I'm going to work, to gather information for a student who is leaving. He successfully made it through the program, and with that his wrongs have gone away—at least publicly they have. No one ever has to know the mistake he made as a youth or where the courts sent him to reside. He has an opportunity to move on and live a fruitful life. I won't say good-bye. I never do. As many past students have learned, I'm with them forever. It's a simple pact I made with myself long before I became an educator: help people. I never reach out to them after the fact. It's a pay-it-forward profession where you never really know how much good—or harm, for that matter—you may have done. They know how to find me if needed. I hope this young man never has to look back.

Another former student, now in his twenties, left me a message this morning. He's unemployed and needs a place to live. I'll do my best to help him, because everyone needs a break in life. As is the case with many of the youths I help educate, he was dealt a bad hand. He didn't venture through life with general, uneventful moments, sprinkled with some peaks and valleys. He was hit with something that's impossible to prepare for, something that a large majority of people are lucky enough to avoid. It's an event that smacks an unsuspecting victim in the mouth on some otherwise uneventful afternoon. It's an event that changes a person's life, influences their perspective, and forces them to question their integrity and the integrity of those they share their life with. I was hit with such an event and I will never forget it.

Part I
LIFE FLASHED BEFORE MY EYES

Chapter One

In the Blink of an Eye

I always show up to work early but on February 8, 2006 I was earlier than usual, cup of coffee in hand. The first thing I did was call my mom to wish her a happy birthday. I wanted to do it from my office phone because she loved seeing Hampton Bays School District on her caller ID. She was so proud that her son was a school principal—with even bigger aspirations. I opened with the same line I've used since moving out: "Mama, its Frank Vetro." It always cracks her up. The simple things make her laugh, make her happy. She never wants a gift. I stopped buying her gifts years ago because they always go to waste. Quality time with her family is all she ever wants, and dinner with her sons always makes her birthday. It was a quick phone call, because I had an extra busy day. I had to cram everything in so I could leave work earlier than usual. My former colleague from Newfield High School, Ms. Quick, was advising me for a presentation called "Rachel's Challenge." Rachel was a student who was killed in a tragic incident at Columbine High School where the "Trench Coat Mafia" killed a dozen students and a teacher and wounded twenty-four others on campus. One of its many messages was to watch what you say. The slightest remark can impact how an individual is perceived, be emotionally scarring, and lead that individual to harm others or themselves. Amen.

There was a peculiar car parked outside my building just across the street. It was plain-looking and neutral-colored, and sort of hovered around all day. I didn't recognize it, and neither did anyone else. That's not the norm in the small hamlet of Hampton Bays, where everyone knows everything about everybody, including what they drive. The locals have referred to Hampton Bays as "the working man's Hamptons" because of its blue-collar stigma. Many community members have forged a living on the water or via another trade or family run business native to the area. It does have the world famous Dune Road and some million-dollar homes. It is a part of the renowned Town of Southampton. However, the Hamptons most people think of begins about eight minutes farther east, in the actual towns of Southampton and East Hampton, to name a couple. That's where you'll find the Hollywood stars and powerbrokers of the world. My security guard, Tom, kept his eye on the car, but nothing required any action.

I ended my workday at 4:15 p.m., said good-bye to a group of students enrolled in the evening school program, and left for Sportime, a local fitness club in Quogue. I wanted to sneak in a quick workout before having dinner with my mom. I already changed into my gym clothes: black mesh shorts, T-shirt, and blue thermal. It was a freezing, bitter-cold day. The school property was a ghost town, which is typical during the dead of winter. Very few activities take place and nobody wants to loiter in that brutal weather. Just before entering my car I took a final scan of the property. I don't know what instinctively made me do that, but something was strange. It was unusually quiet, even for that time of year. There was an eerie sense of calm before a storm.

After my last-minute scan I got in my car and drove through town. I noticed the mystery car was driving behind me, and there were at least three strange men in the car. I stopped at a red light at the corner of Montauk Highway and Springville Road, just at the entrance of the Dunkin Donuts and movie theater shopping center. That intersection was always congested at that time of day, but it seemed as though the entire town was there at that exact moment. Community members were honking and waving. I was the middle school and high school principal of the small hamlet and a very recognizable face.

Suddenly the suspicious car flashed its lights. An undercover police car? If it was, it wasn't the Southampton Town Police who generally oversaw the town. It had to be the Suffolk County Police Department. The three men exited the car, wearing plain clothes, and rushed my vehicle as if I were a drug lord or murderer.

"Get out of the car!" I wondered what the hell was going on as I followed the command. As soon as I exited my car he theatrically screamed, "You're under arrest!" Before I could say a word he violently turned me around, shoved me on the car, and cuffed me.

The handcuffs dug into my wrists. "Wait, I'm the principal of the school."

The officer responded with a smirk. "I know," he said, as he paraded me in front of the town for what seemed like an eternity. I looked at the throng of community members. They were shocked, to say the least, as they witnessed their principal in a horrendous situation. I asked the officer to at least remove me from their view. "Don't worry—no one is looking, it will only be a few seconds." He had no concern for the shocked community, not even the young kids who were watching in tears.

I requested an attorney but was ignored, and although no one asked for my permission, they searched my car. I asked one officer what the justification for the search was but he pretended not to hear me. I didn't press the issue. They were going to do whatever they wanted at that moment. There was nothing to find anyway. I made a conscious effort not to make direct eye contact with anyone in the crowd, but I didn't look down either. I stood tall and tried to look as calm and confident as a person could look in that predicament. When they finished their dog-and-pony show for the crowd, they shoved me in the front seat of the police car. The cuffs were tight and digging into my wrists from my body weight leaning back. The quiet afternoon had suddenly gone from zero to one hundred miles per hour. As we exited the town, one officer followed behind in my car. I wanted to drag him out of it and beat the daylights out of him, but it was no time for fantasies. Instead, I politely asked, "Can you tell me what you think I did?" There was dead silence as the officers looked at each other through the rearview mirror with peculiar stares.

After about a half-hour drive we pulled into the seventh precinct in Shirley, New York. The police officer in the backseat leaned forward and sternly said, "Answer a few questions, and we'll have you out in a short time." "You'll have me out? You staked me out all day, outside of my building, just to drive me back to this precinct, one minute from where I live. What was I going to do, escape? Leave the country?"

He didn't like my response, so I figured maybe I should cooperate a little. After all, I knew I wasn't guilty of anything. Before leaving the car I once again requested an attorney and phone call. Once again I was ignored. They dragged me out of the car and escorted me inside the precinct. I could feel deep grooves on my wrists. Evidence of the extremely tight, viselike grip of the cold steel on my wrists. The officer's didn't care, and they were far from done.

They whisked me into an interrogation room, empty save for a small desk and two folding chairs, and handcuffed me to a cold cement floor closed in by four cinderblock walls. After a lonely wait, one officer entered the room. "I'm Officer Heter." He was fairly tall, maybe six foot one, had a crew cut, and was clean-shaven—and dressed a little shabby, to be honest. He smiled and tried to be pleasant. I assumed, based on my brief evaluation, he was going to play the role of "good cop." I honestly planned on trying to reason and cooperate with these guys. I figured whatever was going on, I'd tell the truth, they would see the mistake, and I would go home. No harm, no foul. In doing so, I lost sight of a fundamental principle: when in police custody, innocent or not, you have the right to remain silent and should do so. They are not your friends.

Officer Heter began by rattling off the names of a bunch of women, some of whom I used to work with, and asked me if I knew them. "Slow down. Which one do you want me to answer about first? Did they file complaints?" They couldn't have possibly filed complaints, so there was no point in asking that, but I did anyway. Heter didn't answer me. The questions came fast and furious. I told the truth in a calm, rational, and respectful manner so he could see it was all a mistake.

"Did you ever call them?" I answered yes. I know I called a few of those women many times, and some of them maybe once or twice. At some point they all received a call from me. And they called me, I might add. I had sexual relations with some of them.

"Did you ever say anything inappropriate or hang up?"

"Hang up? What does that mean? Why would I call someone just to hang up? I never hung up or said anything inappropriate."

"When was the last time you called?"

"I'm not sure but I know it was a long time ago." It had been years since I last spoke with some of them. Still in the dark as to why I was chained to the precinct floor, I asked, "Officer, who filed a complaint against me? Can I see the complaint? Can you tell me what I'm under arrest for, please?" I requested an attorney and phone call probably ten more times. I was ignored each and every time.

Heter walked out. In stormed a hotheaded "bad cop," the officer from the backseat of the police car. He didn't seem as tall as Heter, had dark hair, and was a little husky and also dressed shabby, and I think I noticed a very slight stutter in his voice, maybe not. He was arrogant, had a harsh tone, and tried to intimidate me. He refused to give me his name, but I heard someone refer to him as Sergeant. He just repeated the same questions Heter asked but offered nothing to cue me in as to what the hell I was doing chained to the floor. They repeated a cycle of leaving the room for an extended period of time and then coming back. Time slowed to a crawl. The sound of the second hand on the clock that I couldn't even see outside of the interrogation room sounded like a loud cannon being fired off every second—*bang, bang, bang!* I'm certain they realized that the long wait between questioning unnerves a person chained to the floor of an interrogation room. Trust me, it does.

Officer Heter reentered and continued the role of good cop. He said softly, calmly, "Do you want some water?" I shook my head no, and he left. Next was more waiting, and then *boom!* The sergeant rushed in, shoved the door open like it was the gateway to hell, and screamed, treating me not as a decent guy who was a school principal but like a convict with a rap sheet four feet long. I tried to be polite and reasonable but he only became more irate. When he was done with whatever he was saying, he exited as quickly as he had entered. Hours went by, and I just thought of my mom, worried sick because her son never showed up for her birthday dinner.

It continued. They instigated, teased, and spoke to me sarcastically. They said I was leading some life as a young principal, got all the women, and had a great job, nice car. "You're doing okay for yourself. It seems as if you didn't do anything wrong. Things could be worse though. You should cooperate." How much worse could they get? I heard a few others outside the room speaking in an envious fashion, as if I didn't deserve to be in my position. They were so juvenile. I busted my butt to get where I was. They even discussed what a great story it was going to be. What story? I still had no details regarding who had filed a complaint or what I had supposedly done wrong.

The bad cop blasted back into the room. "You're busted Mr. Principal."

He played a cassette recording of what sounded like someone screaming, all of two seconds' worth—literally two seconds.

Something was not adding up. "Excuse me, sir, can you play more than two seconds of that tape? I don't even know the context of whatever that was or who the person was for that matter."

He refused and completely lost it. Spit shot out of his mouth. "It doesn't matter! We have you busted—on tape!"

"Sir, you have me busted on tape? Doing what? Can I read the complaint filed against me?" Again I was denied.

Instead, the high-strung officer exited, and Officer Heter returned to admit the accusations didn't add up.

"Then why am I cuffed in an interrogation room?" No response.

More time passed, and the sergeant stormed back in. He yelled a little more. Then he screamed, "You called Steve Madden!" That's it, in perhaps a comical moment I raised my voice in frustration, "I don't even know anyone

5

named Steve Madden!" He clarified it was a store. "Don't play dumb. You called that store." I was confused. I didn't even know anyone who worked at that store. I didn't even know the store existed. "Sir, what would be the point of me calling the store? For what? What are you accusing me of?"

I looked dead into his eyes. Slowly, politely, and quietly, I insisted, "I really don't know what you're talking about." For a quick moment, even he looked surprised, as if he really believed me—maybe he had arrested the wrong person.

His look was short-lived as he tried to maintain his poker face. "There was an eleven-month investigation!" He slammed down a stack of papers six inches thick. It sounded like he dropped a bag of cement on the desk. "We have records. You called the same woman twenty times in one month!" I leaned forward to scratch my head with my cuffed hand, wondering what the hell he was talking about. Maybe he was just trying to strong-arm me. Varied thoughts raced through my mind as I tried to figure things out in a split second. I have been involved with a lot of women and am not proud to admit I can't remember them all. At that point I wished I could. A few of the women mentioned by Heter had been intimate with me. There was just absolutely no way they filed complaints though. It was a long time ago, and there was nothing for them to complain about.

The sergeant screamed again but I didn't even pay attention. It was all just background noise with a visual of a guy ranting and raving, arms fluttering. I had nothing to say because I simply didn't know what was going on. I didn't do anything.

"Be honest!"

"Honest? You haven't done anything but cause me to distrust you, and I really don't know what you're talking about."

He leaned over the table, real close, and stared me down. I could feel his breath and hear his heartbeat. "Frank, this is kid's stuff. If you were any old Joe, I would slap you on the wrist and tell you to get out of here. But you're a young, good-looking principal. The media is going to be called. It's going to be rough for you and your family."

Media? What did I do? My world was unraveling. Everything I worked so hard to obtain was being threatened. They were relishing in the idea of destroying me and every facet of my life. I didn't say another word. I repeated their words over and over, not wanting to forget how malicious these officers were.

He yelled a little more and walked out of the interrogation room. Both officers returned a few minutes later, but the conversation was over as far as I was concerned. My mom was waiting for her son, who was never going to show up.

Officer Heter quietly said, "Sign these papers and we'll let you make a call." Papers? What papers? He threw down about four pages written without my knowledge and without my proofread. He said it again, with more force, "You have to sign these cards before you make a phone call."
I noticed Miranda rights were written on them. "Wait a second. Now you give these to me? Now you offer me a lawyer? I've been requesting a lawyer for hours, since 4:30 p.m., and it's now almost midnight." They wanted to make it look as if they continually offered me my rights and I voluntarily gave statements. None of that happened. It's not like I confessed to anything though. I didn't even know what to confess to. No question about it, I wasn't thinking straight. I kept thinking of my mom's birthday being ruined and the manner in which I was arrested. I kept seeing the students and community members' tears and looks of horror. I kept hearing the officers' threats. I had no clue what was written on those papers, but surely the officers wouldn't have created charges or a fictitious story. You grow up thinking police officers will serve and protect, not seek and destroy. Wrongful arrests only happen in the movies, right? Think again.

The officer took me to a phone. "Make a few calls." I called Marc Meyer first because I was concerned about my job, my livelihood. We rose through the educational ranks together, eventually both becoming principals in Hampton Bays. I knew he would try his best to do damage control. Next I called my high school buddy, Craig Dolinger. He's an attorney, and I knew he'd do his best to get me representation on short notice. I tried to but couldn't get in touch with my superintendent, Joanne Loewenthal. I assumed she was being bombarded with phone calls. The next call was the toughest. I called my mother to tell her why I didn't make it to dinner. Although I assured her everything was under control, I don't think her motherly instinct allowed her to believe me. My other call was to my former boss Nick Dyno. I'm not even sure why I called him. I explained the situation, what little I knew about it, as quickly as possible to everyone, warning that I might be all over the news in the morning.

After the phone calls they took my fingerprints and shoved me, literally, into a very cold cell. Everyone else in lockup was allowed to wear their long-sleeve shirts, but they made me take mine off, so I was left in my gym shorts and T-shirt. I ignored the cold and stayed awake, still wondering what I was charged with, who filed the charges, and what the officers wrote on the papers. I didn't know how bad it was going to be but I didn't feel good about it. The cell was like something out of a two-bit movie: four brick walls, an iron slab that you were supposed to sleep on, and a toilet in open view that was so dirty and nasty I wouldn't have used it to pee if I could stand five feet away from it. I was by myself in the cell but I could hear the other prisoners in the cells along the row. The stench was unbearable, and the constant back-and-forth arguing between the prisoners and the officers created a cacophony of noise in a world gone mad that I tried to shut out of my mind.

Some of the officers berated the prisoners and, at times, acted worse than the so-called bad guys. They were cruel and enjoyed treating us like dirt. I'm sorry, but I didn't deserve to be spoken to in such belittling fashion. They weren't better than me. When you treat people that way, they are going to come back at you. I knew better than to respond rudely, but the night was filled with yelling and cursing between the prisoners and officers. In that very brief microcosm I could see how the system could be a recipe for failure. I stayed awake wondering how this could happen. The entire night was like a surreal television drama. Unfortunately, this story was real, and I was the star character.

After a bitterly cold night, they woke the inmates early to bring us to the Central Islip Courthouse. They gathered and chained us together, like a chain gang going off to the fields to work until we dropped. As we were about to be loaded in the steal wagon they stopped the line to un-cuff me. A moment of relief came over me. I was being released. Yeah, right. Instead, they placed me in the front of the line and told us to walk. They stopped the line for about a minute just at the exit of the precinct. That was when I got the criminal red carpet treatment. There were news cameras waiting that wanted a nice, clear shot of me, and the cops were happy to oblige. Flashing light bulbs, questions hurriedly yelled in my direction—I never realized I was so important. I was the first one loaded into the claustrophobic steel wagon. The ride to the courthouse was cold and brutal. It felt like the walls were closing in on me. Actually, my whole life was closing in on me. Someone really had it in for me. The question was, who?

When we arrived at the courthouse, it was a freaking zoo—total chaos. People everywhere cursing, yelling, and fighting. It was a combination of a busy day on the trading floor of the New York Stock Exchange and the gladiator days of ancient Rome. I didn't say a word. I just remained as poised as could be. Some of those officers also were relentless and inhumane in how they spoke to and treated us. I wasn't guilty, merely accused. I'm a decent person, not a serial killer. Everything that was happening was wrong—more than that, it was an injustice. After a brief "tour" of the facility, we arrived at central booking and were placed in what they called a holding cell. The place was a shit hole. There must have been twenty of us in each cell, maybe more, and the many cells on the floor were all filled to capacity. That cell, like every cell, was nothing more than a waiting game—a waiting game in a world filled with terrible smells, disgusting toilets, and bologna and cheese sandwiches that wouldn't seem palatable to a prisoner in a medieval dungeon. But as bad as I must have looked at that moment, it had to be good compared to the other "captives."

The officers moved us from one room to another, each filled with maybe half a dozen officers sitting around doing nothing. Some would completely disrespect us before moving us to another room, where the same thing occurred again. It took hours for anything to get done. Every time they moved me, they un-cuffed and searched me, and then I would wait until the next time they un-cuffed, searched, and moved me. All the while they relentlessly tried to find my hot button so they could have their fun until they decided they had taken away enough of my dignity. Unfortunately they never decided they had enough. I refused to fall for their nonsense though. A few of the alleged criminals also milled around, looking for a confrontation. They knew they couldn't do anything about the guards who were treating them like dirt, so another con or alleged con that looked at them the wrong way sufficed. My martial arts training came into play here—not the physical aspect, the mental.

I began practicing Tae Kwon Do, a Korean martial art, in the 1980s. That was when the martial arts had a surge in the United States with the Karate Kid, the Teenage Mutant Ninja Turtles, and countless other martial arts shows, cartoons, and movies. Everywhere you turned it was in your face. With his deep Korean accent, my instructor, Master Lee, always grunted, "Practice hard." If those words were meant for me, they were usually preceded with a slap to the head. However, practice hard is exactly what I did. I don't cheap out on anything. It's one hundred percent—or else why bother? But nothing is simply a matter of practicing hard. I learned that practice doesn't make perfect; perfect practice makes perfect.

9

> *My approach to life slowly changed. I learned self-discipline, to self-reflect and refine my patience. I also began to visualize—to foresee an outcome, understand what action was needed to achieve that outcome, and work to achieve it. I practiced self-reflection and visualization so much that they became subconscious acts. Martial arts helped me become mentally and physically strong. There are those who practice a discipline for fitness and self-defense, and those who practice as a way of life, whereby self-defense and fitness become a secondary result. Martial arts wasn't just a passing fad for me. I no longer practice the physical aspects, but I consider myself a martial artist, and that's a way of life.*

It's a way of life that helped me control myself while being yelled at and belittled by guards and stared down by a few inmates. No worries—I was confident that if I needed to defend myself, someone was going to find out the hard way that this principal was not the one to mess with. I smiled, if you could believe it. Nothing could break me. After hours of waiting, a clerk called me to the front of the cell. He asked me questions so they could figure out my bail amount. It was another couple of hours before I was called again.

I understand there has to be large numbers of guards. I also understand that they have to have an edge to them because of the "clientele" they deal with, but they could have toned it down a bit. At times they literally provoked individuals for confrontations. After they had finally provoked enough and got some disrespect back, they took measures to solve the newly created problem. Sometimes the person deserved it, but honestly, sometimes they pushed too far. I'm not saying lockup should be a pleasant place, because it shouldn't be, but there has to be some respect for human dignity.

Meanwhile the media was bombarding the courthouse and flocking to my mom's house, my house, my neighbors', and Hampton Bays School District. I was all over the newspapers, on every news station, and all over the internet. Of course I didn't realize any of that, because I was sitting in a cell, waiting for someone, anyone, to actually treat me like a citizen of the United States. Finally I was called to be arraigned. I was handcuffed and patted down again, followed by more belittling, and then escorted to the courtroom. When I entered I noticed my family and friends waiting to show their support. My mom was standing in the courtroom in tears as her son was dragged in, in hand cuffs. She didn't deserve that.

I sat on the side bench as a member of skid row and listened to Honorable Judge Hensley issue out the bail amounts for each case. Crimes that were felonies and committed by repeat offenders were given minimal bail or no bail at all. When my turn came, an attorney was waiting for me—my friend Craig came through. As I stood in front of the bench, Judge Hensley said there were seven misdemeanor charges of aggravated harassment. Seven counts of aggravated harassment? Seven people complained against me? For what? He didn't say much else and set bail at $17,500 cash or $35,000 bond! *Are you kidding me?* The bail questionnaire that I was asked while in holding allowed for a maximum of eleven points. The higher the number, the more likely a person was to return to court and the less the bail amount, theoretically. Now, I had a great job, earned a good living, had a strong educational background, owned a home, and grew up in Suffolk County, Long Island; my friends and family filled the court room; and as the judge stated, I had no prior record. I was a perfect candidate to return—as in, not skip out of town. I should have been rated a perfect eleven, the bail should have been zero dollars, and I should have been released on my own recognizance (ROR). Instead I received a score of *seven*! Did they really think a principal of a high school with lifetime roots in the community and a clean record was a flight risk over a lousy misdemeanor?

I have to add that I'm so glad I live in Suffolk County. It must be the safest place in America if the police force can waste multiple officers and an undercover car to stake out a respected principal outside a high school building for claims of harassment. Isn't there something else they could've been doing? So many others are just asked to go down to the station—or, better yet, they are given a warning that there are claims of harassment being alleged so *if* they are doing something, stop. That wouldn't have been humiliating enough. This was an opportunity for a few police officers to go to the bars or go home and brag to friends and family how they were all on television or in the newspapers apprehending the Suffolk County felon of the century. I started to think the arrest had nothing to do with whether I was guilty of anything or not. It had to do with a few Suffolk County Police officers getting a chance to be in the news. It didn't matter that the story could ruin my life; it made theirs.

The court officer un-cuffed me and handed me orders of protection to sign, rapid-fire. I didn't get a chance to read them either. Then he handcuffed me again and dragged me out of the courtroom. Looking over my shoulder,

I saw my mom walk away with tears streaming down her face. She was bombarded by reporters but my friend Leo Baez put his coat over her head so the cameras didn't get a clean shot of her. They placed me in a holding cell while I waited to be bailed out. That cell had a different name but it was just as disgusting as the others I had been forced to occupy. It came complete with an odor from the bowels of hell. And now another pressing problem had posed itself. My family had to come up with the bail or I was going to rot in jail.

An officer immediately asked me for my papers. "What papers? I don't have papers."

"The numbers on your papers are wrong," he said. "They have to be the same, or they'll turn your family away once they come up with the money." What numbers?

"Then forget about me. Find my family before they leave so you can fix their copies!"

Hours went by and I was still waiting. Waiting for bail that was not on the way. Continuing on my lucky streak, they loaded me onto a blue, full-size bus with fenced windows that was filled to capacity. I was sandwiched with the other inmates driving east on the Long Island Expressway. Destination: Riverhead Jail. I was sent to Riverhead while career criminals were sent home on their own recognizance. After what seemed like an eternity, we were taken off the bus and checked in to the jail. They were obviously expecting me because everyone at the jail was whispering, looking, and talking about me, the principal who was all over the news. They issued me a green jumpsuit and I was an official guest.

While the others were being fitted for their jumpsuits, I noticed a phone on the wall in the neighboring room. I drummed up the nerve to sneak over and call my principal friend Marc to see how my school district was doing. "Things are chaotic, Frankie, but they're doing their best to support you." Good enough, I supposed.

It didn't seem as if anybody was missing me, so I pushed my luck and made another call, this time to my buddy Craig. "Hang in there, Frank, the bail is being taken care of, and it shouldn't be long." A gambling man by nature, I really pressed my luck by making three more phone calls to my family. Of course they weren't around because they were trying to acquire bail. Finally my sister Maria answered her phone. "Frank, how are you doing?" She sounded sad and tired. I chuckled to make light of the situation, hoping to reassure her that her younger brother was okay,

"Oh, fine, thanks, and you?" Hearing her voice was nice. It brought me back to childhood, when we would play silly games to keep ourselves entertained—climbing trees, running around the yard, doing any stupid thing together that we could think of. We were close growing up and grew closer as we aged and moved out of the house. That was a very soothing split second but I came back to reality fast to ask her to record the media attention on television. I hurriedly said good-bye. Safe to say I was in enough trouble. She didn't sound good—like an older sister worried for her younger brother, naturally.

I snuck back over in the nick of time. Just seconds later they lined us up for lunch. A very appetizing smell came from the rolling cart. That stale white bread and single piece each of what slightly resembled bologna and cheese was nothing short of five-star quality. The cart was in the corner of the very elegant, empty corridor/dining hall. The guards called us over one at a time to choose from the mouthwatering buffet. When it was my turn I hesitated because I didn't want to eat. The guard screamed, "You have to walk around the pole ... around the pole ... *around the pole!* Are you an idiot?!" I closed my eyes and took a deep breath. I have a pet peeve about the general lack of common courtesy that exists in society, not to mention the extremes that were evident at Riverhead Jail. How the hell was I supposed to know the protocol regarding picking up a dirty rotten sandwich off a cart at a jail when I had never been there before? Second, I didn't even want the freaking thing.

When I was younger I was a lean little guy with a lot of energy. Wherever I was, trouble wasn't far away. I was a good kid who respected authority and did well academically thanks to my parents' emphasis on education, but I hung around an older crowd who happened to get into trouble. Unfortunately, I had a fierce temper, a quick trigger, and zero patience for nonsense, so if someone did me or someone else wrong, I felt a need to fight. There was no in-between; I went from calm to the Incredible Hulk in a split second and would return to normal just as quick. I fought people the same age, younger, and a lot older. I wasn't a bully. I picked the fights that I believed needed to be fought, not the ones that were easy victories. My temper was leading me down a road toward seriously hurting myself or someone else.

13

> *One afternoon I completely flipped out on my mom in the kitchen. I don't even know why, which was par for the course. She looked at me in a way she never had before and never has since. It wasn't fear but more of a helpless "I don't know what to do anymore" look. "Frankie, this person you are becoming—you have to stop. I don't like you." I walked away feeling like I had been run over by a Mack truck. I was angry at myself for putting her in that situation and knew then and there that I had to change. And I did slowly (stress* slowly*) control my temper. It wasn't until many years later that I learned other ways to fight battles besides blowing a gasket and brawling. Although I, like everyone, have moments of weakness, my self-control is one of my proudest accomplishments. My temper has left me with physical and mental scars of a childish mentality that I deeply regret. You never really win a fistfight. It's a loss the second it turns physical. However, in a different sense, fighting the good fight has followed me into adulthood. Sometimes I wish it didn't and I do consider it a curse.*

The Frank of yesteryear would have definitely walked over and beat the living daylights out of that guard. That wouldn't have been a very smart move. So the even-keeled Frank paused, took a deep breath, and just picked up two sandwiches. I stared at the guard as I gladly gave my cuisine to another inmate who wanted them more than I did. He looked like he needed them more too. After about a half hour I was escorted to my cell. The sound of the bars slamming shut was loud and very real. God, it was dirty, small, and miserable, just like all the others. I dropped the gift bag (toothbrush, rules, etc.) they gave me upon arrival and leaned on the bars of the cell, my arms extended out into the hallway. My life was falling apart, and I couldn't do a thing about it. The media was having a field day, and I couldn't say anything to stop them—I couldn't tell them the truth. Thoughts swirled in my head. *What did I do? Who did I do it to?* I envisioned my accusers, whoever they were, and the police high-fiving each other as they watched and read how effectively they were destroying me. I wondered how it must feel to have that much hate in your heart. You have to have a heart before you can answer that question.

My thoughts were interrupted, and I was escorted to the jail psychologist. "Why am I here?"

"They recommended it because your case is high-profile. You're acting different than the others. You're quiet. They want to make sure you don't hurt yourself."

"That's because I'm innocent." I laughed immediately, realizing I just used the standard line said by everyone in jail. The psychologist playfully joined in. That saying is so true, by the way. Everyone is innocent in the big house. "I'm not about to hurt myself. I would never do that to my family—or myself, for that matter."

"Wow, they really screwed you," she said, noticing the bail amount. That seemed to be the consensus and a jail psychologist made it official. She let me make a phone call and I was able to reach my sister-in-law Inmaculada. It was a real quick conversation, only seconds long, and I don't recall any of it except that I asked if she could make sure I get my toothbrush and some underwear because I didn't know how long I would be locked up. Inma is a very thoughtful and caring person. She would do right by anybody and that's why I knew she would do whatever she could for her brother-in-law.

Following that phone call I had a brief and pretty uneventful conversation with the psychologist, and then she sent me back. I was sorry to go. She treated me like a human being. There was still no bail posted and it was obvious I was staying yet another night locked up thanks to the paperwork mishap. Maybe they were having too much fun and realized that if I left, their lives would go back to nothing more than berating and insulting less publicized prisoners in the hellhole.

Eventually I was allowed out of the tiny cell for a short stint. I asked an officer if I could read the vicious headline sitting on his desk, one of many.

"No fucking way!" he shouted. "What if I'm the guy on that page?"

"No shit?" He spoke to me about it for a minute and he was actually quite cordial.

When I returned to my cell, the officer threw the paper in. "Hey, teach, this is for you."

I thanked him and read. The article, directed by lies of incompetent police officers, completely destroyed me. I had imagined total annihilation, and there it was in print to confirm my worst fears. It didn't say who had filed charges against me, either. The identities were not disclosed, because they were "victims". They were *"alleged"* victims! And I was an *"alleged"* criminal—maybe my name should have been withheld too!

The story was also repeatedly broadcast from a television in the seemingly disease-ridden jail. Damn it, I thought. I am not an animal. I hoped everyone could see through the vile-spewing stories. Just over a day ago I was on top of the world. I carefully scripted my life and worked my butt off to achieve my goals. It was all so perfect, and in the blink of an eye, it had drastically changed. I was caught in the muck and mire of a Suffolk County jail, waiting for someone to post bail, as news of me being taken out of a school and off the streets weaved its way through the media outlets. I was trapped in a damp, dark jail cell. Immersed in a world of deception, lies, and publicity-hungry officials who found my conviction more beneficial to their agendas than the truth.

I felt sad for my mom. She didn't deserve it. On her birthday, no less, so she could think about the events over again for the rest of her life. A few hours later, as I stared at the ceiling, a correction officer called to me and passed a note from Jennifer Boyer, a board of education member in Hampton Bays. It said, "Frankie, keep your head up. We're on your side." A tear rolled down my cheek. I think the last time I cried was when I was run over by a car at three years old. I survived that mishap. I would survive this as well.

I vowed at that moment to take a mental picture of all that happened and would happen. I would not soon forget. By the time the night fell, the blitzkrieg simmered to a quiet standstill. I closed my eyes and wandered off. Being locked in a small, dingy cell sure gives a person a lot of time to think. I thought about my life, from childhood to present day, and tried to figure out exactly how I wound up in the mess I was in.

Chapter Two
Back in the Day

My family was like nomads during my early years, moving from Astoria, Queens, to Lake Grove, Long Island, when I was born in 1971. We uprooted to Florida, moving quite a few times in the Miami and Fort Lauderdale areas before moving back to Long Island—downtown Coram—where I officially grew up. I was never a "kid" in the typical sense. I was never interested in birthday parties, the zoo, or sleeping over at friends' houses. Big Bird and the Cookie Monster were not a part of my life. I went to the racetrack and local off-track-betting (OTB) on the weekends. The family trips I recall were to Atlantic City or Las Vegas. The walls of my room were covered with pictures of Charlie's Angels and posters of Gulf Stream, Yonkers Raceway, Belmont Park, Churchill Downs, etc. I was surrounded by bookies, hustlers, and other individuals with pretty shady backgrounds. I swear I had a five-o'clock shadow when I was six. Back then the village raised the child, and although surrounded by shady people, my family provided a nurturing environment that kept me on the straight and narrow.

While in my cell the first image that came to my mind was a picture of me on a tricycle with my mom kneeling over me. Mom has been there for me from day one, and one thing I was certain of was that she would be there for this trying time. She is an amazingly strong person with a breaking point that has never been reached. It's no doubt that I inherited an internal strength and ability to endure both physical and psychological suffering from my mom. In her quiet way, she is nurturing and incredibly resilient, and she sacrifices to prevail in spite of people or circumstances. I smiled again and felt the warm comfort a child could only get from a mother.

17

Me and mom. © Photography by Gina Esposito.

Inner strength is no stranger to my dad, Rocco, a construction worker by trade. Although not physically big, in his younger years he was a mythical figure that everyone relied on and marveled at. As if he was with me in the cell, I could hear him ranting the same lines he's been using since arriving from Italy via the *Andrea Dorea* in the fifties. "Frankie, I was told in 'America there's gold on the streets.' I ain't seen nuttin" and "I made a man's salary when I was eleven." He jokes to this day about coming all the way from Calabria just to meet a Sicilian: "During low tide I could walk to Sicily!" There were no heart-to-heart talks with dad. He taught with his actions and always had a unique perspective on life. For instance, one Friday afternoon he came home from working on the construction site and literally crawled through the house the entire weekend because of his pain. After dinner, as he sipped his espresso, I asked, "Dad, why do you do this to yourself?" His response: "Frankie, there's only one thing worse than working, not working." Monday morning, he stood up and went to work. His actions taught me a lot about pride, courage, and faith in oneself.

My dad made it to the fifth grade before having to go to work for his family, and my mom, in her words, barely made it out of high school. Those paths weren't their choice, though, and that wasn't the path they wanted for their kids. They always worked real hard and pushed us to do well in school so we could have more options. I tried to make a conscious effort to do well in school, not just for me, but for them too. It didn't come easy, but while attending middle school I learned to make lists, and that helped a bit.

Middle school was a pretty chaotic time. I imagine a lot of people can make that claim. The design of my middle school building didn't exactly help out budding adolescents. It lacked interior walls. Lockers and portable dividers barely five feet tall were used to separate classrooms. Everyone could see each other which magnified the problem when something went wrong in a class. If a fight broke out, forget it—total chaos ensued. I felt overwhelmed—meeting new people, changing classes, having seven different teachers, being assigned all the homework, and dealing with everything else that comes with puberty, like zits! For some reason, that I can't recall, I started making a homework list every morning. I'd list every period, even lunch, and write down the assignments and other notes to organize my days. One of my not so academically inclined friends found out and started picking on me something fierce. So of course I punched his lights out and knocked him down the flight of stairs in the Two South wing of the building. Afterward, a teacher took me aside and said, "Making a homework list is a mature thing to do Frankie. Keep it up." I still got in school suspension for that though. Trouble seemed to find me. I've been making lists ever since. Every day I write on a small piece of paper and fold it into my back pocket. If you break things down and organize, overwhelming days become manageable. Students know my lists as "The Hit List." Yeah, yeah, I realize that's probably inappropriate. Everyone is so sensitive.

My lists helped me succeed throughout high school, where I dreamed about going to physical therapy school and becoming a trainer for the New York Rangers. My guidance counselor, Mrs. Rorer, was terrific and determined to help me get there. She was a heavy set Greek who playfully called me the "Italian stallion." In early May 1989, with her deep accent, smiling ear to ear she screamed, "Veeetro, you have been accepted into a physical therapy program, a master's program!" That really was great news, but I turned the offer down. Mrs. Rorer's jaw dropped. She was devastated. "This is a great opportunity! It's what you want!"

How much trouble could this kid possibly get into?

I don't remember my reasoning, but whatever I told her wasn't the truth. When I was a child, my dad worked a lot and wasn't around much, but my older brother Sal was a male presence in my life on a daily basis. I naturally followed the same professional sport teams and had the same hobbies as him. We would always throw around the football or baseball, or play hockey or wiffle ball in front of the house. It was music to my ears every time he would ask, "Want to have a catch?" Everything I did with Sal left a great memory. Of course my entire family was there for my younger brother. My brother Sal and sister Maria were already off to college though, so I decided I wanted to be there for Rocky the same way they were for me. So I was, and I would never in a million years trade the time I spent with him for a college dorm or a billion dollars. The amount of laughs we had together are priceless.

By the time I was about to graduate from Longwood High School I had big dreams and thought I knew it all—until my economics teacher, Mr. Terry, hit me with a left hook. There was some downtime in class, and we were each seated in a student desk. "Frank, what are your plans after graduation?"

I proudly responded, "I want to be a physical therapist. My dream is to be a trainer for a professional sports team."

Mr. Terry, in his distinguished suit and perfectly polished shoes, dressed to the nines as always, became very serious. In a deliberate and stern tone, he insisted, "Don't dream." Uh, what? Talk about taking the wind out of a graduating teen's sails. He said it again. "Don't dream. You can't touch dreams. When you wake up they're gone. Turn your dreams into goals and achieve them." Unfortunately, youth is wasted on the young, and I didn't fully appreciate that practical advice he gave me.

My plan was to attend SUNY Stony Brook and then apply to their physical therapy program after the required two years of undergraduate work. Stony Brook was known for its sciences and physical therapy program, and the price was right since it was a state school. The problem was that Stony Brook was a big university with hundreds of students in a class. We were all just numbers—our social security numbers. Nobody was watching, and nobody cared as long as you paid the tuition. No attendance? See you later. Nobody was checking homework? That was fine with me. Test in three weeks? I'd be back then. Why bother? I had to drive to school, park in the South P Lot, take a bus to campus, and then walk a country mile between classes. I couldn't even understand my teachers. They weren't even teachers. They were researchers from other countries mandated to teach a course or two. Why put myself through the nonsense? When the time came, I would do what I needed to do to be accepted to the physical therapy program. What a stupid kid.

I should have been sitting in the Javits Lecture Center, but instead I decided to make some quick money on the handball courts and billiards tables. My dad owned a bar, R&J Bar, for a short stint, and that's where you would find this kid, "the short bartender," complete with a towel in my back pocket. The local hustler, "Hollywood," with his long, flowing, bleached-blond hair would set me on the pool table and explain the game of billiards. I'm not sure what was stranger: Hollywood teaching me or me paying attention. He played well enough to win, nothing more, and sometimes purposefully lost. His marks always thought they had a chance. That's why they came back, which made Hollywood more prosperous in the long run. I never won by much either, just enough to keep them coming back. Few people saw how much skill I actually had, and they lined up to pay me—uh, I mean *play* me. I didn't consider it gambling. I was betting on my ability, and that was a sure thing.

I could usually get money whenever I needed it. Plus there was always the opportunity for this cocky teenager to parlay his earnings playing cards or wagering on a horse or sporting event. I picked up those habits as a kid, while my dad very briefly dabbled as owner of a restaurant, Rocco's Place. That was where the local bookie, Eddie, would frequent, and that was where I gravitated. Eddie would place a sea captain's hat on my head, and we would be off to the beach every morning. I'm certain he was just using the cute little kid to pick up women. They came around early and often! They weren't the only ones, though. Although I didn't realize at the time, Eddie did some serious "business" on the beach. That's when I was introduced to the world of gambling. Regarding my wagers, I stress the word *opportunity*. Those tips didn't exactly pan out much of the time.

Unfortunately, I had to build a résumé of legitimate work experience. So from May to September, when school wasn't in session, I actually earned a paycheck. My dad wasn't thrilled because he didn't want his children living a life wielding a pick and shovel like him. Nonetheless, I inherited both my parents' work ethic and was ready and willing. One of my first official jobs was at Flower Fields, not far from Stony Brook University. I was part of a grounds crew that maintained tens if not hundreds of acres of land that was infested with poison ivy and hornets nests. Every day I was stung by hornets and acquired a new batch of poison ivy! It was miserable. I was sent to the hospital quite a few times, all for about six dollars per hour. Those damn hornets! Every time I hear that buzz I feel like Captain Ahab. They are my white whale. The others on the crew were lifers who would smoke weed and had no ambition. That wasn't the life I was looking for. I may have gambled and hustled, but I never had an addictive personality, and I always had a drive to succeed.

I left that job, and the following summer I made fifty cents more per hour at Lawrence Aviation in Port Jefferson. It was a sweatshop, a gigantic warehouse filled with huge ovens spewing flames directly from hell! There were sheets of metal everywhere you turned and huge vats of acid with dead animals floating around. The outside looked like a government zone where they experimented with nuclear bombs. The extreme outside temperatures were cooler then the warehouse, way cooler. And the product the warehouse manufactured was titanium. Among other things, it was used for military purposes and commercial airlines. My job was to inspect the titanium for defects and ensure it was ready for the next phase before delivery. I hope the company didn't actually rely on my expertise. I had no idea what the hell I was doing.

That was one dangerous job. The titanium dust that I breathed in, working with no mask, in a building with zero ventilation, probably took years off my life. Some of those sheets were thinner than razors. At some point we had to flip them, and if they started coiling, your fate was sealed. All anyone could do was watch the bloody horror show and take you to the emergency room. The sheets would come out of a red-hot oven, boasting what I believe were thousand degree temperatures. I came about two inches from falling face-first onto one of those and left that room real quick.

Breakfast for the college kid, then off to earn some cash.
Mom already had the pot of sauce on the stove.

One veteran worker demanded I go back to the room—"It isn't dangerous," he claimed.

Oh really? "Then how come the hand you are waving me back with only has two fingers?" Years later, Lawrence Aviation was in the news because of a government superfund to clean up the mess they made. I hope they didn't throw away the lung that I coughed up. I had a few other, more typical college jobs like landscaping, gas station attendant, and cleaning pools. The pool gig wasn't what I thought it would be. My vision of being a cabana boy for wealthy women in the Hamptons was quickly replaced by crazy dogs chasing me out of the yards.

I did manage to charm one woman though. Diane graduated from Longwood High School the year before me. We wanted nothing to do with each other until February 1991, when she showed up to watch her friends play hockey on a team I was a part of. When the game was over we went to our cars. It was very windy and freezing, and I was only wearing a T-shirt and shorts that were completely drenched with sweat. That was when she said, "Frankie, why don't you put your jacket on before you get sick?" It wasn't what she said as much as how she said it. I mean, she really didn't want me to get sick.

It's hard to explain—obviously a lot of people say things like that, but when she said it, it was different, it came from her heart. I became interested. We became a couple, and our relationship lasted on and off for seven or eight years. We got engaged but for the wrong reasons, and it didn't last. When she officially rid herself of me she said something that stuck: "Frankie, you're an amazing man, the best friend anyone could have, but you will not be a good husband." Ouch! She was right though. I wasn't ready for marriage yet. She was a great girl, so supportive and very caring, and I gave nothing back. Zero. We had some rough times but I'm thankful for my relationship with her (I'm not sure she would say the same). I hope her life is great. She deserves it. Hell, there's a woman from my past. Did she press charges? Impossible. I faithfully committed to her and I'd like to think there was a reason for that. Plus I haven't seen or spoken to her in so many years that I can't even tell you how many.

Here's something else that didn't work out: my college plan. My grade point average was so low that the university sent me a letter telling me to do better or get out. I tried everything to make up for my blunder so I could get into a physical therapy program. I did much better academically, and instead of volunteering the required one hundred hours, I approached the one thousand hour mark. I took a ton of science courses above the requirement, assisted in a research lab, and got a job as a physical therapy aide. If I had been that dedicated from the start, I wouldn't have been in that predicament. It wasn't enough. I tried to get into a program for the next couple of years but to no avail. The damage was done, and that "dream" was awoken from. Mr. Terry sure was right.

*Preparing to schmooze a bigwig in the physical
therapy program. That idea didn't work.*

I was still confident, though, and I didn't blink. I regrouped and went to my college advisor, who put both hands on her cheeks. "Wow! You have more science background than a science teacher. Do you want to be a school teacher?"

"Sure, why not?"

All I had to do was student teach and take a corresponding lecture course. I student taught at Sachem Central School District in the fall of 1995. I can't lie—the first time I was in front of the class, I stepped back from the chalkboard and thought it was pretty awesome to see "Mr. Vetro" written on the board. What wasn't so cool was that I also thought I could educate kids. Boy, was I wrong. I learned fast that all the theory and textbook stuff taught in college sounded great but it sure didn't work in the real world. After my first few days, I threw out my notes on theory and classroom management. That stuff would never work unless a person was teaching a class at Utopia High School. I adjusted and had a pretty successful experience. So in December 1995, about 178 credits and six years later, I earned a 120-credit, four-year degree with certifications to teach biology, chemistry, and general science.

Talk about taking the high road. No worries. The tortoise wins the race, and it was time for me to start making up ground. Mr. Terry's advice meant more to me now. I had to be proactive, work hard, and see the big picture. Since that setback, I always set short- and long-term goals. I even set goals for the day. Goals help a person focus and give a purpose. Even the smallest goal creates a feeling of accomplishment and something to build on. I was about to make my mark on education.

Chapter Three
A Pleasure Doing Business

It wasn't easy to find a teaching job, period, let alone find one in the middle of a school year, so I accepted a position as a substitute and then as a leave replacement in the Sachem Central School District during the second half of the 1995–1996 school year. As I taught I sent résumés to every school district on Long Island, and I was hired as a life science teacher in North Babylon School District's summer school program. Boy, did those kids take advantage of a rookie. They drove me crazy. I think I was being punished for all the shenanigans I myself pulled as a middle school student. As I worked I continued to send résumés to literally every school district on Long Island, whether they were hiring or not. I wasn't going to sit back and wait for something to fall in my lap. I got called on many interviews but screwed them up. The questions they asked concerned theory and textbook stuff that were irrelevant to being a quality educator. After several bad interviews, I learned to play the game. I spit out textbook answers on philosophy, theory, and pedagogy. They were concepts that I didn't believe in but knew the interview committees wanted to hear. It worked, and I got offers.

One interview offered some insight on Long Island education. I'll leave the name of the school district out, but it was located in Nassau County. It had a pretty tough student population in what a person might characterize as an undesirable neighborhood. The advertisement was for a high school science teacher with no further specifics. The building was everything I imagined, and I'm not being complimentary. Run-down is an understatement. The science chairman greeted me and sat me down in a classroom, and another science teacher joined us. They explained the position was for chemistry and handed me a New York State Regents exam to complete.

It was a hot, humid August day, and I couldn't answer any of the questions. They came back, and my suit jacket was off, my tie was undone, and I was dripping sweat. "Can I have a little more time?" They smiled and said yes. They came back forty minutes later, and I only had about five problems done—the easy ones such as "What is the symbol for hydrogen?" The gig was up. I grabbed my things, handed them my incomplete test, and apologized for wasting their time. They sat me back down. "Don't worry if you don't know the material. Our students are a tough population, and this school isn't very academically driven. Your résumé says that you're a black belt in martial arts. Just get one kid to pass the state assessment and keep the rest in line, and you'll be a hero. Can you do that?" I shook the man's hand. "Of course." It was the first time I wondered, when it comes to secondary education does education become secondary?

About a week later I decided to accept a job teaching biology in William Floyd Union Free School District located in Mastic Beach, New York. The math and science coordinator, Ms. Palmer, told me I was going to be a great teacher, showed me my classroom, and gave me a tour of the building. I recall she playfully commented that I had a charming "Brooklyn/Italian flavor" in my manner and speech. At one point we walked by one of two faculty lounges, the upstairs lounge. She stopped and with a very serious look stressed that I should not socialize in that room. She said there was another faculty lounge downstairs that was more appropriate. I wasn't sure what that meant and simply nodded in agreement.

When the 1996–1997 school year started, I was, for the first time, on my own full-time as Mr. Vetro. It was a great feeling. I worked hard night and day to stay afloat and become involved. All the coaching assignments and extracurricular activities were locked up, so I volunteered at night with the varsity football coach, Paul Luongo. When Ms. Palmer came into my classroom for an unannounced classroom observation in late September I didn't blink. No pressure—the students respected me enough to clam up and be on their extra best behavior, and Ms. Palmer gave a good review. My days were spent preparing for class and eating lunch in the "appropriate lounge" with my mentor, Alfonse Leonette, and a representative from the teachers union. I think his name was Bill Hennessy.

Everything was great until I walked by the "bad" lounge, where the "rogue" teachers associated. I couldn't resist. It was like putting a skull and crossbones on the door. I had to see what was going on so I poked my head in. The teachers were a little boisterous, not so politically correct, rough around the edges, and they liked to gamble a bit. There was a good time going on in that room. I stuck around and began socializing with these teachers. In time I got to know them, and actually they were not unlike many of the people I grew up with. They were nice people who worked hard, cared about the kids, and, God forbid, liked to have a good time at work.

I guess word got out because around the middle of October Ms. Palmer poked her head in as I shared a hearty laugh with Greg Bradley, a member of this group that playfully called themselves Asshole Island. I might have been handing him a twenty-dollar bill for something but I can neither confirm nor deny that (wink). If looks could kill! She gave me the stare of death and shut the door. A hush came over the crowd as if I had been stricken with a plague. What was the problem? I worked hard, did my job well, and did whatever my bosses asked of me. After that day I was a dead man walking. The administration became sticklers with their classroom observations. They started to make a big deal out of little things that a first year teacher, on the job for only a few months, would naturally have to improve. For example in December 1996 the principal, Mr. Feeney, wrote me up because I made a spelling error during a lesson. The word I misspelled was malpighian as I described parts of a grasshopper. He didn't even realize that error—who would? I'm the one who corrected it after realizing I misplaced the "h." Humans make mistakes. Here's the kicker, when he wrote up his evaluation of my lesson, *he* misspelled malpighian!

I was informed by quite a few insiders that William Floyd had a reputation for getting rid of non-tenured teachers en masse, and once again they were doing just that. Due to my association with the "undesirable" teachers, I was going to be one of them. I wasn't shaken at all. I refused to be pulled down by nonsense. I didn't need Ms. Palmer, Mr. Feeney, or Superintendent Mr. Hawkins, who, during the last week of school, asked me who I was. I said I was one of the teachers his district was letting go, and added, "With all due respect, the teacher quality will be severely downgraded with my departure." I shook his hand, smiled, and chatted with him. I had no hard feelings towards any of my supervisors.

My résumés were already out, and I was getting job offers and happy to leave.

I took away positives from my year at Floyd. The kids were great, the staff was great, and I gained a year of experience. Many times it's just as important to learn what not to do as it is to learn what to do, and I learned some things about being an educational leader. My bosses at William Floyd completely turned off a young, energetic teacher who was willing to do anything for the school. They judged me by the company I kept. When I became an educational leader, I was sure to nurture the untamed energy of a young employee and never judge people by their personal choices. Are they good people? Do they care about kids? Are they professional at work? That's what's important. If people don't learn to separate business from personal issues, they will wind up in a career and life filled with misery. Before leaving Floyd, I said good-bye to Jim Griffin and Claude Fox, and Greg Bradley was nice enough to give me the name of his friend, a principal in Miller Place Union Free School District, Dan Nolan. "He will help you if you need it," Greg assured me. I never reached out to Mr. Nolan, but I periodically heard his name for the next seven or eight years.

Just as the 1997–1998 school year was to begin, I accepted a position teaching biology and chemistry in the Middle Country Central School District, located in the Selden and Centereach areas of Long Island. Yes, back to chemistry, but with some know-how under my belt, I was able to swing it. Within a few weeks on the job is when I met Marc Meyer, a first-year guidance counselor. We were the same age, and, like me, he was positive, personable, and ambitious. I remember having a drink with Marc one Friday afternoon, as was the norm, and he brought up the topic of going the administrative route. He was reading my mind. After what happened at William Floyd, I wanted as few people as possible as my boss and decided to become a principal and superintendent. I planned the next five years of my life to get experience in as many areas of education as I could. I wanted a complete understanding, not just the view from the eyes of a classroom teacher. I began each and every workday with that mind-set.

During my second year at Newfield, my engagement to Diane ended. Some people go on vacation when they are down, some go on spending sprees, and some sit around lamenting in a state of depression. I was sad but couldn't sit like a poor soul. I kept moving. I finished up my master's degree at Stony Brook University in December 1998, and went back to school to earn an additional ninety credits in educational pedagogy. I dragged a colleague of mine, Gilda, to many of those courses. Day and night, weekends, summer—the pursuit was a grind on both of us, but we made the best of it and had a ton of laughs together.

I would get to work so early that a custodian would unlock the door for me. That was when I did my prep work, when no one was around. That gave me the opportunity to make the rounds during the school day. Many teachers stay isolated in their classrooms and don't realize what goes on in other departments or throughout the district. They don't understand all the implications a principal's decisions have on a building. My free periods were spent soaking up information from administrators and chatting with teachers, secretaries, and custodians. I wanted to learn about their thoughts instead of seeing just my perspective as a teacher. I also liked to chat, briefly, with students. They were important to me as people, not just as teenagers that had to learn the subject matter.

I taught biology and chemistry. I stayed late giving extra help, coached various sport teams, chaperoned events, worked at the alternative high school, and taught summer school. I even decided to become a union representative and then a grievance chairperson. I was determined to have a grasp on every aspect of education. My evaluations were always excellent, and I received a Special Teacher Award for my efforts. My philosophy on work was embedded in me as a kid when I asked my dad what his job was: "Frankie, my job is to make my boss's life easier." It's as simple as that, and I went about each day making my supervisor's job easier. I was never one to sit around the rumor mill, not willing to do anything extra because of contractual concerns. That's nonsense that creates an us-against-them mentality and is not conducive to a productive work environment. Professionally I did everything right.

Personally I lead the bachelor life—and then some. If I wasn't doing something work related, I was at the gym, on a date, at a happy hour, or doing something, anything. I was young, energetic, and professional. I kept myself in shape, came from a good family, and, pardon me for saying, had a good personality. I was also always around women by way of the teaching profession and after-hours get-togethers, and that sure made it convenient. Unfortunately, my nightlife and weekend extravaganzas became the talk of the town. People who didn't even know me spoke about what they "heard" I did the night before. Man, some of those stories were so exaggerated, some. Spread rumors, pass on juicy stories that were no one's business, and judge everyone but yourself were the norm at Newfield though.

Downtime at Newfield HS, circa 1999.

It's not as if I went out just to have a good time. I was always working on my agenda and networking to make my way up the ranks. Just like in the business world, many deals and associations in education are formed over a drink. I was a hard worker and extremely reliable. I never took off from work. I was always respectful to everyone. I never lied, manipulated, or forced any type of relationship on a woman. Sure, many of the relationships involved sex, but that was between consenting adults who had the choice to walk away. I won't apologize for being out on my free time. I never did anything illegal, always made conscientious decisions, never jeopardized my health or anyone else's, and never did anything to embarrass my family, my school district, or myself. Certainly it never interfered with my job performance or I would've quickly changed my lifestyle. To be honest, I think ninety percent of men and a decent percentage of women would have loved the lifestyle I was living. Maybe if my coworkers' lives were complete or at least more interesting, they wouldn't have felt the need to talk about mine.

Some say that teachers have too much time on their hands. I could write an entire book about all the screwing around that went on, not just in my school district, but in education in general. I also don't mean just with single people but also married individuals. When it came to having liaisons at Middle Country Central School District it was like the red-light district. The relationships many of the teachers were having were not rated for general audiences. The happy hours turned into feeding frenzies, clothing optional. So many people were up to no good but I never judged them. If the public only knew who was teaching their kids. I could fill an entire volume with explicit stories about a young school administrator in the New York education system, from the Hamptons to Manhattan. At least I was single.

During this same time period I ran into a first-year social studies teacher, Michelle Konik—literally. She was hurriedly turning the corner of the hallway, on her way upstairs, and she bumped into me. She was attractive—blonde hair, blue eyes, about five feet three inches tall, and had an excellent figure. At first, we never spoke—ever. I kept a distance because she was having an affair with Jim, another teacher, and a friend of mine. A skinny, jock type, he couldn't have been more than 150 pounds. He was a real personality and a great friend who would do anything for anyone. No doubt he was an intense, hard worker and very dedicated to the students and the school district in general.

The problem was that he was married with kids. I didn't give a shit. It wasn't my responsibility to monitor their lives, and I was never one to judge someone else. Who knows what's going on in someone else's personal life? I did wonder why an attractive girl with so many things going for her would be involved with a married guy, but I didn't belabor the point. It wasn't my concern.

Jim and I had some ridiculous times together—about three years of total debauchery—and I lived to tell about it. No matter where we went drinking—Mike's Place in Coram, the Beach Bar in Hampton Bays, Lily Flanagans in Islip, Planet Dublin in Stony Brook, the Fifty-Six Fighter Club in Melville, Popei's Clam Bar, or any other place that served drinks on Long Island—the stories always made their way back to work. Unfortunately the affair between Jim and Michelle became very public. The workplace already was a breeding ground for sexual rumors, and the ones about them topped the charts. Hey, those rumors at least temporarily knocked me out of the number-one spot. For a short stint I didn't have to hear how I was sexually involved with women in every building of the district—including central office.

The nightlife didn't get in my way professionally. When it was time to work, I never missed a beat. I forged ahead with my plan of becoming an educational leader in the fall of 2001. After securing exceptional recommendations from two of my supervisors, Sue Bove and Mike Tesoreiro, I walked into my principal's office to discuss my intentions. Mr. Ross shook my hand. "Mr. Vetro, you're a great teacher and hard worker. I think you will be great at anything you do. Follow your heart." I was back in school, this time the Queens College Administrative Program. My administrative internship brought me the longest days imaginable. I would get to work around 5:30 a.m. to prepare for my teaching day. Immediately after the final bell, I coached varsity football up until about 4:30 p.m. From there I would go back to the building to supervise at the alternative program. My day ended around 8:00 p.m. unless there was a board of education meeting or I was assisting the district office with a project. I enjoyed where my life was, and in October 2001, I met a great woman named Suzanne. It was her first year in the district. And no, I didn't sleep with her. I liked her and wanted a legitimate relationship.

Suddenly it hit the fan with Michelle and Jim. Rumors were flying, and everyone was speculating. I couldn't and didn't believe any of them, because I witnessed most of their escapades. It escalated—fast. In November, Jim told me he wouldn't be at work because he called in sick to go to the dentist. The next thing I knew, I, along with many others, was called into the district office to be questioned for a massive investigation into their affair. The assistant superintendent for personnel, Richard Herman, questioned me. I didn't want anyone in trouble and truthfully explained everything I witnessed: consensual adults, whether morally right or wrong, had an affair. I witnessed nothing else, and I was around to witness more than anyone else. Nobody did anything wrong other than have a personal affair.

I never learned what the investigative findings were, but Jim wasn't allowed to return to work. I never saw him again. He literally disappeared into the wind. The rumor mill churned as to what may have happened, but nobody really knew, and I don't listen to gossip. By December 2001, Jim was gone, and Michelle remained. That was a really crazy time, and one result that I do know of was that my budding relationship with Suzanne went south just about overnight. She didn't need a reason to be on the administration's radar as a first-year employee, and when I got caught up in the middle of that scandal, we kind of drifted apart. I can't figure out any other reason it didn't work out between us. Even then Suzanne and I were always on good terms, so I can't imagine her pressing charges against me. Why would she? Then again, why would anyone?

Michelle and I began to speak in 2002. I asked her about the details with Jim, but she said she was trying to forget about that part of her life. I figured I would respect that. It wasn't like I thought she was innocent in the affair. I saw her as a person who made a mistake. We all have that moment in life that we don't want anyone to know about. Think about it. Out of your entire life, there has to be something you're not proud of. What if everyone knew that lowest moment you had and they constantly judged you by that, every day? Would that be fair? Would that be a true evaluation of your character? The body of work should represent an individual, not their weakest moment in time. And that was how I approached the situation. Nobody wants to be judged by his or her worst moment in time.

Michelle was about twenty-eight years old and living with her parents. She told me her life was in disarray and asked me to help her out. The kennel that she said she owned in Coram was run down, and I helped her clean it up. I suggested a financial planner and someone to help her with her taxes, both of whom I knew personally, and both helped her out. I motivated her to go to school so she could earn credits and get pay raises. I didn't think she had friends, so I invited her to spend time with mine. I honestly felt bad for her and enjoyed helping her. I would have done the same for anyone else.

I helped her so much that she gave me a CD recording, "In Your Eyes" by Peter Gabriel on which she inscribed, "Made especially for you." I was careful in accepting that gift. She was a friend but I did not want her as a girlfriend. I was honest with her, sometimes brutally so. I just wanted to be single, have a little fun, and focus on my professional goals. She was in complete agreement and wanted to get her life in order anyway. Of course, nothing is that simple, and it did eventually turn sexual. How was

I, a single guy, to resist an attractive body, and a woman who didn't mind being just friends and having sex? The old phrase "friends with benefits" described us perfectly. I continued to see other girls. Michelle accepted it and showed appreciation for our friendship with notes thanking me for being an inspiration in her life, a wonderful person, and her very dear friend.

We were a great team, and our friendship was by no means a one-way street with sex as the sole and final destination every time we were together. Michelle also helped me out. She was an electronics whiz, and I was (and still am) technologically challenged, so she helped me do research, create PowerPoint presentations, program my cell phone, and do anything else related to computers or electronics. She would cook and do many other things. I never once asked her for this help. She was glad to do it, and I was very appreciative of everything. I realize I should have resisted the physical aspect of our relationship. Few men in my place would have resisted this sexual genie in a bottle. I know that's not an excuse. Hey, as crazy as the relationship may sound, it worked for us. Michelle might be the best friend I ever had.

After that situation with Suzanne didn't work out, I was at it again with other women in the district. Allison Engstrom, a well-endowed math teacher, was one of them. I discovered she was well endowed first hand during a happy hour but I will resist telling just how I made the discovery. I personally never found Allison attractive. The drinking had a lot to do with our conversations. She seemed like an easygoing, nice enough person though. My first encounter with her was at a bar, Irish Times. Allison and her friend, another math teacher, caught a ride with a social studies teacher named Kelly, who had to leave early. They asked me if I could take them back to their car, and since it was on my way home, I obliged. Allison sat in the passenger's seat while her friend gave me a sensual neck and back massage. But I decided it was time to leave shortly afterward. I had another agenda. It was harmless and uneventful.

Some time went by, and we both found ourselves at another bar, Mike's Place, for happy hour. A lot of drinking and of course a lot of sexual bantering went along with it. As the night progressed, everyone left, but I stayed behind to have a drink and chat with some other people I knew. Allison also stayed a bit longer, and eventually we were driving toward Huntington to go to a gentlemen's club. Yep, it happened that fast at Newfield High School. I hate strip clubs (I swear), but she said she wanted to go and I thought it would be interesting if she got a lap dance from a female stripper. After spending some time at the club she asked me to pull my pants down so she and a stripper could check me out. I nearly spit my drink out trying to control my laughter. Enough had been said, and the eventuality was obvious to both of us. We decided to go to the Commack Motor Inn.

When we got to the room, I was barely in the door and her breasts were up close and personal. We got down to business, but I couldn't actually go through with having intercourse with her. I wasn't that drunk, and honestly I just wasn't attracted to her. Both the beer and I really just wanted to go to the strip club with her, and both the beer and I decided it was time to get the hell out of there. I made up some story about my truck being broken into. Go figure—her and her beer fell for that, and we left.

One other time, at an establishment located in Blue Point called Cavanaugh's, she invited me to meet her and her friend out, but I respectfully declined. Allison came out to happy hour on October 31, 2003, after my last day at Newfield, and we spoke on the phone a few times after, but it never amounted to anything more than that one sojourn to a strip club and a motel where nothing much happened. For the life of me I couldn't think of a reason she would file a complaint against me. She couldn't have.

Around the same time period I became very social with another woman, Ada. She was awesome and we became good friends too. Not much else I could say about that. There's no way in hell she filed a complaint, no way possible.

Continuing down memory lane, Michelle Rogak was a science teacher at Newfield. When I first met her, she told me she worked at Hooters which was strange because she was not the least bit endowed. She was attractive and had a cute body. During the summer of 2002 I had to tend to some business at my district's other high school, Centereach. On my way out, I paid her a visit to congratulate her because I heard she just got engaged. When I congratulated her, she shrugged off the conversation and changed gears by inviting me to go to the beach with her. Uh, what? I didn't go.

When the 2002–2003 school year started, I asked her if she wanted to work at the districts evening school for at-risk students. I figured she probably needed some extra cash for her wedding, and we needed a science teacher. She agreed, and she did a great job. It wound up giving us more time to talk too, and we got to know each other a little better.

One night the usual group was having drinks at Mike's Place. Rogak approached me because she wanted a ride home. No problem. During the ride, she wanted to show me the house that, she said, she and her fiancé were going to live in. If I remember correctly it was somewhere in or near the H section, in Coram. I took the tour and she grabbed my hand to slowly guide me from room to room. I didn't take the bait, suggested we leave, and dropped her off. It was still early, but I had enough for the night. The year went by with a lot of the same nonsense, but I avoided being involved with a woman who was engaged—not that that's something to be proud of. A person is supposed to avoid that stuff.

Meanwhile, the friendship Michelle Konik and I shared created an unstoppable team. We were helping each other accomplish our individual goals. There was nothing we couldn't do, and both our lives were better for the assistance we provided each other. On February 19, 2003, Michelle once again showed her appreciation for our friendship, giving me a book with a personal note inside that said things like: You are amazing, you inspire me every day, there is no one like you, and my one in a million guy. I was hoping she didn't mean that last one literally, because I didn't plan on being anyone's guy.

When the school year ended in June 2003, a coworker, Keith Hasek, had an end-of-the-year party at his house. Michelle Rogak was there, not wearing her engagement ring. She told me her engagement was off. I didn't expect the games to begin so quickly, but things always escalated real fast at Newfield. When I excused myself to go to the bathroom, Rogak followed and closed the door behind her. That's where everything came to a head.

She came over to my apartment many times during that summer. She was cool with the understanding that we were just having fun together, and she really was a lot of fun. I liked her. We continued whatever you would call it into the next school year and then just stopped speaking after I left Newfield. I did see her out and speak with her a couple of times. One night, while at a bar/club called the Crazy Donkey, she told me her engagement broke off after I left Newfield. If that were true then she lied to me and was still engaged when we screwed around. Either way I never had any issues with her. Maybe she was disappointed about how things panned out between us? But even then it was so long ago and disliking me would have nothing to do with having me arrested. I couldn't begin to explain why she would file a complaint against me. She couldn't have.

In 2003, I made a solid push to get to the next level professionally. Of course, my peers had to be the most negative influence possible, with comments like "You'll never get a job as an administrator" and "Why would you leave such a safe, secure job?" I knew then and there that I didn't belong in the district anymore. The negativity was immense. The district offered me an opportunity to gain some experience by appointing me as the principal of the summer school program and head of the science department. I was very appreciative of the opportunity and wasn't going to let it slip away. I committed myself to making sure I ran the best department and summer school program the district had ever seen. I made sure to tap into my resources. Ken Stanton, the summer school principal for many years prior, was always happy to answer any question I had. He was a great mentor and would not let me fail.

When the 2003–2004 school year started, I was approached by John Ried, the assistant superintendent who appointed me summer school principal. He shook my hand, "Frank, that was the most successful summer school we ever had. Congratulations and thank you." I thanked him for the opportunity.

I acquired some experience and was drawing some positive attention. But the more I thought about it, the more I realized I wouldn't feel comfortable as an administrator in a district where I had so many personal relationships. It was time to leave my mistakes behind and get out of Dodge. That was why I had already sent résumés all over Long Island. More often than not, the only way to move up is to get out.

One of the districts I applied to was Hampton Bays, in the Southampton Township. They were looking for an assistant principal for their secondary building, which housed grades seven through twelve. It was a small school with only about eight hundred students for all six grades. I was familiar with the town because I had spent a lot of time there, albeit partying. I knew the makeup of the community pretty well and thought the school and I would be a perfect fit. The downside to becoming an administrator in large schools like the ones I had been associated with is that you can easily lose touch with the students. In Hampton Bays I could be an administrator and yet still know and understand the student population in a meaningful way.

They called me for an interview in early September, and unlike the many botched interviews I had out of college, I was ready. It was a pretty grueling process, three rounds of interviews in front of almost twenty people, but my presentation became stronger each round. I was hired about three weeks later and couldn't wait to get there and build the work environment that I had always envisioned. I wanted the positive rapport with students, teachers, and staff that I thought was missing in the school districts where I worked. I couldn't wait to introduce my blue-collar, roll-up-your-sleeves-and-get-dirty attitude to work with teachers, not against them. I intended to create a positive atmosphere where everyone in the educational community supported one another to achieve a common goal. I was certain I could accomplish this.

My last day at Newfield was Friday, October 31. On November 3, 2003, I was to begin a new life in Hampton Bays. I received many heartfelt cards and letters from my superiors, students, and faculty members. I'm not naïve, though—I'm sure others were happy to see me go. Not everyone is going to like you. Unfortunately, there were a few students who thought I quit on them. One card read, "Mr. Vetro, you always taught us to never quit, and now you quit on us in the middle of the school year." That made me sad. I always preached about believing in yourself and never quitting. I wish that student and all the others who felt that way understood I would never quit on them or forget about them. Overall it was a nice departure, and the cards and gifts continued to show up at my office in Hampton Bays in the months to follow. My Newfield students were great. They drove me crazy at times, but that's what teenagers do.

I would like to think I was a positive influence on them. One of my strong points is discipline. I am quick to enforce rules, but only because I care. I always felt that schools didn't prepare students for the world. There are too many safety nets. Yes, I wanted my students to learn science and do well on the state assessments, but to me that was secondary. The process by which they learned was more important than what they learned. That's why I tried to use positive reinforcement when they did the right things. That's why I took time to chat about their interests. Character traits like respect, pride, integrity, etc. are what I wanted to instill in them. After all, we forget the facts as we move through life. It's how we learn the facts that shape our lives forever. I showed an interest in their lives and took time out of my day for them. Sprinkle in some discipline, some science knowledge, and a few laughs, and I think I did an okay job. After hearing the news of my hiring in Hampton Bays, Michelle gave me a card:

Baby, what can I say? You are amazing. I am so proud of you. I am so excited just knowing you are going to be the best thing that ever happened to Hampton Bays. I've told you a million times how much I believe in you. I will

never stop. You, to this day, are still the most inspirational
person in my life. I love listening to you. I respect and
admire your dedication, motivation, and passion to be the
best at all you set out to do. The best thing is that you are
mine now! And I love you!!!

That card illustrated the number one reason I had to leave. I wasn't in
the mind-set to have a girlfriend, and I was not all hers. If we were going to
remain friends, then it was best for me to leave. It was worth it if it meant
keeping our friendship. My district could not contractually give me a leave
of absence. That was fine, because I knew I wasn't returning. I was leaving a
very cushy job with a ton of job security to take a chance on a new position
in a new district. My fellow union members thought I was crazy to leave
on those terms without the security and a safety net. "What if you don't
succeed?" Add that to my list of reasons for leaving. I didn't want to wind
up with that complacent, don't-want-to-take-a-chance mentality. Tenure
and job security were not going to stand in the way of a challenge. I learned
early that if I didn't believe in myself, nobody else would either.

*When I was in Longwood Middle School, the administration
and my guidance counselor refused to put me in a foreign language
class. They told me that course was for capable students. Between
the troublemakers I associated with back then and the fact that I
was called to the principal's office for my forays into "boxing," they
thought I was too immature and would fail. They didn't believe me
when I said I would work hard and do well. Thankfully the Italian
teacher, Mr. Samperi, put his neck on the line and successfully
lobbied for me to be in the class. I was never averse to hard work,
and I was determined to prove my detractors wrong and make Mr.
Samperi proud of his decision. It wasn't hard to do. Mr. Samperi's
lessons were so hands-on, so hysterically entertaining, and so over
the top that you couldn't help but remember them. I loved him and
his class, and so did everyone else. I excelled so much that I was
placed in the accelerated course the following year. Mr. Samperi
spoke to me about the entire situation: "Frankie, believe in yourself
and your ability, because people are negative and will try to hold
you back." Those were powerful words for a middle school kid, but
they were well taken.*

41

Like my days on the handball courts, I was betting on myself; therefore, it was a sure thing. On my last day at Newfield I sat at my desk and reflected on a conversation I had with a veteran teacher during my first year. We were both in the science office when a student came to me with a very nervous, needy look on his face. He wanted to talk, but I just yessed him to death as I scrambled to get materials for my next lesson. He walked away with a halfhearted "Thanks, Mr. Vetro." The veteran teacher explained that during my career, there would be moments when I wouldn't have time for students, but sometimes I would have to make the time, because many students don't have the support of friends and family. He sadly said he had a similar situation his first year teaching. "Frank, the student I ignored went home and killed himself, and to this day I wonder if I could have made a difference."

I scrambled to find that kid. I couldn't reach him and was a nervous wreck and couldn't sleep. The next day I made sure I found that youngster as soon as he walked through the doors. Thankfully his dilemma wound up not being serious. I wonder to this day if that story was even true, but either way I learned my lesson. It's a lesson that everyone should learn. We all have to be better listeners. We should not just hear someone, but listen.

I endured many positve and negative experiences in my short career as a classroom teacher and appreciated all of them for what they taught me. I learned a lot about what to do as an administrator, but maybe more importantly, I learned what not to do. I often think about that interview when I couldn't answer any chemistry questions on the state exam. My instincts that day were correct. Education is filled with bureaucracy and hidden agendas. Many people lose sight of the real purpose of education: the students. Indeed, education becomes secondary. I walked out of Newfield High School on October 31, 2003, Halloween, and didn't look back.

I suppose my approach with Michelle Konik and the lifestyle I was leading with so many women, many of whom haven't even been mentioned, does not shed a positive light on me. That's fair, and I accept it. But I can look anybody in the eye and say I never placed myself in the life of someone who didn't ask me to be there. I was a young man who had been in a faithful, monogamous relationship with one woman my entire adult life, and when that ended, I simply wanted to have some fun. No doubt I could have done some things differently, but that doesn't make me a criminal— which is why I couldn't figure out the reason I was sitting in Riverhead Jail.

Chapter Four
The Only Way Up Was Out

My extended family already thought my parents had moved us to another planet, all the way in the suburbs of Suffolk County, an hour from New York City. If they only knew I was about to commute another forty-five minutes east. November 3, 2003, was one of the best days of my life. I woke up, put on a new suit, and headed toward Hampton Bays. The song playing on the radio was "Dreams" by Van Halen. I used to play that song prior to my martial arts tournaments, and I took the fact that it was on the radio as a sign that things were going to be great. The ride to work, although longer, was much more relaxing. Driving into the sun and taking a more scenic ride on Long Island's south shore, toward the Hamptons, had a different feel compared to when the sun was at my back driving to Newfield in the center of Long Island—perhaps further symbolism that my life was headed in the right direction. It felt good making a fresh start.

Four new administrators were hired in the district. The superintendent, Joanne Loewenthal, was brought in to get the district moving in the right direction. She brought her colleague from upstate New York, Nicholas Dyno, to be the secondary school principal. Two assistant principals were hired to help him, me being one of them and Linda Anthony the other. My close friend Marc Meyer had also recently become the elementary school assistant principal. Nick Dyno was a very intelligent man. He was well spoken, and loved to throw around educational jargon. He spent a lot of time in his office and, at least to me, always seemed on edge. I always thought he was going to have a heart attack. It was a shame he didn't socialize more, because he was a pretty funny guy and easygoing. He had a strange way of going about things. His approach seemed so chaotic, but in the end it all came together. His mind was the epitome of organized chaos. He did a great job though and had some real good ideas for the building.

I was his perfect complement. I had the energy and the roll-up-your-sleeves, blue-collar mentality he wanted. I was the disciplinarian he was looking for, the person who could be everywhere all the time, who could dole out consequences to wrongdoers while still earning their respect. Sometimes I felt like I was his bodyguard, protecting him from the dangers of the community. Whenever things got out of control, I would step in to buffer him from the situation—a sort of administrative secret service. We had very different styles that when combined formed a terrific team. I loved working with him. He trusted me and gave me a lot of leeway to act on my own and learn. I knew that if I needed help or made a mistake I had his full support. It was so much work, but we had a ton of fun working together—a ton.

On the first day of school, I entered the building and asked myself, "Now what do I do?" I pretended I knew what I was doing for a few days while I settled in. I stationed myself in the main lobby as teachers began to arrive. That's something I made a habit of doing. The first teacher that walked into the building, Barbara, showed no emotion, just a blank, zombie-like stare. She looked at me, said, "We need you," and kept walking. I didn't know what to make of her comment. As more teachers and students entered the building, I noticed a peculiar dynamic. The teachers were fed up, while the students acted as if they owned the school. They didn't respond to the requests of adults and lingered in the halls with absolutely no intention of ever going to class. They had a false sense of entitlement. The hallways seemed to have more kids in them than the classrooms. For such a small school, the building was very loud and chaotic.

I learned fast that the district had absolutely no structure to it at all thanks to constant administrative turnover and no stable leadership. Principals and assistant principals only stayed a couple of years at most before moving on. They either couldn't last or chose to move on to what they thought were better opportunities. As a result, there was no vision, no educational philosophy, no policies, nothing. The veteran teachers had seemingly thrown in the towel, and the younger teachers had no structure or leadership to learn how to be an effective educator. The morale could not have been any lower at the school, and there was very little, if any, trust between the administration and the teachers union. Years of downward spiraling in both discipline and leadership left the district, in my opinion, on the verge of a state takeover. I was scratching my head after the first week, wondering what I had gotten myself into.

I went home and had a drink or two—or three. I had never seen a school so disorganized. I don't know how anything ever went right there. I had only been associated with very large districts to that point, and there is no doubt in my mind that if those buildings were as chaotic as Hampton Bays was, there would have been assaults, riots—you name it. It would have been a war zone.

That's the funny thing. Nothing really bad was actually happening among the students. Yeah, they did a lot of dumb things that every teenager would do if undisciplined or unsupervised, but I was used to much worse. In fact, growing up I definitely hung around with much worse and maybe even did worse myself. For change to occur, the philosophy had to change. We had to reel the entire building back in.

I spent the weekend gathering my thoughts and figuring out what my game plan would be and how I could help make my boss's life easier. I thought about my vision and the events and lessons I learned in my life and career. I went to my old reliable and made a list—a list of the standards I lived by, what I liked and disliked about my former bosses, and what I thought a school system should be. I figured out how I could apply my approach to life toward a better future in Hampton Bays. When I was done, everything seemed much clearer. It wouldn't be easy, but at least there was a plan that could be systematically carried out. Of course, my plan meant nothing without the approval of Mr. Dyno, but as was the case most of the time, we were in complete agreement and would use each of our strengths to balance the other's weaknesses.

It was Nick's building, he had to oversee everything, including my performance. It's hard to detail what a high school principal and assistant principal do on a daily basis. It's literally nonstop—the phone calls, the meetings, and the amount of fires you put out with the students and teachers, and the balance of the staff. Throw in the community members, and you really can't plan on five free minutes. You're on call every second of every day, and you always have to have your A game. This doesn't include the paper work that had to be done. It was impossible to get anything done during the day. Lunch? What lunch? When the day ended, it was important for me to attend after-school activities because they were important to the students. Of course, all this is done when the job is being done the right way. My responsibility was to bring structure and order to the building, create

45

policy, build morale and a mutual respect throughout the educational community, and maybe, most of all, discipline the students. That was something that had not been done effectively in years. Whoever coined the phrase "The tail is wagging the dog" must have worked at Hampton Bays.

Together, Mr. Dyno and I embarked on a long-term working relationship to accomplish our plan—every day for twelve, fourteen, and sometimes even more hours a day, sometimes seven days a week. It was a slow go, as there was resistance. The teachers were abandoned so many times and reluctant to trust someone who had just showed up on their doorstep. Twenty years of neglect was not going to be erased in a month. Simply put, I gave my life to that district. I was hired to help turn the ship around, and I didn't want to let them down. Regarding leadership, you can have a ton of great ideas, but if people aren't willing to work for you and with you, then it doesn't matter. If the teachers weren't going to come aboard, then we would be failures. We had to win their trust.

I was the first one at work every morning and the last one to leave. I ran around like a mad man, through the building, in the parking lot, through the fields, or in town. I was compelled to be everywhere at every second. Whatever the issue, people knew their concern was my concern. It was some workout. There are hundreds if not thousands of events that take place throughout the school year. I attended almost every one of them— sporting events, practices, plays, musicals, etc. I also helped organize and/ or participated in tons of fundraisers and charities for the community. When nothing was going on I worked out with the kids in the weight room or jogged around the track or over the Ponquoge Bridge to Dune Road. I spent time in the town, went to Starbucks for a cup of coffee, and chatted with community members. I wanted to understand the culture of the community. I didn't do it just to win people over. I did it because I really cared. I wasn't going to be yet another fly-by-night administrator at Hampton Bays. My personal life became secondary to the educational community.

As the boss, I had to give directives to much older, veteran teachers who were set in their ways and had tenure and job security. It's a tough way to manage and a tough balancing act. I didn't want to give the impression that I was a pushover. I had to be firm and flexible at the same time. Even with the stress of the tremendously high-energy building and the extremely long hours, I loved it. I could succeed in any school district—or profession, for that matter—but that town for some reason seemed like the perfect place for me at that time in my life. The school needed so much time and effort, more than others. Nick Dyno and I began to take huge steps and pick up a full head of steam to move the school in the right direction. It's a funny thing—the higher I moved up the ladder, the more I became a servant to the community I was leading.

Softball fundraiser in Hampton Bays. Terrible batting stance.
© Photography by Gina Esposito.

47

The staff was beginning to have faith in the administration. Teachers learned they had my support as long as they worked hard and were professional. I didn't have to like the individual or agree with his or her personal choices. I also didn't always agree with them professionally, but they came to understand that it wasn't personal and I always had good intentions. When I was wrong, I was the first to admit it and quickly apologized. I ignored the gossip and rumor mills. I didn't want the building to be like that. There's a saying that administration 101 is a course that teaches future administrators how to divide and conquer the staff. I didn't want that crap. I wanted everyone to be one happy collective, working toward a common goal and being part of something bigger than each individual. I wanted staff to be friendly and enjoy working with each other. Work could not only be more pleasant but also a little more productive. As I suspected, by and large the teachers were fine. They just needed to trust again.

As far as discipline was concerned, I had a ton of heated battles with students, and community members. Parents all want discipline until it's their kids being disciplined. Hampton Bays was definitely not used to discipline but I was not going to back down. It's not easy to discipline yet still have the students appreciate you, but I think I accomplished that. By the end of the first school year, the community began to understand that I cared for their well-being. They were more accepting of my disciplinary measures and began to accept more responsibility for their actions. It didn't make me the bad guy. It made me the guy who finally gave a damn.

In fact, during Senior Awards Night, after the graduating students received their awards and scholarships, they presented me with a plaque for my effective and caring approach to discipline. The plaque was titled with my theme for the year: Eight Basic Rules. Its purpose was to refocus on very basic, daily routines throughout a school day that were no longer seen as important. It was nothing revolutionary as far as disciplinary philosophy—why reinvent the wheel? I just put common sense principles to work for me and remained consistent with their implementation. It made me feel good that the very students I disciplined and at times had expelled from school understood and appreciated why I did it. It's one of my proudest moments.

Hampton Bays was much different from Middle Country School District. Many times when you work in large school districts, you get lost in the mix, whether you're great or terrible at your job, with no one seeming to notice or care either way. That didn't happen in Hampton Bays. Most importantly, the women in my life and the mistakes I made with them were gone, left back at Newfield.

Michelle Konik remained an excellent friend. I didn't see her at work every day, so that made our friendship easier. In February of 2004, she gave me a letter describing how all of my words had affected her life in a positive way. It read, "To Frank, my true friend, your words will stay with me forever." It concludes, "Thank you for touching my life. You continue to inspire me each and every day." Shortly after, she gave me a book with a note: "Frank, you will go over the top! Congratulations. Love, Michelle." I know I shouldn't have continued to sleep with her, but we never had any real tension. We remained great friends and were always there for each other.

In fact that same spring, she called me extremely frightened, claiming an individual was outside her house, on drugs and harassing her. I dropped what I was doing and drove over her house. When I arrived, she was filing a report with the police, and there were no signs of him anywhere in the vicinity. I gave her a warning. She didn't exactly live in the best neighborhood. She was a small, single woman and needed to be more careful about who she let into her life, let alone her house. Maybe I was a little stern that day, but although I may not have been in love with her, she's my dear friend, and I still care about her. As we discussed the situation, an eleventh grade student of hers, Stephanie Veraldi, entered the room. She apparently helped out at Michelle's kennel. Michelle claimed it was strictly professional and school sponsored and that Newfield High School knew about it. That sounded pretty strange—as in not legitimate. I happened to speak with a Newfield High School administrator who was aware of the community service involving Michelle. All I could say in response was that Newfield had better be careful. As an administrator I would never have approved such community service.

I was rarely at Michelle's kennel. I didn't like the smell of the bichon frise dogs. There were tons of them. Plus, my friend Leo Baez was fixing up her house/kennel, and I didn't want my friendship jeopardized with either of them if the business arrangement soured. It was best I stayed away. The times we did see each other, Michelle drove to my house. She was always very appreciative of my assistance to her. In the beginning of 2005 she gave me a book about famous speeches in history with a handwritten note: You'll be in the next edition, I'm sure of it! Love ya.

Shortly after, in February, Michelle called me from the annual Westminster Kennel Club Dog Show at Madison Square Garden, the world series of dog shows. Michelle had won her group and was moving on to the next round that evening. Nick Dyno told me I should leave work a little early and attend the evening competition. I didn't want to send Michelle mixed messages, but I went because it was a major accomplishment for her and big news in the dog breeder world. I knew how excited she was and figured no one else would show up for her.

I grabbed a train to the Garden, but when I arrived I wasn't happy. It was a school day, and her student Stephanie was there. Michelle already had a questionable attendance record because she took off to go to dog shows, and now she had taken a student out of school to attend an event. What if something terrible happened? How would Michelle or the school explain it? Michelle swore to me that Newfield had sponsored the event as a part of the community service. "Michelle," I asked, "how can a dog show for your personal hobby be a school-sponsored event?" Anyway, Newfield had procedures in place to detect illegal absences. I know because I was on the district's attendance policy committee when I worked there. If it weren't legit, and they were doing their job, red flags would have been raised as to Stephanie's absence.

I actually thought about being in a committed relationship with Michelle but April came around and the thought quickly left my head. Instead, I went to Las Vegas as I did every April. In June 2005 I attended the retirement party of my former principal at Newfield, Mitchell Ross. Evidently I overreacted with regard to the Stephanie issue. I was told there was nothing to worry about and after graduation she was going away to college. I was pleased to get that news since those instances when I saw her did fester in my mind. And by late June 2005, even to my surprise, I gave it the old college try and made the commitment to Michelle. After all, she really was a tremendous friend to me over the years. She was attractive, professionally stable, and kindhearted. It was time to put up or shut up. We got along great too. The month of July was a pleasant surprise to me.

That same month Nick Dyno informed me that he accepted a position as principal in the neighboring school district in Southampton. This really took me off guard, because usually he kept me in the loop regarding even his most secretive life issues. The word spread fast in Hampton Bays. His departure came just as they were starting to believe in an administration again after years of instability. His leaving was going to create a huge void, and although most people wished him well, a few really felt betrayed. I stood by him the way I thought he would've stood by me. He had to do what was right for him and his family, and I don't think he felt right in Hampton Bays. The district was scrambling and wondering what to do next with the new school year quickly approaching. I learned a lot working for Nick, and I was going to miss him, but at the same time I saw it as an opportunity. I let the emotional aftershock of his departure settle down, and about a week later I called his secretary, Grace McGuire.

During the years of turmoil at Hampton Bays, Gracie was a constant and had her finger on the pulse of the building. We had a very good relationship, and I was banking on her support. She was upset, having been through so many principals over the years, and now another was added to the list.

"Gracie, if I were to become principal, would I have your support?"

She said the words I wanted to hear. "Frankie, I would definitely support you if you were the next principal."

I then spoke to Nick Dyno, who said he would support me 100 percent and even recommend me to the superintendent and board of education as the next principal. After soliciting the support of other key people in the district, the next step was to explain to the superintendent, Joanne Loewenthal, that I was the person to take Nick's place. I didn't promise to have every answer at my fingertips. I promised to be the hardest-working, most compassionate, strong-willed, and dedicated person in the district— which I had been since my arrival. She brought my request to the board of education, and they supported me. My efforts as an assistant principal were well documented and much appreciated. It's a nice feeling when your hard work doesn't go unnoticed.

In August 2005, I was unanimously approved to be principal of Hampton Bays Secondary School. Why not? It wasn't rocket science. It's not about knowing all the answers; it's about knowing how to get the answers. During the same time period Michelle asked if we could go to Stephanie's graduation party. She said Mr. Ross, my former boss, would be there, along with other adults from the Newfield community. I agreed, because it's not uncommon to make a brief appearance at a student's graduation party. We went, and I socialized and had a beer with the adults, but I felt strange. There were a lot of teenagers and former students there. They were good kids, but it wasn't my thing to drink and socialize with teenagers. I wanted to leave, and Michelle agreed. We wished Stephanie luck and said our good-byes. Michelle and I were doing great and were off on a very last-minute trip to Disney, where she had a time-share.

That trip wasn't good. We didn't get along very well being alone together for an extended period. Plus, my psyche was a little off, because while we were at Disney, I discovered someone hacked into my voice mails. It didn't put me in the mood for fun. When we returned from Florida, I pretty much stayed away from Michelle. We really did not get along that well spending a lot of time together as a couple. Great friends is what we were in my mind but not couple material. Plus I was busier than I had ever been. A lot of things had to be done to get the school year started. I spent night and day at work, 7:00 a.m. until 10:00 or 10:30 p.m., seven days a week. I was mostly with my computer aide, Patricia McGovern, because we still had to finish the master schedule for the school year. And on top of all that, we still needed to hire someone to fill my assistant principal position.

My superintendent wanted to hire an experienced, retired administrator. I wanted a young person with energy and ambition. I agreed, though; after all, she was the boss. The search was narrowed to two individuals, and that was when I joined the interview process. After the first candidate finished, the second candidate walked in. He was a distinguished-looking man in his upper fifties with a full head of grey hair and about six feet tall. Unlike me, he looked every bit the image of a principal.

"Hi, I'm Dan Nolan. Thanks for having me."

Dan Nolan? The man I heard so many good things about over the years had a face. To go with his look, he also had the jargon down pat and played the role real well, too. But I knew more about him than he thought. He was a normal, ordinary guy, my kind of person. My opening question was "Do you know anything about 'Asshole Island'?"

He seemed as if he didn't know how to respond, but when I laughed, he quickly joined in. He was well versed with my past colleagues. We took a walk around the campus to have a more casual talk. I knew he was the guy to hire. Prior to opening day, after not seeing Michelle for a bit, she gave me another card:

> Baby, I never thought I could love someone as much as I love
> you. I am so proud of you. You are going to be incredible.
> I'm so excited for you, I can hardly stand it. I hope you have
> a great opening day. With all my love, your #1 fan.

I didn't even acknowledge the card. She may have felt neglected, because she came over to my house and mentioned that her new principal, Gordon Brosdal, introduced himself to her in the school's distance learning lab. Michelle said he commented on her defined triceps, and said he loved dogs. I met Gordon quite a few times. He was an English teacher in the Middle Country Central School District when I was working there as a science teacher. Gordon is somewhere around twenty years older than she is and I laughed hysterically at her obvious attempt to make me jealous. "Michelle, in no time at all you'll be sleeping with your new boss."

When the first day of school arrived, there I was, standing in front of the faculty as principal. It was my building. I sure didn't fit the typical mold. I was young and spoke as if I had stepped out of a scene from the movie *Goodfellas*, and to quote Joanne Loewenthal's playful words, "Frankie, you walk and talk like such a jock." There were people from Newfield who thought I couldn't be an administrator, but within two years of leaving them, I was now a principal, and had surpassed many of my superiors. My parents were so proud. Although they never had a chance themselves, they strongly believed in education, and now their son was a principal. I wasn't done yet. I was going to continue my rise through the ranks.

I didn't prepare an elaborate speech for the first day—or any other day, for that matter. I hate to be scripted. I had some notes, but I like to speak to people, not read to them. What I said came from the heart. I vowed to work hard, but I wasn't about to be a one-man show. Instead, we would be a team, working together to achieve a common goal. Teachers were encouraged to take risks and try new things. If something went wrong, I would take the heat, and when something went right, I would give them all the credit (it's really such a simple formula). If they weren't successful, then I wouldn't be successful. It wasn't about individuals. It was about the school, the community, the big picture. Maybe we could have some fun along the way.

Someone who sure wasn't having fun was Michelle. She came over my house about a week later, unannounced and looking and sounding terrible. I was really concerned and asked her if she needed help with anything. She couldn't explain it to me but admitted something was wrong with her. She asked if Stephanie was the reason that our brief relationship was over, gave me her phone number, and asked me to speak with her. I was at a loss for words. I didn't expect to ever hear that name again. I initially refused, and didn't understand why she wanted me to make the call. I explained there was no way it would have any bearing on our relationship. Michelle started to cry and asked again. I don't recall a time when Michelle ever let herself go, but I have to say she was really troubled. As I stared at her unusually unkempt self I reluctantly agreed to call Stephanie at her college. If for nothing else, maybe Michelle would get herself back on track.

The conversation was about an hour long. Stephanie went on and on talking about things that I couldn't even tell you about because I wasn't even paying attention. I guess she caught on to my indifference, because she said she was insulted at my unwillingness to reciprocate with conversation. She suddenly shouted, "Michelle hates you, and she will never talk to you again. I got what I wanted!" I hung up and blamed myself for making the call. I didn't have time for nonsense. I told Michelle that she was a great friend and person, and plenty of guys would love to have her as a girlfriend. I also suggested that maybe she should go to therapy. I meant it sincerely.

I resumed a lifestyle of going out late at night and partying hard. I'm not saying that to brag or because I consider it a badge of honor. I'm simply stating the facts. I was living the life—a life beyond my means, but it didn't cost me anything extra. Every time I went out to an upscale establishment in the Hamptons, there was somebody there working a side job who either worked in the education world or was looking for a job in the education world. If it was thirty-five dollars to park the car, they did it for me—"No problem, Mr. Vetro." It cost $400 for a bottle of vodka and table service, but hey, someone needed something, so "Here you go, Mr. Vetro." I was partying with the wealthy folk, and it was costing me minimal money. Of course, I knew they were using me, but what did I care? I guess I was using them too. I enjoyed showing up, having my car parked, and being welcomed with a kiss on both cheeks by a beautiful woman. The nights were wild, no question about it, and they stretched from the Hamptons to Manhattan. But as always, when the workday started, I had my A game, and there were no hints of my personal life. My job and responsibility to the educational community, especially to the kids, always came first. From September 2005 through January 2006, my professional career could not have been scripted any better.

Now that I think about it, this is also when my personal life began to slowly collapse. I had to cancel my credit card, and I was receiving letters from creditors telling me I was delinquent on bills I never knew I had. My America Online account had a recent contact list of about five hundred e-mail addresses. I didn't even own a computer and only went online maybe once a week, when I used my brother's computer. When I called AT&T

Wireless in late September to inquire about my bill, the representative told me I could go online to view my account.

"I don't have an online account." The woman not only verified that I did but gave me different e-mail addresses where my bill was sent. I assured her I never set up an online account. I didn't even own a computer. I immediately called three credit bureaus and put passwords on my bank accounts, retirement accounts, mortgage, etc.

In October, Michelle called me at work, crying again, to tell me Jim was in her driveway. Jim? Come on. It was late at night, and I was still at work. I told her I couldn't leave Hampton Bays yet and I would call her when I was done. I honestly didn't believe her and thought she just wanted my attention. She appeared at my house uninvited a few days later on October 22, 2005, during a family celebration. When my family went home, Michelle told me we couldn't be a couple. Now that really confused me. I thought I already made that decision.

"Uh, okay," I said. "If that's what you think will be the healthiest thing for you, then you should follow your heart."

As she was leaving, she stood in the doorway and told me that she loved me. Now, I have faults, but lying to someone is not one of them. I wasn't going to tell Michelle I loved her just for the sake of trying to make an extremely confused individual feel better. "Michelle, have you considered my advice and sought therapy? Because you don't look well." I said it sincerely. She just stood in the doorway without responding. I felt helpless. She helped me so much over the years, and I wanted to help her. I didn't know what to do or say.

Not long after, Stephanie's brother, Nick Veraldi, paid a visit to my office.

"What's going on with you and my sister Stephanie?" he asked. "What? I don't even know your sister or you for that matter. Why are you here?"

He caught a little bit of an attitude with me, and I have to tell you I wasn't happy either. I was at work. I had a life and things that had to be done—important things. I had no time or patience to be wondering about some girl I didn't even know or visits from her freaking brother.

"It seems everything died down, anyway, so I guess it's over" he concluded. Over? I didn't even know what he was talking about. Not wanting to make a scene, I smiled and just wished him luck as I walked him out. I had a school to run. Was Stephanie behind my arrest? In hindsight, something wasn't right with her.

In November I went out with a friend of mine from Hampton Bays, Saverio Naclerio. We went to a bar, *Irish Times*, in Holbrook, Long Island, to watch the New York Yankees playoffs. Some old colleagues from Newfield High School were there. One of those colleagues, Gilda, I had not seen since leaving Newfield. I approached her to say hello, and we caught up over a drink for about fifteen minutes. Allison Engstrom was there, and I think Michelle Rogak was too. Allison joined us for the drink. After finishing, I decided to leave with my friend and said good-bye. There were other places to watch the game. I never had any bad feelings for Allison or Michelle Rogak, but I didn't need even a potential for a headache given our history.

A few weeks later, I attended the Longwood High School football playoffs. I was invited to the game by a Longwood Board of Education member, Dan Tomaszewski. While watching the game from the sidelines, Allison left a message on my cell phone saying that she thought I was a dick. Where did that come from? Shortly after, I had a phone conversation with a Newfield chemistry teacher named Gayle. As we were catching up on old times in the Newfield science wing, she said that Allison Engstrom and Michelle Rogak were angry with me. "What? Why? I just saw both of them at a bar. I literally had a drink and a conversation with Allison for about fifteen minutes." Gayle didn't have any specifics and I didn't bother to press the issue. I just chalked that nonsense up to the soap opera that was Newfield High School—something I was glad to be away from. Were they in on my arrest? For the life of me I can't see how. No way.

The fact is, in the fall of 2005 I was very enthralled with my career and life in Hampton Bays—maybe too much. My personal life was not as important to me as my job, so I ignored the childish crap and nonsense that surrounded my life—until December 2005. That's when I received a phone call from a friend's wife. "What the fuck are you trying to do?" she screamed. She didn't sound well and was frantic and short of breath. She was far along in her pregnancy, too. I really thought she was going to lose the baby. That was how bad she sounded. Evidently someone put e-mails on her husband's car from my AOL account with a cover letter suggesting I was the father of the unborn child. Of course, it was all a lie. My friend paid me a visit, and we quickly cleared things up, as he saw through the evil forgery.

However, the very next day I went online while I was at work and discovered that someone signed me up for an account on a website called Reunion.com. Not only did an account exist in my name, but someone also used it and spent money to search for the whereabouts of a female acquaintance of mine. My secretary helped me figure this stuff out and we cancelled the account. I had a strange feeling, so I called this woman to let her know what happened. Thank God I did because the next day, she intercepted a letter that was sent to her husband via certified mail, from me, from my home address! The letter introduced me, my profession, and where I worked before confessing I was having an affair with his wife! I suppose a good guess is that whoever was behind that incident was also behind the reason I was sitting in Riverhead Jail. After that, on December 17, 2005, I went to the seventh precinct in Shirley to file a report of identity theft. The officer told me that if no money was stolen then my identity was not stolen. He refused to listen to me or take a report. I suggested that he write it up anyway and call it whatever he wanted to call it. Just write down what I was reporting. He refused though. I wasn't happy. That same day I changed my cell phone number.

Meanwhile Michelle called me to tell me she was going to China to take care of some business regarding her dog breeding. She asked me to go with her but I had my own problems and couldn't focus on her business. I had work anyway so that was a good excuse. About a week and a half later I had a woman over my house, and Michelle barged in at 12:30 a.m., screaming and crying. My friend went home very afraid that night. I decided to drive to Michelle's house to try and talk sense into her. Shortly after I arrived, Stephanie appeared. I didn't want to see or talk to her, so she left, but not before calling me a piece of shit. I asked Michelle, practically begged her, to see a therapist. Her mental state seemed to be way off. She was also interfering with my social life. I felt helpless because I really didn't know what to do for her.

Professionally I remained strong. The minute I arrived at work, I was the leader of the building and had to act accordingly. I had a plan for my school and goals for myself. I had to see them through. And while my personal life was in complete disarray, my career was as solid as ever. Morale in my building was the highest it had been in years. Generally speaking, the Hampton Bays community appreciated my energy, honesty, sincerity, and desire to truly make a difference in the school district.

We had a long way to go but were making progress—so much that at a December board of education meeting, I was honored as a dynamic principal. The president of the teachers union commented on my leadership skills, and the superintendent followed by claiming I was a "dream team administrator." The board of education presented me with gifts, including a book, *What Great Principals Do Differently*. Inside, the board members and superintendent wrote about the great job I was doing and how I was the future of the Hampton Bays School District. A small celebration was held at a local establishment, JT's, following the meeting. The experience was not only a great highlight in my educational career but also a signal that my approach to leadership was right on the money.

So many people thought I couldn't be a successful administrator and expressed their thoughts to me. I was glad they did. Throughout life, people will tell you that you can't do something. Don't listen! I wasn't done by a long shot. I had accomplished some of my goals, but I had more. To think I was born into a family with limited traditional education. To think that my ancestors came to America from Italy so their future generations could become educated and lead better lives. Not only was one of their own educated, but he was also an educational leader and making a name for himself. They were so proud. Why would I do anything to ruin what I was accomplishing and shame my family name? The answer is simple. I wouldn't.

Michelle lingered, though, even though I asked her to back away. I have to be honest though, full disclosure, I was a part of that problem. On Friday, February 3, 2006, at around 9:00 p.m. while I was at Mike's Place having a drink with Dan Nolan and his sons, Michelle invited me to her house, which was about two minutes away. The next day, Michelle stopped by my house unannounced. I should have stopped associating with her cold turkey and didn't. I was weak and stupid, and continued to have meaningless sex with her. I swear that somewhere beneath the sex I was concerned about her well-being. I know it might be hard to see that and I accept any and all ridicule that may come my way. Toward the end of the night, out of nowhere, Michelle began to cry and apologize. She just kept saying that she was sorry. I asked her to elaborate because it made no sense. It was so random. She never did, the night didn't end well, and she went home at my request.

February 5, Super Bowl Sunday, I was preparing for my annual party, which Michelle was not invited to. I had a phone conversation with her just before my company was due to arrive. During the conversation I asked about her behavior the night before. She spoke in a manner that I have never heard her speak before. She was aggressive and began to push my buttons. At that point we both became a little heated but eventually calmed down, and Michelle changed the subject by asking me to go with her to a therapist she began seeing. I had no clue why she wanted me to go and how that would help but I was happy to see that she decided to see a therapist. I told her I would call her during the week to set an appointment.

As promised, on Tuesday, February 7, I called Michelle at about 10:30 p.m. I was on my way home from a board of education meeting. It was another of my many long days in Hampton Bays. I explained that after the busy week I was in the middle of, I would be able to accompany her to her therapist if she thought it would help. I thought maybe going with her would be the catalyst for us to amicably distance ourselves from each other. And I wanted her to be healthy as that happened. We both helped each other out tremendously over the last four years, but it really was time to move on. I reached a point where I was ready to settle down, leave the late nights out on the town behind, and start another chapter. I grew up surrounded by a large family, and I was ready to start one of my own. This portion of my life definitely would not include Michelle. As I hung up the phone Michelle said that she hoped we could work things out.

Part II

THEN CAME THE KILL SHOT

"If all the world hated you and believed you wicked, while your own conscience approved of you and absolved you from guilt, you would not be without friends."
— Charlotte Brontë, *Jane Eyre*

When one person makes an accusation, check to be sure he himself is not the guilty one. Sometimes it is those whose case is weak who make the most clamour.

- Piers Anthony

Chapter Five
The Enemy Showed its Face

"Hey, principal, let's go!"

If there was ever a second where I thought this could turn out to be a bad nightmare, it was quickly put to rest.

After my delayed response, the guard yelled, "Get the fuck out of the cell!"

"Yes sir." It was not a nightmare. It was very real. Sometime around 8:00 p.m. on Friday, February 10, I was finally being bailed out. Everyone sat around in every room doing nothing though, so it wasn't until about 10:00 p.m. that I was officially released. To add insult to injury, when I got my belongings back, I noticed $1.50 was missing. I guess one of the guards had to stop for a cup of coffee as they were thinking of insults to hurl at me. For someone who had been sitting around doing nothing, I sure felt like crap. My body was sore all over. That cot showed no mercy. My hair felt like steel wool, and my teeth felt like mold was growing on them. I just wanted to get home, take a hot shower, eat, and get a night's rest. I exited into the waiting room and saw my family sigh with relief.

I could hear their exhale as they ran over to me. My brother Rocky led the way and gave me a big hug, and the rest of my family followed suit. Rocky is just over nine years younger than me but we spent a lot of time together growing up. I tried my best to teach him and be a positive influence in his life. I hated that he had to see his older brother in handcuffs. My friends Jon Boswell, whom I met at the titanium plant when I was in college, and his wife, Lesley, put up the entire $17,500 cash bail. The money had been acquired over a day ago, but my family was indeed sent away because of that initial mistake with the numbers on the paperwork. That "mistake" cost me an extra night in a godforsaken jail. Something tells me that "mistake" wasn't a mistake. The reunion didn't last long. My family wasn't too happy with the inefficiency and incompetence they had to deal with while I was being held hostage by the system. My brother Sal spoke so anyone could hear: "Let's get out of here before they lock me up!" The arrogant guard agreed with him. Thus, we all hurriedly exited before something else happened. Not unlike when I left Newfield for Hampton Bays, I didn't look back. Here's an aside: I learned a great weight loss plan—twelve pounds in two days! You'll just have to get arrested and have your life destroyed in the media. Is anyone that vain?

When I got home, I decided to make journal entries. I took diligent notes every day, regarding the events, the people I spoke with, and anything else I learned.

February 11, 2006

I called a few attorneys, it was tough to get in touch with a lot of them because it was the weekend. I scheduled a meeting on Monday February 13, with Nick Marino, the same attorney who represented me at my arraignment. I decided I would call Michelle after that meeting. I had a lot to catch up with over the next few days first. She couldn't have been doing well with me being all over the news. I was sure Newfield was buzzing with the news, maybe she heard something of importance. I really wondered if Stephanie was the one behind my arrest. Although I didn't know how she could be, she was the only person I could think of. I was certain Michelle would find out for me.

My brother Sal and sister Maria gathered the media coverage. The police sergeant wasn't kidding when he said he was going to ruin my life. Reports filed locally, statewide, and nationally informed the world that after a thorough police investigation, Frank Vetro had finally been caught. The world got a glimpse of the predator who had hidden under the guise of a New York educator. The statements couldn't have been further from the truth, but, hey, they made for a good news story. *Newsday*, the *New York Daily News*, the *New York Times*, the *New York Post*, *Southampton Press*, *The Independent*, and other outlets in print media, on the internet, and on television were relentless. The press acted as court stenographers, typing without questioning or exercising any sense of caution or due diligence. Did they ask the authorities for proof before going to print? It was the Wild West of free speech.

A few of the many included a *Daily News* writer, "HS principal in sex harass rap". He opened with "A HANDSOME high school principal terrorized former female colleagues, random retail clerks and even an ex-student from a Suffolk high school where he once taught, cops said." *Newsday's* catch line was, "Nabbed at School", "Principal charged with making sexually explicit phone calls to teachers, a former student, other women". "HS BIG IN PERV ARREST", "Sicko sex calls" was courtesy of the *New York Post*. "PRINCIPAL WITHOUT PRINCIPLES?" "Also Accused of Stalking Female Neighbor" was the cover of the *Independent*—apparently yet another woman named Michelle had claimed I was following her around town. I believe she even got airtime on *News 12*. I didn't even have a neighbor named Michelle! The arresting officers lied, and the reporters, whose job is to create headlines, tell juicy stories, and sell papers, were misled. The libel kept coming. According to The *New York Post* the police said Frank Vetro "Spoke to his victims in a sultry, creepy voice, pelting them with graphic and perverted sex talk, sometimes laced with violence." And "the evil educator would disguise his voice." Phone calls? Stalking? A former student? Man, anything to sell papers. It went on and on. I really wanted to see the complaints filed against me.

Students and staff members at Hampton Bays and my neighbors said a lot of good things about me, but the media didn't bother to air much of that. The juice of the story was that a principal in Hampton Bays was a mad man. There was no need for anyone covering the story to spend a moment's thought on whether I was guilty or innocent. Being innocent wouldn't have sold papers or made a good opening tagline for the late night news.

> *One of the best lessons I ever learned was taught by my middle school reading teacher, Mr. Hartman. His classroom was in the middle of that building with no walls, and he was sitting with me and a few other students at a circular desk. I felt like I was under a large microscope being watched by aliens in a* Twilight Zone *episode. The lesson focused on words used by the media to influence or mislead the public. In particular he mentioned* virtually *and* practically. *Given my current predicament, he should have included the word* alleged. *I recall him warning us to be careful of what we saw, heard, or read in publications. He suggested, in middle school language, that we sift through the words and numbers because everything was not as it seemed and should be taken with the proverbial grain of salt until*

> *further review. Although there are quality news reporters out there, there are also a ton of biases and way too much self-promotion. He wanted his students to think on their own, form their own opinions, and not blindly follow what they read or heard.*

A distorted image of me was created, and I hoped everyone could see through the nonsense. The judge at the arraignment, Judge Hensley, was cited in one newspaper as saying the strength of the prosecution's case worked against me in terms of setting bail. Strength? What strength? Was he even supposed to see the evidence against me? Did he see it? I didn't even know the details of my arrest yet. Although the media took great liberty in publicly destroying me, they skillfully left the names of all the alleged victims out of the immensely one-sided story. Either way, quantity doesn't mean quality. To be honest, of all the things said, the worst was that they made it sound as if I was preying on one of my students. I would give my life for those kids. Guilty until proven innocent—the American way.

It got better, well, worse. I checked out the press conference at Suffolk County Police Headquarters. Lieutenant Joanne McLaughlin, Police Commissioner Richard Dormer, and the commander of the seventh precinct, Inspector John Meehan, were among those on hand. All the heavyweights of law enforcement in Suffolk County were involved in this high-profile case of a principal gone mad. There was no hamming it up for the cameras, of course not. Every time inappropriate phone calls are *alleged*, all the top brass in Suffolk County become involved. Sure they do. Is it Adolf Hitler who is associated with the expression "The Big Lie"?

I vaguely recall another famous expression: "The bigger the lie the more they'll believe it." Is that Joseph Goebbels? Obviously the authorities wanted to win the case in the media. They lied to their superiors, who relayed the misinformation to the press, which transmitted a further distorted message to the world. It was a sick and out-of-control game of telephone, and the objective was to see how sick of an individual Frank Vetro could be portrayed as. As promised, the arresting police sergeant who refused to give me his name, Michael Cosgrove, had his personal, albeit ridiculous, quotes for the papers. Lieutenant McLaughlin's statements were such that you could have put question marks at the end of every sentence. She had no clue what the truth was or what the hell she was talking about. The head honcho in Suffolk County, Police Commissioner Richard Dormer, was quoted in one paper, "This is terrorism, and we take this very seriously, especially because of his position."

He essentially called me a terrorist! Here's a tip for the commissioner and lieutenant: do some homework before taking the podium in front of the media.

Dormer, with his most earnest camera face, urged all women who had ever received a suspicious phone call to come forward. He really needed to take it down a notch. I'm surprised I didn't have several thousand more complaints filed against me. Who hasn't received one or more of what would amount to a prank phone call? The arresting officers were hoping for bulk because they had nothing. They couldn't have possibly had anything. I suppose they thought all sorts of random people would see the news and call in saying they too were victims of Frank Vetro. The police department's phone never rang once, not even with a prank call.

Unfortunately, I figured Dormer's theatrics would cause a major problem. A police commissioner who goes on the news and essentially calls someone a terrorist has backed his department into a corner. Dormer couldn't admit a mistake had been made and that his department had failed to do any police work to determine if the charges were warranted.

I figured they would play dirty pool and do what they could to lie, cheat, and draw this case out because the police would refuse to admit they were incompetent and fear going before the same press to retract their statements. Lost on the first day was that magic word, *alleged*. You don't destroy someone off allegations. I was innocent until proven guilty, right? No, not when the six o'clock news stuck microphones in their faces. Furthermore, why was it more serious? Is the law prejudiced? Where in the New York Penal Code does it state that a principal must be judged more harshly by the law than anyone else?

There was also an underlying motive. The District Attorney's Office in Suffolk County, the town of Crookhaven—I mean Brookhaven—is very political. The chief prosecutor, Thomas Spota, built his reputation and political campaign on taking down corrupt politicians and school administrators—and here was a chance to throw Frank Vetro into the boiling oil along with all the other corrupt felons. As one of many assistants under Thomas Spota, the way to make a name is to take on some trials, do well, and gain experience. What better way to impress then by being aggressive and taking down a high school principal in a well-publicized case? This would surely put a notch on a young prosecutor's belt. That was for sure one reason they came out full throttle. However, I was certain they would soon realize they had no case, draw it out, and hope that I crack and take a plea. Out of all of the criminal charges and after all the publicity, they would have to convict me of something, or they would look foolish. I predicted they would threaten, intimidate, and stall to make my life as miserable as possible and wait for me to give up and accept a criminal record.

February 13, 2006

I entered the law firm of Russo and Pedranghelu and formally introduced myself to Nick Marino since we hadn't officially met yet. I wasn't sure, but I imagined he was in his late forties or early fifties. Honestly he wasn't very personable, but that was irrelevant. Nick was known to be excellent in the courtroom, and I hired him for a trial, not to cut deals, make a plea, or be my friend. We immediately got down to business and he asked some background questions. The most interesting question was when one of the partners of the firm asked if my dad was in the mafia. "Um, no," I said. "Why? Would you treat me different?" After a few basic questions, a handshake, and some exchange of money, the formality was over. Nick handed me an envelope and told me to read the statements filed against me and gather my thoughts with regard to them. Judging by the media blitz, I was going to need more than innocence to clear my name. It's a legal system, not a justice system.

Since my case was high profile, I planned on retaining another attorney, Lori Horowitz from Tuan and Cho LLP. And it wasn't because I had all this money lying around. In fact, I didn't have any money. My career just started to take off and I was just beginning to get ahead in life. Lord knows my family didn't have extra cash. Han Tsien Tuan, one of the partners of the firm, said Lori Horowitz had a lot of contacts in the system and could work on the public relations aspects of my case to combat the negative publicity. She wasn't cheap, but I thought having a woman at my side might look good to a jury. I was thinking everything through with one thing in mind: trial. I didn't know how I was going to take on the monster called the State of New York, my resources didn't add up to much.

As the day ended, I sat down to read precisely what I was charged with and who filed the complaints. Pulling the statements out of the envelope, the names jumped off of the first three statements: Michelle Rogak, Allison Engstrom, and Stephanie Veraldi. I didn't even read them. Instead I put them and the remaining papers down and just sat back for a moment, confused as to why or how they had developed such hatred for me. After a moment my curiosity kicked in again. I picked up the small pile of complaints and turned to the next one. I don't have words to describe the shock. I began to sweat. *It must be a mistake,* I thought. I turned back to the other complaints and quickly realized the same name was referenced over and over again, completely stabbing me in the heart.

I read further, scurrying back and forth between the pages. How could she have done this? How could all these lies have been told? Sometimes when you're caught up in the middle of something, instincts become fuzzy, especially when an attractive person is involved. I didn't see it coming. Superman had his kryptonite, Achilles had his heel, and I had a woman who did a great job convincing me of her friendship and using her body as a sacrificial lamb to follow through with a devastating plan. She claimed to love me and be my friend. It was all a charade, and she was the master illusionist. Years of nonsense and character flaws that I was too blind to see suddenly smacked me in the face. Six complaints stemmed from her, and she personally filed a seventh! She didn't let me separate from her. Michelle Konik convinced others to separate me, an uncontrollable human being, from her. I slammed the papers down.

I'm a strong person, and although the events swirling into my life were upsetting and beyond belief, I knew I could handle them. The truth would be found out, and this would end like all bad nightmares do. But what Michelle, the police, and the poisoned media were doing to my mother made my blood broil. What did Josephine Vetro do to deserve this despair at seeing her son treated like a disgusting animal? All my mother ever did was show kindness, generosity, and love, not only to her family, but to everyone she has come in contact with. My dad is tough as nails and prides himself on always being in control and doing what is needed to keep his family safe and together. Now he was confronted with a plight he couldn't control. Together they showed their kids how to work hard and be honest, and now their son was being ripped apart in headlines across the state as some kind of mad man. The depth of Michelle Konik's hatred for me was to the point that she didn't care who else she hurt or damaged with her malicious lies.

We grow up thinking justice is being served in this country, but that isn't always the case. There are hidden agendas out there and I couldn't help but think someone on the inside had one. Something just wasn't adding up with these statements. I felt immense anger and betrayal, not only toward

Michelle, but also toward the police, who are supposed to fulfill justice and protect the innocent. Perhaps the police wanted to flex some muscle for a pretty blonde. How long was this in the making? I decided to save my quarter—no use calling Michelle to ask about her therapy. I'd have my day with her.

February 14, 2006

I met with my superintendent, Joanne Loewenthal. Nick Marino thought I was crazy not to resign, because he was certain I was going to be fired. Bob Smith, my representative from SAANY's (the School Administrators Association of New York), agreed and said I should turn in my resignation. I refused to resign. It was my career and I would not just walk away from it. Then what would I do? Who would hire me after such a public arrest? I stuck with my gut feeling, and at the end of the day I was correct.

My superintendent gave me a hug and smile. She had the police documents and began by stating, Frank, this is bullshit. You were set up. She said when she told the authorities that the district was supporting me, they expressed displeasure. Why? Police are supposed to hope justice is served, not have personal vendettas or make personal judgments against a person they don't even know. But my not having a job would've helped them justify their very questionable arrest and forced me into a plea deal when my finances ran out.

As the meeting progressed, I asked if I could read one particular letter that was written by a member of the Hampton Bays community. I never made it through the letter. It was very touching, and my superintendent stopped me before it became too emotional. When the meeting ended, I was still employed. As our discussion came to a close, everyone left the room, and my superintendent closed the door and gave me another hug. She assured me that I had the support of the district. I was placed on paid temporary leave to get my stuff in order.

February 15 to March 2006:

I took this time away from work to do a preliminary breakdown of the case against me. I began by reading the statements again, and noticed the officer's names from the seventh precinct: Officers Heter, Benson, Lutz.

With just a quick glance any half-witted individual could see that the case was ridiculous. All the police did, like waiters in a café, was write down what someone told them and act on the information without a moment's thought as to whether it made sense or not. I thought there was an investigation that took months to complete? Didn't anybody see anything peculiar? There are a great number of questions that one would think a thorough police investigation would have easily uncovered. I didn't think there was an investigation.

Within minutes I realized the officers weren't even smart enough to cover their foibles. I was arrested at 4:30 p.m. There were Miranda cards. The first card, accompanied by the initial statement, has no posted time on it. The second Miranda card shows it was 8:30 p.m. when they read me my rights and I stated I wanted to speak to an attorney. However, the officer still wrote two additional statements after that up until about 9:45 p.m. Of course, that's not at all how it happened, I was grilled until about 12:00 a.m., and the cards were given to me all at once. But 9:45 p.m. is still over four hours after being cuffed, interrogated, and threatened. The point is these guys didn't even hide the fact that they violated my Miranda rights.

What the hell are these statements that *the officer* wrote on my behalf anyway? Why wouldn't they want me to write the statements myself? That way there could be no debate. I wouldn't be able to deny they were my words and thoughts. I have been in a few car accidents, and each time the police showed up, I wrote the accident report with my own mind, in my own handwriting. These statements were manufactured, not taken from my words. Then again, my words and thoughts would say something totally different and would not have helped their cause. Common sense dictates that it doesn't take seven hours to write four statements that are a few paragraphs—not unless you have to go in another room and think creatively to piece together a story from fantasyland.

I reference the shoddy work because as a principal, I made decisions that affected the lives of individuals. I made sure documents were precise. The names, times, dates, incidents—everything had to be accurate or else they may have been invalid. I also made sure everything was thoroughly investigated before acting. I was obligated to question everyone (including the person accused). Please tell me that when the police arrest someone and destroy a life, they're held to a higher standard than a principal disciplining a student for cutting class.

The Accusatory Instruments

The case seemed open-and-shut in the media. The evidence was overwhelming. There was a thorough investigation involving many random women. Police officers are honest and only look to see that justice is served. An innocent person pilloried in the press—that only happens in the movies, right? Think again. The misdemeanor information is basically the same on each complaint. *According to the police*, each "victim," being duly sworn, stated that I wrongfully, knowingly, intentionally, recklessly, and with criminal negligence committed the offense of aggravated harassment in the second degree. The conduct extremely annoyed, threatened, and alarmed them. The arrest was based in part on recognition of the defendant's voice and/or Cingular Telephone Company trace results. Below are notes and a summary I jotted down for my attorney.

Michelle Rogak's (Statement Date: December 10, 2005)

1. In March of 2005 I started getting calls from a male voice. The voice would whisper.
2. The voice sounded familiar and *I couldn't quite place it* until an ex-student Stephanie told me she was getting harassing phone calls also. She said she recognized the voice as an old teacher that worked at Newfield High School named Frank Vetro D.O.B. 10/18/71. He is now the principal at Hampton Bays High School.
3. Michelle [Konik] approached me … and she told me that Stephanie Veraldi told her that Frank was harassing her on the phone.
4. Frank and I dated for about two weeks. Frank was still dating Michelle Konik at the time. Michelle [Konik] found my phone number in Frank's phone.

Preliminary Notes

1. The *alleged* calls lasted six months, March to August 2005, yet she did nothing. She complained four months *after* they stopped. Was she annoyed by the calls or because they stopped?
2. On her statement the police said the arrest was based in part on recognition of the defendant's voice. Rogak never said I did it

though. She could have easily *placed* my voice, but didn't. There's a good reason for that.

3. Stephanie told Michelle Konik, who told Michelle Rogak it was me? Do police officers actually give credence to such crap?
4. I wasn't dating Michelle Konik or Michelle Rogak. In fact Rogak was engaged at the time she says we dated. And if she knows my birthday, she was stalking me.
5. How could Michelle Konik see Michelle Rogak's phone number in my phone? I haven't called her in years. Plus when did Michelle Konik have my phone anyway?

Stephanie Veraldi's (Statement Date: December 17, 2005)

1. I got a hang-up call on my cell phone. It was the same male voice whispering.
2. I recognized the voice as one of the teachers at my old high school. His name is Frank Vetro. He is now the principal at Hampton Bays High School.
3. I know Frank personally. I know his voice through Michelle Konik, who I work with at her house.
4. I heard Frank was calling other teachers and pranking them … so that's why I decided to make a police report.

Preliminary Notes

1. She claims she was harassed for two weeks in early August 2005, but waited over four months *after* they stopped to file a complaint? You have got to be kidding me.
2. Was it a hang-up or a male voice whispering? She *does not* know me personally and *couldn't ever* recognize my normal voice in August 2005, never mind me whispering for a few seconds.
3. Michelle gave me her number in September 2005, and she had a sixty-four minute phone conversation with me a month *after* she *claimed* to know I harassed her.
4. She filed a report because she heard I called other teachers? So she filed on their behalf? Stephanie didn't hear I was calling them. She wrongfully told them I was calling them.

5. She works at Michelle Konik's home? Is this a normal student-teacher relationship?

6. Her complaint was filed the same day I attempted to file my own report of ID Theft. My report would have meant no pictures or quotes for the authorities.

Allison Engstrom's (Statement Date: December 19, 2005)

1. It was a male voice that called and was whispering ... I handed my phone to my girlfriend. She kind of played along with him, and we laughed and joked about it.

2. In July 2005 my friend Don shouted, stop fucking calling. That was the last time the voice called my phone. I never called the police because I didn't feel threatened.

3. ... Around early November 2005 ... Michelle Konik said that her boyfriend Frank Vetro, who is a former teacher at Newfield High School and now the principal of Hampton Bays High School, was the one making the telephone calls.

4. I don't really want to press charges for what he did to me, but calling Stephanie Veraldi is a bit disgusting.

5. I was with Frank one night.

Preliminary Notes

1. She didn't feel threatened? She didn't really want to press charges? They played along and laughed and joked about it? The *alleged* calls lasted from July 2004 to July 2005. One year and she did nothing? When the caller was told to stop, s/he did. Harassment? Whoever called entertained her!

2. Allison also could have easily recognized my voice. She didn't for a reason. Michelle Konik told her it was me. Of course Michelle didn't tell her, or anyone else, that she had sex with me, the madman, for three months after she was spreading the lies.

3. I had a drink with Allison in October 2005. Two weeks later, she called me. Why didn't she ask me or say something? Why would she speak with a man who harassed her?

4. Allison didn't want to file a complaint, but *if* I called Stephanie, something should be done? That is a big if.

5. She was with me one night? We went to a strip club, she got a lap dance, we went to a motel, and she took her clothes off. If you're going to sing, use all the lyrics.

Christina Impastato's (Statement Date: January 11, 2006)

1. I worked at the store (Steve Madden) since the week of 10/17/05. About 3 days after my first day ... at around 9:30 at night I got a very disturbing phone call.
2. He said, hi, who is this? I told him my name.
3. On December 23, 2005 at 7:45 the same guy called back. I'm pretty positive that on January 2, 2006 at around 8:15 (she references another call).
4. This girl came into my store and approached us ... and basically said she knew this sounds crazy, but she wanted to know if we were getting harassing phone calls. Like, how would she know ...?
5. She went on to tell us how she recognized his voice and that he was her old teacher at Newfield High School. She told us his name was Frank Vetro.
6. He is now the principal of Hampton Bays High School. I wish I got her name.... You guys need to talk to her.... She sounds like she is really being harassed a lot.

Preliminary Notes

1. Not one of the times she references receiving a call leads back to me. Not one!
2. The girl who approached her at work was, of course, Stephanie Veraldi.
3. Stephanie walked into a crowded store, with extra staff during the holidays, and asked the exact girl who was receiving phone calls if she was getting such calls? What a coincidence! That's because Christina admitted giving her name to the caller. Stephanie knew exactly whom to go to.
4. Christina never said I did it. How could she? She couldn't have ever heard my voice. Stephanie told her I did it. How would Stephanie recognize a voice that was calling someone else? Better yet, who would believe this garbage!

5. She couldn't even remember Stephanie's name but remembered everything about me?

Michelle Konik's (Statement Date: February 7, 2006)

1. I told him not to call me anymore.
2. The conversation of him yelling at me and me defending myself lasted about 10 minutes.
3. I am involved with an ongoing investigation with Officer Heter.
4. I am afraid that if I go through with it and press charges that Frank will come after me. You don't understand—he is going to blame all of this on me and come after me.
5. He scares me.

Preliminary Notes

1. She told me not to call her? We had literally hundreds of phone conversations from the time the first complaint was made until the arrest. We had over seventy phone conversations, some over one hour long, between January and the first week of February 2006 alone. Plus e-mails and tons of intercourse.
2. My phone records show that the conversation she's referring to was twenty-seven minutes long, not ten.
3. I would blame all this on her? All of what?
4. According to all the other statements, she knew I was harassing people but allowed it to continue? She's an accomplice at best. Maybe it wasn't a crime she innocently discovered but a crime she maliciously committed?
5. As a teacher she is supposed to protect her student. If she knew I was such an animal, why did she give me Stephanie's number? Either she used Stephanie to set me up, or knowingly put her in harm's way. Either scenario doesn't play out well for her.

Nancy Maletta's (Statement Date: February 8, 2006)

1. Around the beginning of August, I started receiving hang-up calls. The calls continued for about the whole month. The person who was calling *never said anything*.

2. My daughter Stephanie Veraldi had been receiving harassing phone calls from an unknown male caller. Police Officer Benson told me that while investigating Stephanie's complaint they were able to identify the guy hanging up on me, and his name was Frank Vetro, one of the teachers at Stephanie's high school.
3. I have felt harassed, annoyed, and alarmed by these calls, and I want to press charges.

Preliminary Notes

1. The caller never said anything, yet somehow I was identified? How's that logical? It's not and that's why Nancy never said I did it. Officer Benson told her I did it. Who the hell is he and how the hell would he know?
2. The time on her complaint is 9:00 p.m., when I was already chained to the precinct floor. I guess to stockpile complaints.
3. Was she really alarmed, annoyed, and harassed by the alleged hang-up? She waited six months *after* being hung up on to file a complaint.
4. I don't even know her. Why would I call just to hang up? I don't get it.

Rocco Veraldi's (Statement Date: February 8, 2005)

1. The beginning of August 2005 I began to receive hang-up phone calls. I received 5-10.
2. The caller would hang up when I answered the phone. I later found out that my daughter Stephanie had been receiving unwanted calls ... from a male caller.
3. These calls did annoy and harass me, and I want to press charges.

Preliminary Notes

1. Can we please get the date right? The date should be February 8, *2006*?
2. He received five to ten hang up calls in August, and six months *after*, he decided he was annoyed? Although it didn't happen, a grown man in his fifties was harassed by this?

3. If the caller never said anything, how could he have identified me? That's why he didn't!
4. Why would I call just to hang up?
5. He complained at 9:45 p.m., as I was already chained to the floor. Pile it on, guys. Something has to stick.

Summation

Stephanie is referenced in six of seven complaints, and Michelle Konik is referenced in five. And coincidentally they were the only ones who actually accused me. I thought it was random women? They're all related! Why did these "victims" continue to interact with their "alleged" harasser and never mention anything? Also, the police claimed an eleven-month investigation. After eleven months, not one audio exists of me saying sexual things to these so called victims? And if the complainants live in the sixth precinct jurisdiction. Why were the complaints filed at the seventh precinct? The statements all have a nice theme to them to; Frank Vetro former teacher at Newfield High School and current principal in Hampton Bays. Plus, I'm not stupid. Even a two-bit crook uses a throwaway phone for criminal activity. I wouldn't have left an easily obtainable phone record. No one would—unless they wanted a phone trail for the clerks at the police station. And where are these so called "trace results" and phone trail anyway?

> *At midnight on August 12, 2002, I received a call. The caller whispered so I couldn't make out if it was a man or woman. "I'm standing, naked" and a few other perverted things were said before I hung up. I laughed it off as a stupid prank. The next morning, I left for my administration course and saw my truck and the fence had been vandalized. There was also a note under my windshield wiper that included more perverse content (I still have that original, partly decomposed note).*
>
> *A stupid call is one thing, but this person knew where I lived and vandalized my truck and neighboring property. The vandal knew my life pretty well, because they didn't touch the car I drove for years although it was parked right next to my vehicle. Instead, they walked up a long residential driveway and headed right for the white Chevy*

> *Blazer I just purchased. I was concerned and decided to file a police*
> *report within the week. Then, on Wednesday, August 14, I received*
> *another, more alarming call, and it was definitely a male caller. I*
> *didn't recognize his voice, but I remember what he said: "Frank, I*
> *know you're a teacher at Newfield High School, and I'm going to*
> *spread rumors about you." The caller abruptly hung up. This was*
> *no longer a stupid, perverse prank call. This was my reputation and*
> *career being threatened. This was no longer an incident to report to*
> *authorities when I had an opportunity.*
>
> *I went to the police that day. There were two counts of aggravated*
> *harassment filed (the phone calls), and one count of criminal*
> *tampering (the vandalism). I still have the reports, none of which*
> *were ever investigated by the way. By the end of the week I not only*
> *had a new phone number, but I also got rid of my landline phone*
> *altogether and bought a cellular phone.*

To this day I don't answer private calls or numbers I don't recognize. I was a thirty-year-old man, in very good physical condition, and could take care of myself, but I felt alarmed, threatened, and harassed. I didn't want it to continue for even another day. When you feel threatened and harassed you do something about it. You don't let it go on for months or years. Michelle was in that same administrative course I was taking even though she wasn't going to school for her administrative certification. A strange coincidence?

While I was in Riverhead Jail, my employees Pat and Virginia, aware of my lack of technological prowess, did some homework by searching MySpace and Webshots.com. They found some things and instructed me on how I could navigate through on my own. I didn't own a computer so others printed things out for me. Here's a summary of my findings (I tried not to alter their bad grammar). Meet the victims.

Stephanie Veraldi's MySpace Accounts

I typed "Stephanie Veraldi," and a picture of a Bichon Frise appeared. Her account opened with Michelle's business name, Doriann Bichons, bragged about the business as if it was hers, and included pictures of Michelle's dogs. The following popped up:

Headline: Bichons!
Gender: Female
Age: 35
Profile updated: October 31st, 2005
About me: We have been breeding Bichons for over 20 years. We are known for breeding healthy, exceptional dogs.

Stephanie had another profile under the name Stefania. The following popped up:

Advertisements

- Wednesday August 3rd, I am having a party at my mom's Aug 4th ... call if you wanna join. [She posts her name and phone number on the internet.]
- Saturday, February 19th, PARTY. Both my parents are away that means two empty houses and double the parties! Leaving me and my two brothers to ourselves is not a good idea! Never trust three Veraldi's.

About me: My dogs are kinda my life! Lol yeah that might sound pathetic but not if you got to experience what I have over the past two years! ... I work for a breeder so I am always around my puppies and I also show dogs so I learned how to care for them. Bichons are the best! Message me if you are interested in buying a Bichon. Yeah so my best friend is like twice my age! Get over it. She is the best ... the most amazing person I have ever and will ever meet in my life! She is so strong and so brave and has taught me so much. I am who I am because of her and will become whatever I become because of her. She changed my life. She's beautiful and smart and STRONG!! I would be happy to become half the woman she is!
Interests: cops, and hot teachers
Books: S&M, Female Domination, Fem Dom, Dominatrix ... hahaha.
Hero: A great friend of mine who changed my life forever [Michelle Konik]
Occupation: groomer when I go home
College major: Secondary Social Studies [like Michelle]
Groups: Bichon Frise Lovers Only! I Love Bichon Frises! and Bichon Frise are the Best!
Status: She changes this between single, lesbian, in a relationship, and swinger.

Pictures on her profile included:

A. Michelle with her dogs, described by Stephanie a hottie;
B. Michelle shooting a gun. Stephanie's friend Mallory comments, "Way to put up pictures of your lesbian lover";
C. Stephanie drinking, and references to smoking marijuana;
D. Stephanie (underage) with Michelle, holding bottles of beer; and
E. A creepy picture of Stephanie. I thought it was Michelle—spitting image. It was no wonder she was being referred to as Mini Me.

Her profile states (the spelling was left as is):

A. Oh and I wouldn't fuck with me cause I get people arrested.
B. Stop this *try*.
C. I have no tolerance for physically, mentally, or emotionally abusive men and will do everything in my power to keep [my friends] away from that … I have succeeded.
D. Stephanie is a liar who u should never trust.
E. Steph will do anything for her teachr, friend, big sis, and luv
F. Stephanie was brainwashed! Lied to. Recruited?
G. Blondy plans ahead. 3 victims from Newfild? Can 3 lives B Ruine!

Stephanie's Webshots.com account included the following pictures:

A. Stephanie, about eighteen years old, drunk at Oneonta College, drinking with friends, family, her dad's girlfriend, Michelle Konik, and another Newfield teacher named Beth. She claimed her dad, Rocco Veraldi, was a pimp who liked to get everyone drunk.
B. Stephanie at college with male strippers, biting their G-strings, posing suggestively, making inappropriate remarks, referring to Michelle as a hottie, and referencing lesbian and female lovers.
C. Stephanie with the Suffolk Community College soccer team at a hotel, posing with a case of Bud Lights in her arms.
D. A "mystery person"—it's Michelle Konik in disguise, posing in her very recognizable house, and wearing a cheerleading jersey from Newfield High School.

Allison Engstrom's MySpace

Pictures on her profile included Allison:

A. Posing provocatively with captions that reference playing spin the bottle
B. Partying with Michelle Rogak, who left a comment saying she loves being dirty
C. On her back, her hands placed on another woman's groin while being straddled
D. Wearing a shirt with the words, "I'm too pretty to do math"
E. Standing in front of and pretending to pee in a men's public urinal
F. With a guy she references as "Dr. Howie felthersnatch" (say it fast over and over)

Her profile states:

A. Allison would like to meet…ANYONE who isn't fuckin retarded!
B. Her student commented, saying, "Hey Ms. Engstrom!!!! How's your summer?" [That's why a teacher shouldn't display this stuff.]

Michelle Rogak's MySpace

Pictures on her profile included Rogak;

A. Provocatively posing with a caption that says: Wow, it almost looks like I have boobs;
B. Posing with friends, showing off their asses and playing a game: Guess the Bottom;
C. Drinking alcohol with friends and teachers, squeezing Allison's boobs; and
D. Strategically placing her head over a painting of a penis.

Her profile states:

A. Rogak referred to herself and Allison as sluts as they converse over a picture of a naked guy.
B. Rogak, an earth science teacher, stated her favorite movie was *Earth Girls are Easy.*

Note: Two of her former students referenced her being a fucking cock tease and reminisced about making many prank calls! I swear.

Christina Impastato's MySpace

A. There are photos of Christina in provocative poses at eighteen years old, working as a shot girl and drinking alcohol.
B. One phrase claimed: You're only as strong as the tables you dance on, the drinks you mix, and the friends you roll with.
C. There was a group, Sean [name] is a Pimp. It claimed: This is how we start gangs and cults.

Christina's Coworkers (MySpace)

On October 25, 2005, at about 4:22 p.m., Christina was sent a message on MySpace from a coworker that said Christina will start work on October 31, 2005, at 3:00 p.m. (Christina claimed to receive a call at work the week of October 17, 2005). Was she even working there when she claimed to receive a call? Christina's complaint also mentions two of her coworkers, April and Jessica, who claimed to get calls similar to what Christina claimed to receive all the time. On MySpace, guys commented about having sex and phone sex with them. Their pictures could have been in *Playboy*. The lingerie and poses were not rated for kids. April had nude pictures.

Of course dressing provocatively or having consensual phone sex does not make them deserving of being harassed, if they were. I'm just trying to note the culture of their work environment, and perhaps figure out how and why they received these allegedly harassing phone calls.

I also would like to know how Stephanie's mom would feel about all this. Stephanie admitted she couldn't be trusted and liked to get people arrested; referenced a dominatrix lifestyle and smoking marijuana; displayed lewd pictures of herself with male strippers; referred to her teacher Michelle

Konik as her best friend, a hottie, mentor, and big sister. Stephanie's friend Mallory referenced Michelle as Stephanie's lesbian lover. Stephanie proudly told the world that Michelle was everything and that she was growing up to be just like her. She posted pictures of her drinking alcohol with friends, family, Michelle, and others. Michelle was everywhere, but what couldn't be found anywhere was one picture, word, or reference to her actual mother—not one.

February 18, 2006

My buddy Leo asked me to stop by his job site. He sounded like he really needed to speak with me. Leo was the one who helped Michelle when she needed extensive work done on her home/kennel, from August to early winter of 2004.

When I arrived at the site, Leo got right to the point. "Frankie, the student mentioned in the paper—is her name Stephanie?"

"Yeah, how did you know?"

Leo yelled, "Damn it! Do you remember when I asked you if Michelle was bisexual?" I did remember that, but I just brushed off the question as guy talk and didn't even think to ask why he would ask. Leo continued, "Stephanie was always at Michelle's house."

I interrupted, "The entire time, as in multiple days, weeks, and months? Because she was a student at that time."

"I'm sorry Frankie. How could I know? If I did I would have said something. Do you want me and Joe (his employee) to be witnesses or something? Because we saw things that did not seem appropriate."

"Like what?"

"I have young kids in school, and I would not want them as close with their teacher as this girl was."

I stopped him for a moment so I could get something to take notes with. Here is what they claimed to witness:

1. Michelle and Stephanie were in Michelle's bedroom on a Saturday for about two hours.
2. Stephanie took showers at Michelle's and always had a bag with a change of clothes.
3. Stephanie was there late at night, sometimes alone, other times with other young girls.

4. Michelle drove Stephanie around in her car.
5. Stephanie was at Michelle's house alone while Michelle was still at work.
6. Stephanie didn't just help with the kennel. She did yard work, cleaned the house, etc.
7. Stephanie drank beer at Michelle's house.

Shortly after, I spoke with my brother Rocky. After he learned who Stephanie was, he told me he saw her with Michelle on Thanksgiving Eve in 2005 at a twenty-one-and-over club called Port Jazz. Stephanie was only eighteen years old. Rocky also discovered I was the subject of "away messages," messages users post on their computers and appear when others attempt to contact them. These messages were being left under Michelle's screen name, *Isis7Isis*, and Stephanie screen name, *Rocks-Daw-Da*.

I didn't have a computer. Others monitored the messages for me, and there were instances when I was told there was no message. For example my friend Mike Loftus confirmed he was not able to see certain messages that my brother Rocky could see. Michelle didn't want everyone to see the messages of her showing remorse, but messages that bashed me were open to the world. There were hundreds, probably over a thousand messages left for over a year, but I did not include them all. The song lyrics they quoted often times referred to abuse, abusive relationships, and loving someone that you can't have (merely my interpretation). There seemed to be a form of communication between Michelle and Stephanie in some of the messages. The entire situation was juvenile, but the police believed them. The bad grammar is theirs, and the dates are pretty much on point.

Away Messages

Stephanie (December 5): Michelle, I can't wait for the day you wake up without him on your mind, Love, Steph. [This was actually handwritten, on an index card]
Stephanie (February 6): This is going to be one memorable weekend!!! ... Home.
Stephanie (February 6): One day he'll wake up and realize how much he needs her, and she'll be waking up to a guy who already did. Luv my big sister. [This was on a lot of the messages.]
Michelle (February 12): He could have had it all.

85

Michelle (February 14): How can certain people lie straight to your face and feel no remorse?

Stephanie (February 14): Five words … I got what I wanted … He'll remember them forever. He could have had the best life but he lost her.

Stephanie (February 15): He ruined his own life … he lost her!

Michelle (February 15): I wonder if her husband knows where she was yesterday? I just can't take it. Is it possible that everything I thought is really true? A visit on Valentines Day … hmmm. [This is related to the letter that was mailed to a woman's husband in December 2005.]

Stephanie (February 15, in response): She was there to let her son see his real daddy. Is it possible that everything you thought is true?

Michelle (February 15): Newfield knew long before February … no one said a word … know who your real friends are. ["Know who your friends are" is a line I always said.]

Michelle (February 16): My heart is broken. I can't take this. Why did this have to happen? Love is blind.

Stephanie (February 16): Eat shit and live!

Michelle (February 17): Does he really think I gave him the only copy of the nipple cream tape? When will he learn that I am not dumb? [The nipple cream tape was actually a voicemail left on my phone by an employee I was sleeping with at Newfield. Michelle said a cassette tape of it was left in her mailbox. I'd bet she is the one who accessed my voice mails.]

Stephanie (February 17, in response): She's so fucking smart … and I'm a her in training. No wonder your so fucked!" [Michelle manipulated/trained her student to hate me.]

Michelle (February 17): Out of sight out of mind? … Wishful thinking

Stephanie (February 17): Oh and orange is sooo not his color … it doesn't go with creepy blue eyes! [Referencing prison jump suits.]

Michelle (February 18): I don't understand how a heart can love no matter what … that is unconditional.

Stephanie (February 18): I hate you … go to jail already. [They taunted a man they claimed to fear.]

Michelle (February 18): What will this week hold? It didn't have to be this way. [No it didn't, she could have left me alone.]

Stephanie (February 18): And I'll become what you became to me. [Song lyrics.]

Michelle (February 18): Have you ever loved somebody so much that you was just to blind to see passed, all of the pain that they was causin you, Destiny's Child. [Song lyrics]

Michelle (February 27): Who gets into fights at weddings? [A drunken man did start a fight with me at a wedding. How did she know?]

March 2006

The architects of my set-up seemed to have accounted for everything. What they didn't count on was that when the smoke cleared from the nights in jail, the media, and the humiliation, I was not going to just lie down and become a victim of their spite. I had support and was more than happy to take them on. There's nothing like family—nothing. My immediate family, of course, was behind me all the way. The students praised me to the media, saying that I was a role model whom they respected and looked up to. Students wore T-shirts saying, "Free Vetro. We want him back." This support never made news outside of town, of course. The story made better press when it was all about a principal being a terrorist. The fact that students, teachers, administrators, and everyone including the town drunk realized the charges were trumped up didn't make as good a story.

I received tons of cards, e-mails, and letters of support, from people I have never met. Maybe they met Michelle. Inspired by the events that emerged, one student named Kieran wrote an article for the school newspaper centered on how the media would cross the line at times and how people were portrayed as guilty before being given a chance to defend themselves. People came out of the woodwork to show support—from the sheriff's department, administrators from other school districts, attorneys, local firemen, and even officers from other precincts.

Even my old school district, where some of the complainants work offered support. My former principal, Mr. Ross, and his wife, Kathy, who I believe were friends with Stephanie's dad, Rocco, wished me well. The math teacher I was pretty close with, Gilda, who was also friends with Allison Engstrom, shared kind words as she handed me a character reference. The fact that close friends of the complainants offered support spoke volumes.

The generally positive response I received was in two forms. People told me I was a great guy who did a lot of good and they didn't believe the accusations. It was also said that regardless of whether I was guilty, I didn't deserve what was happening. My body of work was enough to show that I was a 99 percent solid person and citizen, and I shouldn't be judged by 1 percent. Although I appreciated the latter statement, I reminded those people that I was indeed innocent. Their point was well taken, though, and I agreed. It just had no context with me at that moment. I, like everyone else, have that small percentage that isn't something to be proud of. But the claims Michelle and her coconspirators made are not where my personal faults lie.

My assistant principal, Dan Nolan, was put in charge of the day-to-day operations of the building. I was carrying out the other administrative duties from central office, which was only about one hundred yards from my actual office. My secretary, Grace McGuire, made sure I stayed grounded and had my finger on the pulse of the building. Both she and Dan made frequent visits to keep me in the loop, raise my spirits, and assure everyone that I was the leader of the building. Marc Meyer, whom I considered not just a friend but also a brother, always made a point to be at my side at all public events. Diane Albano, my Superintendent's secretary, was someone I knew I could trust. I appreciated everyone's warm words. Suffice it to say so many people in Hampton Bays—most of them—made me feel at home and offered words of encouragement at a time when they were needed. It was tremendous and made me feel good about myself and what I accomplished.

Not everyone was supportive. Some "friends" decidedly cut off communications with me, but those details aren't worth the time or my ink. Generally speaking, Hampton Bays was a town that appeared to be very loyal and supportive. Although I didn't live in the town, they treated me as if it was my home. My superintendent even offered her help. She took notes from her conversations with the authorities and the media. She said she would share them with my attorney and would love to take the stand on my behalf. She even called my old school district and dropped Michelle's name to ask if she had any history. She said Len Adler, the superintendent there, verified that Michelle did and that there was more to the story.

When I saw her, I asked, "Ms. Loewenthal, what is her history? Can we find out more details?"

She said she would keep me informed as she found out details. Before leaving my presence, she had a question for me. "How can we get Jim back in town?"

"What do you mean?"

"I'm a superintendent. I know a lot of things." I was happy but not sure why. It seemed there was something out there that could help me. I could only assume it had something to do with the affair she had with Jim years ago. Jim and I may have been kindred souls. But even if there was something he could help me with, how was I going to get a hold of him?

Chapter Six
The Hunt Continued

It was as if he heard my conversation with Joanne. The very next day, Jim found me. My buddy Marc called me from the elementary school. "You aren't going to believe who just called and left a message with my secretary." I didn't even have a chance to throw out a guess. "Jim called and left a number for you to call back. He said you would know the reason for the call." I took the number, thanked Marc, hung up, and called Jim. It was a phone number from another state. I left a message, and he quickly called back, not even a minute later.

He cut right to the chase, no formalities. "Hey, Frank, I heard the news and knew right away that Michelle Konik must be behind the whole thing." "How did you know? And what happened to you in 2001?" That was when the dump truck filled with bricks unloaded on me. I'm not sure I was ready for what I was about to be told.

There's an old saying of being "played like a violin." It turned out Michelle could have had her own orchestra. She was that good and we both fell for her antics. Jim blew me away.

"Frank, if you remember, you and I didn't speak to each other much during my last few months at Newfield. I didn't trust anyone at that time. My personal life was falling apart, and Michelle was playing it off as if she was my best friend."

I interrupted, "But I thought you guys were done."

"Frank I tried to end it and get away from her, but it wasn't that easy. I know the rumors going around were that I was harassing and stalking her, but that wasn't the case at all. I can and will prove that to you. Michelle is adept at dividing and conquering. She had me believing she was the only one on my side, but all the while she was the one planning my demise.

Frank, she's ten steps ahead of you, brother. That affair took too much of a toll on my life. I knew I made a mistake and felt guilty for what I was putting my wife and kids through. I wanted to salvage what was left of my family, so I demanded an end to our relationship. That's when Michelle claimed that I was harassing and stalking her. That was just another means she used to reach her goal, and it worked. Everyone in the school district thought I was guilty of something. Michelle created an entire illusion about me, and she was so good at her craft that no one understood that it was all nothing but lies."

"Damn, Jim, in all of that Michelle turned to me for friendship." "Yeah, Frank, her plan worked to perfection. She couldn't have me, yet she couldn't stay away from me, either, so she made it so that she wouldn't have to be near me."

"So, that's when your classroom was moved across the building, away from Michelle's?"

"Yes, and that's when a few individuals associated with Michelle actually came to the school and approached me during football practice. It was crazy."

"Listen, Frank, I called in sick to go to the dentist."

"I remember you told me you wouldn't be in that day."

"If you recall, I lived about forty minutes east of the school, and Michelle lived within minutes from the school. Yet she actually approached me at a state park where I lived, and that's when she claimed that I lost my temper and hit her. Why would she travel forty minutes east to a place to meet me if she was afraid of me?"

"That's a damn good question. There seems to be a pattern here." "She had me arrested, accused me of assault, and had an order of protection placed against me. They wanted to arrest me at school, but Mr. Ross asked the police not to arrest me there. I turned myself in."

"But Jim, there was an investigation at school."

"Yeah, I'm well aware, and that was bullshit. I have documentation from that investigation. I was suspended from school, and it should have been the other way around."

"So what happened to the criminal charges?"

"The charges didn't stick, and my suspension was completely unwarranted. I couldn't fight it, though. I wound up moving out of state. I had to get away for the sake of my wife and kids. I didn't want any part of working with Michelle or be in a climate where people would talk behind my back for God knows how long. That's why I just disappeared after that suspension."

"It's no wonder she never answered when I questioned her about the whole saga."

"Oh, no doubt, Frank. You were already caught in her web, but you didn't realize it. There's a ton of paperwork I have to show you. It will help. In hindsight I wish we had stayed in touch. This may have been avoided.

"Frank, the woman who fell for me in about five seconds completely turned on me in the same amount of time and with the same amount of intensity."

"You're right, Jim, she would do whatever you wanted. I saw it with my own eyes. She would have taken a bullet for you."

"Frank, the truth of the matter is that Michelle wasn't the victim—my wife and kids were the victims and I wanted to try to make things right."

"Amen, Jim, amen. And I'll add to that and say she's not the victim now."
"I believe you. I know you, Frank, and I know her. It's called fatal attraction. Do you still go to Las Vegas during spring break?" "I do, and I will be going."

"I will be there too, so why don't we meet up and talk a little more?"
"Okay, that sounds like a great idea. Thanks for reaching out, and let's stay in touch. Take care."

It was a very nice phone call, and I was glad to see that he landed on his feet. I always knew him to be a stand-up guy, a great friend, and one hell of an educator. He also moved up the educational ranks and moved on to better things for himself and his family. I thought—hoped—we were the only two guys who could truly understand how believable, and evil, Michelle could be.

In hindsight, it was clear that the warning signs were there. I wanted to see the good in Michelle. She seemed to be a good person, at least outwardly. But as nice as she could be, I was learning that there may have been two personalities in one body. I believed I was learning that in a most difficult and destructive way. As her newest prime target. She got everyone else to hate Jim when she realized they couldn't continue, and she planned to do the same to me. She tried to turn my friends and family, my coworkers, and every girl I ever spoke with against me. She failed at that but had no problem going this far to accomplish her goal.

It may have been too soon to draw conclusions but I made an analogy that being involved with Michelle was like being in the mafia. Once you were in, you couldn't get out. She didn't let you. She would manipulate things in such a way that a situation was created. Once the issue was born, your fate was already cemented. Meanwhile you didn't even know there was an issue, because there really wasn't. All the while she had you convinced she was the only one you could trust and that it was everyone else who was against you. Every rule has an exception, and my take on Michelle back in 2001–2002—"No one wants to be judged by their worst moment in time"—seemed to be way off.

I was still employed and could weather this storm. That's why I thought Michelle and my new found adversaries wanted to finish the job. For someone who feared me and had an order of protection against me, she sure was trying her hardest to see and/or communicate with me. Everyone knew, including Michelle, that I jogged, and one of the places where I jogged for years was my old high school, Longwood, four minutes from my home. Michelle never jogged, and in case she decided to jog, she lived a few miles from Newfield High School, in the district she graduated from and worked in. That school had an even better track than Longwood's.

That was why I was in shock on Sunday, March 19, 2006. As I was jogging, training for the Long Island Half Marathon, Michelle approached me on the track. Why would she drive out of her way to go to a track where she knew I would be? Why chance seeing someone you were afraid of? I immediately thought about what Jim told me regarding when he took off to go to the dentist in 2001. My heart started to pound. She started crying and said something about how she didn't want this to happen—blah blah blah. I nervously walked away, afraid. She followed me to tell me she was confused and didn't know what to do. She said if I ever loved her I would not be speaking to Jim after what he did to her. Why would she just throw that out there? How did she know?

I called my attorney, Lori, and was told not to worry about her and focus on myself. What?

Away Messages

Michelle (March 2): He said in a message ... I know you are ordered not to talk to me ... I understand ... thank you for supporting me ... [I said that exact quote to a Newfield "friend."]
Michelle (March 5): ... from Hooters? Why would anyone say that? [Perhaps it was her fake breasts.]

Stephanie (March 6): Where do we go nobody knows. Don't ever say you're on your way down, when ... god gave you style and gave you grace so put a smile on your face. [Song lyrics]

Michelle (March 7): So it was said, so it was written ... he and the ostrich together forever ... [Michelle called the Newfield employee who left me the "nipple cream" message the ostrich.]

Stephanie (March 9): Memories back when she was bold and strong and waiting for the world to come along. Swears she knew it and now she swears he's gone. [Song lyrics]

Stephanie (March 11): He's so done.

Michelle (March 11): I just don't get it. Why pick me? I loved so much ... I would have given my life for him ... for what? For someone who didn't care ... Pretended to love ... Who made out with students ... who slept around ... who harassed women ... I have one question ... why pick the one person who loved him the most ... why me? [Those were lies and libelous. Loved me the most?]

Stephanie (March 13): When your too in love to let it go. But if you never try you'll never know just what your worth' Cold Play. [Song lyrics]

Stephanie (March 13): I'm afraid no one will love me as much as my dog does.

Stephanie (March 13): Bladdy blah blah blah stop your fucking bitching I'm ok I'm just on drugs yeah yeah.

Stephanie (March 14): So how many illegitimate children does this guy have ... Thank god she's away from him.

Talie (March 14, a reply from Stephanie's friend): By any chance does the guy in your away message own an orange suit? Lol.

Stephanie (March 16): Jail jail jail ... oh and orange is so not his color. [Would you want your daughter to antagonize a man she fears?]

Michelle (March 17): Happy St. Patty's Day at Irish Times!!! [Irish Times is a local bar I frequented. More importantly, she never frequented it.]

Stephanie (March 17): She'd never lose her nerve, she's more then you deserve. She's just far better then me Shakira. [Song lyrics]

Michelle (March 18): I remember this day a year ago ... At the parade 'hey guys, we are going to leave' 'yeah, if I had a woman like Michelle I would leave to.' Little did they know he dropped me off and went to the bank instead ... Yeah, happy St. Patrick's Day Hampton Bays ... do you really know him? Too bad he was so fucked up ... we could have had the best life! [I did take her to that parade, and I did drop her off—to get rid of her!]

Michelle (March 20): How could you love him? What is wrong with you? Everyone knew what kind of guy he was.... Don't judge me

93

because I loved someone I believed in I'll always love that person. [Pretending to care and play the innocent victim.]

Stephanie (March 20): She loved him yeah, she didn't want to leave this way. [Song Lyrics]

Michelle (March 21): I don't want to hear anymore stories about him!!! I don't want to cry anymore. You would think after all this time and all these stories I would stop caring, I can't. [Please, stop caring!]

Stephanie (March 23): Since you think you're ten steps ahead ... print this one too! [Thanks to a judas Hampton Bays guidance counselor, she discovered her messages were being printed out.]

Michelle (March 24): There's so many things I wish I could have said ... If I only had the chance. [Is this why she kept following me around?]

Michelle (March 25): Nice to see you're doing your research ... here's another one for you ... I should have always listened to my gut ... [I never responded once to these messages.]

Stephanie (March 29): Out with some HU babes ... DRUNK I will be drunk!

Stephanie (March 30): I'm drunk what U gonna do about it nigga!

Stephanie (March 30): Live while you can, don't you see your dreams are right in the palm of your hands. Vanessa Carleton. [Song lyrics]

April and May 2006

It was humbling. Although Hampton Bays was for the most part behind me, it was tough to not be in my building. I loved those students, and I couldn't be with them and help them with their problems. I enjoyed the camaraderie of my colleagues, but I couldn't work with them. I was allowed to attend extracurricular activities, but only if I was with someone, namely Dan Nolan. I had to run the building from central office. Teachers came to me, and meetings were held at my new location. There was the added pressure of being constantly asked what was going on with the case. Nobody understood how the criminal justice system operated, including me. I had no answers. I wanted a quick resolution too, but the wheels of justice turn very slowly.

On a personal level, I was a little uneasy when I went somewhere, wondering if someone would say something or recognize me. I always felt like people were staring. When I saw a police vehicle, I became nervous. Forgive me for being a little uneasy around police officers given my circumstances. Not to mention I was always on the lookout for Michelle. I was told to stop thinking about it so much and that I was too fixated. I thought I was taking it well. I was working, productive, and enjoying life as much as possible. It was a tough balancing act. I had to be very careful about how I approached things, because I didn't want Hampton Bays to be in the news. I was still very much in the spotlight, and I knew that authorities were trying to dig up dirt, albeit unsuccessfully. My life was dangling by a thread, and I was concerned about protecting Hampton Bays. It was just like me to put others first, even in the worst of times.

On April 10, after one of my meaningless court appearances, I packed and went to JFK airport for my annual trip to Las Vegas. It was about 5:39 p.m., and as I went through the metal detector, my phone rang. It was a 702 area code—Las Vegas. My parents had recently purchased a condominium in Nevada, and I thought it was my mom calling. I quickly answered and asked her to call right back because I was going through the metal detector. I didn't even wait for a response. A few minutes later my cell phone rang again. It was about 5:44 p.m., and … it was Michelle! The actual number was 702-310-6697. Why would she want to talk to me and continue to call me? I asked her to please stop. Thank God I had to board the plane. It was a great excuse to get off the phone without making her angry. Obviously she had the police eating out of her fake breasts—I mean the palm of her hand. I didn't need her concocting more stories.

The next day, April 11, at about 1:30 a.m., my phone rang. Michelle again! The number on my caller ID showed 702-310-6704. She continually asked about my prior relationships and said she wanted answers. She attempted to keep me on the phone, cried, and told me she loved me. I hung up the phone, but she called back six minutes later. It got worse. On Wednesday, April 12, I was walking around the Monte Carlo Hotel and Michelle was in the main lobby. She had an order of protection against me. Why would she come near me? Better yet, why did she travel about two thousand miles to run into someone she feared?

During the same trip, I met Jim at the New York New York Hotel as we had planned. We shared Michelle stories, and it was very creepy hearing what he had to say. There was a definite pattern with her actions and even her words. Now that I think about it, Michelle could've been spying on both of us as we spoke. I only went on a short trip because I didn't have the money to stay longer, thanks to attorney fees.

Back in New York, on April 16, my family was spending Easter Sunday at my brother Sal's house. Before I went I figured I would go running around the Longwood track to burn some calories before consuming thousands at the Vetro Easter Sunday dinner. I told my parents where I would be to protect myself. Guess who showed up at the vacant and obviously desolate track again? I couldn't believe it. Michelle wouldn't let me leave as she followed me to the parking lot. Thank God my parents eventually showed up as I had hoped they would. Parents can sense when something is not right. Seeing them, Michelle ran away crying. What the hell was she up to?

My attorney, Lori, once again told me to stay away. I was trying to, damn it! I requested that my attorneys subpoena all the videos of the encounters. I also wanted an order of protection placed against her. I knew Michelle was trying to set me up for the kill, but my requests fell on deaf ears. I was going out of my mind. When would this "public relations" component from my attorney take effect?

On April 22 at about 9:30 a.m., I was leaving Sportime Gym after my Saturday workout. I was en route to the Hampton Bays groundbreaking ceremony at the site of the district's new middle school. As I drove into town, I received a phone call from Michelle's therapist, Anne Rudolph. She warned me to stay away from Michelle.

"Um, yeah, no kidding."

She said she heard good things about me, that I was a nice guy, and she was only trying to avoid me getting arrested again. She said Michelle loved me, but it was a dangerous love, and I had to be careful. She feared for my safety. When that conversation ended, I called my attorney, Lori. A therapist calls someone to confide in details regarding their client? That only happens if the person they are warning is in immediate danger or their client is a danger to themselves, if it happens at all.

That day, Michelle left a slew of computer messages in hopes of contacting me. That night—actually, the next day, because it was around 12:25 a.m.—Michelle called from a pay phone in my own neighborhood. The number was 631-345-0487. She frantically said it wasn't her idea for her therapist to call me and she didn't want that to happen. She was crying hysterically and said she had no more coins for the phone as it went dead. The next afternoon, April 23 at about 1:47 p.m., I told Lori once again. "Stay away," she told me. Yeah, no kidding, Lori! The months of April and May consisted of me trying to dodge Michelle at every corner, and my attorneys did nothing to stop her. Little did I know, the unthinkable was about to happen.

Away Messages

Michelle (April 1): I don't want to hurt anymore. Kryptonite. [She called me her kryptonite.]

Michelle (April 1): I don't want to hurt anymore ... That's my kryptonite ... why did he do all those things to me? There is still so much to say but nothing can be said ... now all my strength was sucked out of me.

Michelle (April 2): Your face it Haunts, my unpleasant dreams. Your voice it chased away, all the sanity in me. These wounds won't seem to heal. This pain is much to real. There's just to much that time cannot erase Evanescense, My Immortal. [Song lyrics]

Michelle (April 2): Going to Longwood for some air ... [That's where I ran]

Michelle (April 3): I feel like I'm dreaming ... I am so confused.

Michelle (April 3): My head is about to explode ... I have so many questions, Time is not on my side ... I just wish I had the truth, the answers, some truth ... something to explain ... I am going to think ... somewhere.

Stephanie (April 4): 2am and she calls me cause I'm awake ... Can you help me unravel my latest mistake?'Anna Nalick. [Song lyrics]

Michelle (April 5): OK ... I'm going!!! By the way ... the male visitor was really tall and likes dogs??

Stephanie (April 5): Vegas = hot guys that you will never see again.

Stephanie (April 5): I miss my dogs.

Michelle (April 6): What happens in Vegas, STAYS in Vegas.

Michelle (April 6): Make me believe ... what happens in Vegas stays in Vegas.

Michelle (April 7): 5am! See ya! What happens in Vegas stays in Vegas.

Michelle (April 8): I am happy to go but it brings back memories. What happens in Vegas stays in Vegas. [Memories of when she was there with me.]

Michelle (April 15): Back home! Thinking a lot ... Looking forward to Easter Sunday ☺.

Stephanie (April 16): Does it kill, does it burn, is it painful to learn that it's me that has all the control Maroon 5.

Michelle (April 17): If I listened long enough to you, I'd find a way to believe it's all true. Knowing that you lied straight faced while I cried ... still I look for a reason to believe Rod Stewart. [Song lyrics]

Michelle (April 17): S.O.S. Please somebody help me. It's not healthy for me to feel this. YOU are making this hard, I can't take this, it don't feel right. S.O.S. please someone help me, it's not healthy for me to feel this. YOU are making this hard, you got me tossing turning can't sleep at night Rhianna. [Song lyrics]

Stephanie (April 18): She's better then you.

Michelle (April 18): Love, I don't like to see so much pain, so much wasted and this moment keeps slipping away. I get so tired of working so hard for our survival. I look to the time with you to keep me awake and alive ... Peter Gabriel. [I still have that CD she made for me.]

Michelle (April 22): Morning- not my idea ... I did not want it to be like this ... is it possible that no one understands me? I am not going to do anything. [The day her therapist called me, she posted a string of messages in a panic.]

Michelle (April 22): NOT MY IDEA ... I am not doing anything ... NO ONE understands ... NO ONE.

Michelle (April 22): Is it possible that there's no one worth trusting? Even the pro's? I will do the 'right' thing ... all on my own ... no matter what anyone fills my head with ... I need to know something.

Stephanie (April 24): This is going to be the best thing for you and your gonna recreate yourself from this Jefferey Wands.

Stephanie (April 24): One day he'll wake up and realize how much he needs her, and she'll be waking up to a guy who already did.

Michelle (April 24): It seems like everyone wants something from me ... but they don't want what I want from me ...

Stephanie (April 26): And I'll try not to destroy you baby even though we both know I can, oh you know I can The Pierces.

Michelle (April 27): You are still devoted to him said a man in charge. [Her principal got close with her ... in the biblical sense.]

Stephanie (April 28): I'm a silly mess hehe☺.

Stephanie (April 28): How does she do it all??? She's amazing that's how! Oh and her class competition is going to be amazing too!!!!

Michelle (April 29): You would have been so proud of me ... running the first ever class competition single handedly! It was an amazing night ... I did it on my own. [I ran a class competition five months prior in Hampton Bays. She used my ideas.]

Stephanie (May 4): Its funny how you don't even think I care ... do you even remember what I said to you Christmas break?? [Was there a lover's quarrel?]

Stephanie (May 4): See your not what I expected but you're the only one who knows how to handle me and your such a great kisser and I know that you agree Maria Mena.

Michelle (May 4): To think I believed again ... Should I still? [Michelle went on a string of about twenty-five messages saying the same thing over and over.]

Stephanie (May 5): Can you say photo op!! she is the shit.

Stephanie (May 5): Winners dog and winners bitch!!! Best in show coming u! Yeah baby! [She was referring to Michelle's recent victories as a dog breeder.]

Michelle (May 6): I guess I am the fool once again ... why?

Stephanie (May 8): And now you wanna ask me why? ... It's like why does your heart beat and how do you cry? [Song lyrics]

Stephanie (May 9): Head over heals in lust.

Stephanie (May 10): I miss my dogs and my 'big sister.'

Michelle (May 12): Sad ...

Michelle (May 13): I guess I am the fool once again ... thank you for reminding me ... will the hurt ever stop ... I guess for one of us it already did ... that's nice. [Was I supposed to want her after being arrested? I didn't want her before that!]

Stephanie (May 13): Last weekend at Oneonta, perhaps me and mal will get arrested?? [Mal was her college friend.]

Michelle (May 15): I will never forget this ... [Neither would I.]

Michelle (May 16): Will I ever get the answer I need.

Stephanie (May 17): I miss my dogs so much.

Michelle (May 19): How? Why? I can't take it anymore ... how many more things am I going to find out. [She went on and on for weeks with similar messages.]

Michelle (May 22): A little confused ... but what else am I supposed to be ... I have no answers ...

Michelle (May 26): Thinking ... confused ... sad.

Michelle (May 26): I don't know what to do.

Michelle (May 30): I don't know what to do ... I am so confused ... Just your presence and I second guess my sanity. Rhianna. [Song lyrics]

Michelle (May 30): I don't know what to do ... I am so confused ... I remember the Star Wars marathon ... just your presence and I second guess my sanity. [We watched every Star Wars movie together a year prior.]

Michelle (May 31): Ok!! Just your presence and I second guess my sanity.

"It is better to risk saving a guilty person than to condemn an innocent one."

— Voltaire, *Zadig*

Chapter Seven
The Crucial Blow

June 2006

On June 1 I accompanied my superintendent, Joanne Loewenthal, to a luncheon for all the valedictorians in Suffolk County. I was well received by all the other principals and superintendents. My superintendent leaned over and said, "Frankie, we're going to get through this." It felt great. Soon after, I noticed a guidance counselor I used to work with from Newfield, Helene Flynn, was there, along with the principal, Gordon Brosdal. I had an excellent working relationship with Helene, so I went to say hello. When I did, Gordon literally jogged—didn't walk fast, but jogged—away. Strangely, Helene wasn't too warm to my conversation either. She didn't even look me in the eye. I just walked away.

I left the luncheon early, because I had an appointment with my attorney, Lori. On my way home, the unthinkable happened. The sixth precinct left me a voice mail: "When you receive this message, call the sixth precinct immediately."

I called my attorney Nick instead, and he called them before calling me back.

"Frank, they said you violated the order of protection against Michelle."

"No, I didn't. She's been contacting and approaching me for months, and I've been saying this for months, after each time it happened!"

Nick said I had to turn myself in. Arrested again! Didn't anyone involved in this have a conscience? Just on her word, and nothing more? The police didn't want to hear it and ordered me to turn myself in, and they wanted me there fast. It was a tough drive home. I was still in my suit, and I knew it was going to be a long night in jail and another long day in court. I stopped at my parents' house. My mother didn't say anything. All she could do was cry and hug me. I assured her I would be fine. I had so much hate inside me for what these people were doing to me and my family. I called my brother Sal to let him know I wouldn't make the softball game that night. On a lighter note, it was my turn to bring beer to the game, and as usual I still came through. Even in the worst of times I own up to my responsibilities. I took a shower and gave my mom a hug and kiss good-bye. As I walked out of the house, my brother Rocky said in a sad tone, "I'm sorry, Frank." I stayed positive, not wanting to add to their misery.

When I arrived at the sixth precinct I asked for the officer who was looking for me. I expected him to treat me like shit, but to my surprise he was quite pleasant. He shook his head and told me he felt really bad. "Sometimes the person accused of breaking and order of protection is wrongfully accused, but it's no-questions-asked in Suffolk County." He never even cuffed me, and I think he really did feel bad.

"Is there going to be another media blitz?" I asked.

"If so, it's not going to be me who starts it," he responded. He did my paperwork, shook my hand, and wished me luck.

The sixth precinct was much different from the seventh precinct. It was a bit cleaner but had the same types of cells and accommodations. However, the seventh treated the alleged criminals like animals. They spoke down to them, insulted them, and completely disrespected them. As a result, the alleged criminals spoke back, yelled, and acted like animals. I think it's all a part of a self-fulfilling prophecy that exists in many people. They blindly form an opinion of a person without any firsthand knowledge. Miraculously, that someone becomes exactly what the person expected them to be, whether good or bad. Generally speaking, people will live up to or down to your expectations. The expectations at the seventh precinct were as low as could be.

The sixth precinct personnel, on the other hand, showed respect and used words like *please* and *thank you*. They treated us like human beings, and as a result they were treated courteously in return, for the most part. Now, I'm sure it's not always that smooth, but it has to be a better approach to the job. The seventh had too much of an edge to them—a recipe for failure. I realize I'm basing my descriptions of the two precincts on one-night encounters, so it's to be taken with a grain of salt. It's what I experienced though.

After another long night it was back in the paddy wagon and off to court. There weren't any cameras at least. The courts were fairly empty that day, but the officers were up to their old tricks again, treating us like total shit. I actually witnessed them entice one alleged criminal to the point where he mouthed off to them. They came in and dragged him out. Like my last visit, I didn't say one word. I just took the verbal abuse and logged it in my memory bank. When I was finally called to the courtroom, Nick was waiting. It was the same judge, Hensley.

"You are an educated man," Judge Hensley said. "Do you know what order of protection means?"

"Yes, sir."

He banged the mallet and let me go without bail. Released on own recognizance (ROR).

On Saturday, June 3, the media got me again. They couldn't get any of the facts straight from the first arrest and wrote complete lies about this one. They said I pulled into Michelle Konik's driveway and rolled the window down to threaten her. Where did they get that crap? More importantly, where the hell was my defense? I always read quotes from other defense attorneys helping their clients with all the negative press. Where was my help?

I met with my attorney, and he gave me the newest statement filed against me by Michelle Konik. She claimed I pulled in her driveway and told her that I could make her happy. Make her happy? I never even wanted this woman. God, the extremes her sick mind would go to, because she could not handle rejection, is off the charts. She also said I had thirty-seven letters that could ruin her and that she recognized my car. Thirty-seven letters? And yeah, she would know my car, because she came with me to buy it in November 2005, while she was running around and planning my demise. Where did they get this nonsense from? I didn't violate!

My superintendent set up an appointment to meet with me on Friday, June 9. To be safe I contacted the Hampton Bays union representative, Joe Kolarik, prior to the meeting. He said he spoke with Joanne, the board of education, and my representative from the state administrator's association. Joe told me I was well supported, would be treated fairly, and he felt no need to be a part of the meeting. He asked me to call him afterward to ensure it went well.

Joanne opened by saying there were still a lot of people backing me. But she also said because of this latest arrest, the state put a hold on my education license. That made no sense to me, being that the first seven complaints didn't affect my employment. What was the point? Even if I were guilty, there wouldn't be a violation of commissioner's regulations regarding moral character. So my licenses were never in jeopardy.

Joanne said I had to temporarily separate myself from the district. "But Joanne, what will I do for money?" I asked. Joanne said that I had to separate, there wasn't a choice. I couldn't work until the state education department cleared me to work, and I would be reinstated as soon as that occurred.

We spoke about the district, its future, and the different administrative positions that were opening up and being created. We made an agreement, and decided to meet periodically to coordinate my return as principal or possibly in a central office position, which did interest me. The board of education was well aware of the agreement, as was my administrative union.

Joanne tried to reassure me by saying people step away temporarily all the time. She said nobody wanted to end my career. I called Joe Kolarik afterward and everything seemed to be in place. There was more to the meeting but I don't want to veer too far off topic. Separating myself from the district, albeit temporarily, was a major blow. Although I didn't want my current problems to interfere with the lives of the teachers and students, I also didn't want to stop earning a paycheck. I wasn't happy, but it was out of my control, I guess. Talk about being under duress.

I was thirty-four years old. The circumstances surrounding my separation were so public. Who would hire someone in the middle of a messy court case? Why would a young principal want another job? There were no jobs to be had, anyway, especially with the economy so bad. It was only a misdemeanor crime involving *alleged* prank calls—prank freaking calls! It just didn't add up. What else did they want from me? Not having an income was going to seriously jeopardize my defense, which I already couldn't afford. This was just what Michelle, the rest of the complainants, and the criminal justice system wanted: to cut me off from any sources I had to defend myself so I couldn't survive the grueling process. They planned to force a bogus plea deal to save face. I was going to continue on as long as I could, no matter how difficult it became. I was going to give this fight everything I had.

I warned my attorneys that Michelle was not through and kept approaching me, calling me, and communicating to me, but they never listened. My attorneys should have said something to the authorities, the media, or the DA's office. Their job—and, for that matter, the prosecution's job—is to protect everyone involved. I read that order of protection many times. It was a "refrain from" communicating, not "stay away" order. I could drive by her house if I felt like it—or camp out in a lounge chair in front, for that matter. I just couldn't communicate with her, and I didn't.

Upon further review, I saw that the orders of protection were designed in hopes that I would violate them. There were seven in all. Six of the complainants lived and worked in very close proximity of me. Four lived within two and a half miles of me. Three lived a few blocks away. I didn't even know what three of them looked like, and two of those three lived in my neighborhood. The point is that I could've violated the orders at any given time without even realizing it if it was just their word that was needed and nothing more. The least the least they could have done is supply me with pictures so I could know whom to avoid at the local convenience store. The absurdity was off the charts.

Away Messages

Michelle (June 3): Sick to my stomach and miserable. [Because she knows I'm innocent.]

Michelle (June 4): Completely numb.

Stephanie (June 4): Cradle your head in your hands and breathe just breathe. It never ends! What are the chances? Am I in a twilight zone? It's sick! Its beyond my comprehension! Do you have even the slightest idea? Every day, everyday ... It never fails. My life man, my life ...

Stephanie (June 8): Coulda had it all.

Stephanie (June 10): Belmont baby. [Referring to Belmont racetrack, another place I frequented, and another place Michelle went to with me.]

Michelle (June 12): I just want to wake up and realize it was all a nightmare.

Michelle (June 17): Completely numb.

Michelle (June 20): Sad ...

Stephanie (June 24): You got to take big risks if you want big rewards. [Like break the law and frame someone?]

Stephanie (June 24): She's finally happy and waking up to someone else on her mind.

Stephanie (June 25): You've lost her for good now. [I never wanted her!]

Stephanie (June 27): You could say she's safe.

Stephanie (June 29): Finally waking up to someone else on her mind!

Stephanie (June 29): Today was the greatest day of my life!
Stephanie (June 30): My jaw hurts from doing this ... ☺ and it's not even my life! [What exactly was she doing that her jaw hurts?]
Michelle (June 30): Am I dreaming?

July 2006

There was no light at the end of the tunnel. If there was, it was the light of an oncoming train. Nick made discovery and demand motions, requesting, in the spirit of full disclosure, everything the DA had as evidence. That included the procedures used by the authorities, any evidence or witnesses against me, and any evidence that could actually help me as a defendant, otherwise known as exculpatory evidence or Brady material. That seemed like a fair enough request, given that this is the United States of America, right? The DA's office had other ideas. They claimed that they had been ready for trial since the onset and they still hadn't answered his questions or turned over any evidence. All I had were the bogus statements—but I kept my frustration inside, trying to stay focused and positive.

A few incidents occurred over a two week period. My childhood friends Pete and Kim Giery, who stood by me the whole way, stopped by. Pete was another person who, as a favor to me, helped out Michelle when she needed someone to landscape her kennel's one acre property. Anyway, they brought a gift, "Frank, this defines you." It was a martial arts charm that my Aunt Rose had bought me many years ago. My ex-fiancée, Diane, kept it all those years and asked them to pass it along and wish me well. It was a very nice gesture and typical of something she would do. It was nice to know that the one girl I ever completely let into my life showed support. It made me think, and so I went back to the place that changed my life years ago: my martial arts school. I got a rush of energy visiting my old friend, Xristos Gaglias. We had countless, grueling sparring matches against each other in our younger years. After being hit by him, I could honestly say I was hit by the best and I never went down. The hits I was taking at the moment wouldn't drop me either. I rekindled the inner strength and power that comes when a person focuses their energy into a specific goal.

Two days after that visit, I was talking to my younger brother, Rocky. "Frank, they obviously don't know you very well. I wouldn't want you mad at me." My mom added, "Don't they know you will never stop?" That same weekend, I ran into a childhood friend I hadn't seen in years, Carlo. "Frank,

I believe in you, you're a great person who taught me a lot about competing and being the best I could be as we were growing up."

Perhaps the most unexpected event occurred on a Thursday night. I was sleeping on the couch when I received a phone call from a very popular, local priest with ties to Hampton Bays, Father Frank Pizzarelli. He reassured me not to feel bad if I had to point out someone's character flaws to save myself, as long as I was honest. Of course, I already knew that, but it was nice to get reassurance from a priest. I only hoped I could outlast the delays. I didn't want to let my supporters down.

I spent my days writing, investigating, and trying to make sense out of what was happening. My life was quite different. Instead of jogging over the Ponquogue Bridge to the beaches on Dune Road, I would run in Coram, the dead center of the island. Instead of going for coffee at the Hampton Bays Starbucks, I made a cup of coffee at midday. Instead of working out at Sportime, I went to Aspen Fitness in Centereach. Instead of seeing the peaceful sights of the bay on Dune Road, I had to look at the pond in the middle of the Central Islip Courthouse. Instead of spending time with students and teachers, I spent time with attorneys and court officers. It was tough. It was the biggest competition of my life—the sixth and seventh precincts, the DA's Office, and seven complainants versus Frank Vetro. Some people may have assumed I had been wounded to the point where I would just accept my fate. That wasn't happening. I was determined to save my name, my reputation, and my life. I visualized every day how the case would be presented so that when the time came I would have already won before the prosecution ever started. There wouldn't be a person even close to understanding this case the way I did.

On July 7 I went to my office in Hampton Bays to grab some extra clothes, and a couple of other personal items that I kept in my office, because I basically lived there. I only stayed for a brief moment and before leaving the premises, I had another nice conversation with Joanne, as she offered me all the support in the world. She said the town loved me and I'd be back in the Bays in due time. I met Dan Nolan, his sons, and Marc at Tiderunner's, a casual bar/restaurant located on the canal, one of my favorite spots in Hampton Bays. It was a beautiful day, and the beer went down easy. After Dan left, me and Marc drank a little more as patrons sent food and drink over to us as a gesture toward their appreciation for our commitment to the town.

During one of my meaningless court appearances this month,

Stephanie showed up. I don't know why; she definitely didn't have to be there. I noticed something very interesting, though. Michelle Konik had a tattoo of a butterfly on the inside, calf area of her leg. Stephanie was wearing a skirt and as she walked by with a mischievous grin on her face, I thought I noticed a very similar tattoo on the same part of her leg. She seemed to be a clone of Michelle.

On July 10 Stephanie drove by my folks' house. I planned on staying there just for a bit while I figured things out. She approached slowly, gave me a sarcastic smile, and waved. If I had done that I would have been arrested again. What were the chances that the timing could be just right for her to catch me outside? I wonder how many times she, and Michelle, came near me. How did she know I was even there? There was no need for anyone to ever drive by my mother's house unless they were visiting someone on the block. It's not a shortcut to anywhere and is not an outlet street. You can believe me on that. I lived there for twenty-three years, and I was there again.

A hell of a note: spend your whole life trying to be successful and an asset to society, and in just a moment of lies, hate, and deception you end up right back where you started. As far as surviving, I got by. I tried, daily, to find even a menial job in the interim, but it was impossible. Why would a successful young principal be looking for a job after working his way to the top? It's not the 1980s, and with the internet age there are no secrets. Plenty of lies, but no secrets. It was hard, because I knew I was under a microscope. In a flash I went from being a young, promising principal to barely staying afloat—barely.

Away Messages

Stephanie (July 1): I couldn't wait for the day and now it came ... so happy for her!
Michelle (July 10): S.O.S. please someone help me, it's not healthy for me to feel this way. YOU are making this hard, you got me turning and tossing can't sleep at night Rhianna. [This was just after I caught Stephanie driving by my mother's house.]
Michelle (July 20): Thinking and remembering how it was ... and trying to understand how we got to this point. [I rejected you, you lied, and set me up. That's how].
Stephanie (July 23): Just a year ago life was hell ... but now everything is so ...

Stephanie (July 28): Something about this relationship feels other worldly to me, like it was designed by a power and a hand greater then my own. Whatever this friendship is, it's been a great ride. Oprah.

August 2006

Almost seven months after the arrest, my attorneys finally met with the assistant district attorney, Adina Weidenbaum. She was a young, petite brunette with signs of baby fat still showing. She was accompanied by her supervisor. Maybe the district attorney's office thought having a young woman on the case of a man accused of harassing women would play to a jury—or maybe they thought my case didn't deserve anyone with real experience. After all, it wasn't a murder case or anything, unless you consider murdering a man's reputation a crime. Lori clued me in on a few key points resulting from this "confidential" meeting. And from this I can assure you my defense was not prepared. Understand this is secondhand information, because I wasn't allowed at the meeting. God forbid the man accused, the man being destroyed, would be allowed his say. I'm sure everyone involved will deny my claims. Let them.

First off, they turned over evidence, my phone records from April 19, 2005, to about November 23, 2005. I commented, "That's it. They better have more than that." I also asked when they acquired the records and how were they acquired. For all I knew they just received them and had absolutely no evidence when they arrested me accept those absurd statements. There was no way I was about to trust the authorities. I never thought they were going to play fair. Nick said, "I guess we will have to find out." The prosecutors said they were aware that Michelle caused someone else to get arrested before and didn't care that she had a suspect history. Not only did they not care about the implications on my career, but they also conceded it wouldn't have happened the way it did if I had not been a principal. Are you kidding? We all know how the law works and that life is not fair, but the arrogance to flat-out admit they were treating me differently was over the top. The law is not supposed to prejudge. Lady Justice does wear a blindfold, right?

The prosecution also bluffed the hell out of my attorneys by telling them there would be fifty more complaints coming down the pike. I couldn't stop laughing. Not one or two more—fifty! It was already six months after my arrest and a year after any alleged call would have taken place. What merit would anybody give to a person who needed this long to be convinced they were harassed? Jesus Christ, it was so easy to see this was all bull crap. My attorneys should have told them to get lost, and when I told them so, they just stared at me with blank faces. Blank freaking faces!

After an uncomfortable silence, my attorneys relayed more contentions. The prosecution was surprised when my attorneys told them Michelle was contacting me. They told my attorneys if they could prove this, they would consider taking steps to protect me from future encounters. We could have had not one, not two, but three videos that showed the encounters! Why didn't my attorney listen to me and get the videos when I requested them? Also, what about all the contact via the internet? I gave copies of those communications to both my attorneys way before my second arrest. What about my phone bill with the times she called me from Vegas? If they had properly prepared and had their A game, they would have already presented the material. After voicing my displeasure, I was met with more blank stares.

Simply put, no one put in the necessary time—or any time. The ball was dropped, and there was a lack of understanding of how important those videos were. Hell, I knew they were important. Now the DA's office said they were important. Everyone sure paid attention to detail when money was due. That's how the system works. Attorneys only care for as long as the money lasts. It's a crazy system that very few can comprehend. Here's something I could comprehend. If someone had put a stop to Michelle Konik, I'd be working! My attorneys ended our meeting by telling me that I was too focused on Michelle. That just showed they did not know the issues involved. The prosecution also offered a deal. They offered to drop four of the eight charges and give me sixty days in jail. I started cracking up. Admit to four crimes, have a criminal record, and spend sixty days in jail? I told my attorneys to deliver a message to the DA's office: "Go screw yourself." Yes, it was not the finest in the King's English, especially for a high school principal. What was I supposed to say? "Thanks"?

As I walked out, I made a statement that I truly believe to this day. Although one did not exist, even *if* there were a full length audio and video of me doing the things these women claimed, I am still 100 percent innocent. There's no crime in having sexually explicit dialogue between people consensually engaged in those conversations. Simply put, the complainants were not harassed—not by me in person, and not by me on a recording created in fantasyland.

Meanwhile Stephanie left Oneonta College for her sophomore year and stayed home to attend Suffolk Community College. Also, my prediction of a year ago was correct. Michelle was "officially" in a relationship with Gordon Brosdal, her current principal. That's right—a third relationship, at least, with someone in her building, this time her boss, who was old enough to be her dad. Hell, at least the new relationship would keep her away from me. Maybe this could explain my strange encounter with him on the day of that luncheon a few months back? Perhaps that was why he ran away? Maybe he knew what was about to happen. It was no wonder she was left unscathed professionally. If Middle Country Central School District tried to take action she could always claim sexual harassment by her boss. Jim was right—she was ten steps ahead of everyone.

I vowed to myself that no matter what these coldhearted people did to my life I would try my best to remain respectful and civil. I couldn't let them turn me into a monster.

Away Messages

Stephanie (August 4): I'm getting a phone call right now from a private number ... should I.
Mallory (August 4): Yeah, answer it.
Stephanie (August 4): Hello? panties? What? Your naked? Hangs up oh well it's not like it was anyone important.
Mallory (August 4): Yeah it's like hello? Panties? ... no, this is president Bush.
[Destroying my life was just a game to them, nothing more.]

September 2006

On about September 18 I went to court for another meaningless appearance. As always, when I approached the big red brick building from Carleton Avenue, I became a bit tense. It could have been the nicest, sunniest day outside, but as soon as I turned left into the courthouse parking lot, the day turned very gray. I parked and waited in line with everyone else. It was always backed up well outside the building. The crowd would stand there like cattle waiting for slaughter. After what seemed like an eternity, I went through the metal detector and walked upstairs to the dungeon known as courtroom 45D. Please allow me a moment to boast by saying I was once again the best dressed in the building. Today's appearance was nothing more than my attorney requesting an adjournment. I was told by Lori that by the next court date we would know if there was going to be a trial.

"The end is near, Frank."

"No way, Lori, not if we sit back. I want a trial but have no money to outlast them if we don't push."

About six days later, on September 28, Nick called to let me know the court had scheduled a Huntley hearing for October 6, without consulting with him. This hearing concerned admissibility of statements and my Miranda rights. The date conflicted with his schedule, and I was disappointed to know that it would be delayed further. I mentioned the prosecution would be unwilling to cooperate and suggested that evidence would be withheld in violation of my rights. The prosecution was playing this card game as if they had a full house, but I knew they were holding a pair of twos.

October 2006

On October 3 I had a meeting with my attorneys, another waste of our time and my money. They questioned me relentlessly regarding my possible guilt, but for that I gave them the benefit of the doubt. If I were defending someone in a criminal case, I would test him every now and then too, to be sure that I was defending a person who was stable in his thoughts and was a solid defendant. I questioned them about their knowledge of the case and the reason we weren't being more aggressive. Lori was not cheap, and she was doing nothing in terms of PR. As for the criminal aspect, I knew I was 100 percent innocent. I had to face it, though—neither my attorneys nor the prosecution would ever know the case as well as I did. They had many cases, and until mine went to trial, the details would not be understood. Therein lay the problem. My life was rotting away while the truth was being ignored. As I left the meeting, Nick told me, even though I made it clear I was against it, that he was scheduling a meeting with the prosecutors within the next two weeks. What was the point? I warned of more delays.

On October 6 I had to appear at my favorite brick building for no other reason than to get another adjournment to November 17. Nick told me that was when we would receive a date to begin pretrial proceedings. I loved that, and I really wanted them to push for as soon a date as possible. An interesting observation was when I overheard the assistant DA speak about another case with the judge. She made a motion to either drop an order of protection or put one in place because of communication via the internet. It's not important what the motion was. What is important is that there was communication that should not have taken place between a complainant and a defendant that impacted an order of protection. It made me wonder again what would have happened if my attorneys told the ADA that Michelle continually contacted and approached me. I am one hundred percent certain I would not have been temporarily removed from my position in Hampton Bays.

That evening I met up with a woman I was seeing, another Lori, at that local bar *Irish Times* in Holbrook. She was a young, single mom, with two very young daughters, obviously a vulnerable situation. But she, like anyone else with commons sense, knew the issues surrounding me were total nonsense. When I arrived, around 7:00 p.m., I noticed about ten or twelve people from my old school, Newfield, and also from Dawnwood Middle School, where I think Stephanie's mom, Nancy, worked. I thought about leaving, but none of the complainants were there. I greeted my friends and was approached by a few people from my old school who were very friendly and asked how things were going. One gentleman, a math teacher named Tim, bought me a drink, and we caught up on things. Shortly after, two other women from Middle Country Central School District, told me to leave. I rolled my eyes and walked away to chat with Lori.

As I spoke with Lori, those women gave her dirty looks. "Frank, why are they staring at me with such looks of hate?" She had been there for over an hour, and they had had no problem with her then. It was obvious that she was talking to me, and that was all they needed as a reason not to like her. There was always a little tension with those women because of our past dalliances, or should I say "mistakes" that I left behind when I went to Hampton Bays. Although they never really knew me, they disliked me and anyone I associated with. We moved farther down the bar to avoid those malicious women. They didn't stop. They began yelling at her, calling her a "fucking cunt" and "bleached-blonde whore"! I couldn't believe how classless those women were—to drag this poor woman, a totally innocent bystander into it showed their true colors. She didn't deserve that or what was about to come.

I decided to leave, and as I was saying my good-byes I heard her scream, "Frank!" I turned around to see one of the worst sights I could imagine. Violent, vulgar women who were drunk out of their minds, were dragging Lori by her hair across the bar! These women were not kids. Lori was bleeding, and her face was swelling. I broke up the fight with help from another teacher, making sure it was obvious I was doing nothing but stopping the melee. I didn't need another headline saying I was in a bar beating up women. An interesting comment was made by one of the assailants: "Michelle Konik ruined Jim's life, and now she ruined your life. I hope one day someone ruins her life. You all deserve it." I was literally run out of the bar. I now understand how people can develop rage in their hearts when they are unfairly judged or treated. Their hatred was unfathomable. It was hard for me to sometimes keep a reciprocal hate from consuming me.

On or about October 11 I met with my superintendent, Joanne, for lunch at a local establishment in Hampton Bays called Buccachinis. It was nice to be back in town, and we had a nice get-together. She told me again that she would take the witness stand on my behalf as we spoke about the timeline of my case and my reinstatement.

November 2006

I was looking forward to Friday, November 17, but I received a phone call from my attorney on Thursday, November 9. The ADA was going on her honeymoon and her supervisor was on vacation for two weeks, so they couldn't meet. There was another adjournment, and the meeting would be scheduled upon their return—a meeting that I didn't even want to take place. This didn't sit well with me. My attorneys told me on October 3 that a meeting would be scheduled within two weeks. According to my math, that would have been around October 17. Obviously the prosecution knew they were going on vacation for two weeks and that the ADA had her honeymoon scheduled. It was simply unacceptable.

I met with them on November 16, and it was pretty heated. I suggested yet again that the prosecution would string it out as long as possible and force me into submission. If they didn't then they would be screwed. It would look bad for them, as it should, if the case fell apart. It should have from day one—actually, from before day one. It was all a game with Frank Vetro, a pawn, a piece to be moved ever so slowly across the board game of the criminal justice system.

My attorneys just didn't seem to take my case that seriously. Every time I asked about speedy trial regulations, I was ignored. I paced across my house every day playing out the trial scenario, coming up with questions and considering every possible response they could have on the stand. I knew the complainants were not preparing and neither was the ADA (or my attorneys). I wanted them to be aggressive, because I thought we had ammunition to attack. I didn't think my attorneys were doing everything they should have been doing. I warned again that the delays would continue as long as they allowed it. I looked into other attorneys, but because of my inability to muster up the money needed to take on this goliath, it didn't make a difference. The truth shall set you free? No, the money shall set you free!

Meanwhile, I added a few people to my potential witness list. On Tuesday, November 21, at about 8:08 a.m., I received a call from a teacher at Newfield High School named Toni. Another teacher from Newfield also gave me some information, as did a Hampton Bays teacher who used to tend bar with Michelle Rogak. But perhaps the most disturbing information was given to me by a former student of mine named Joe while I was working out at a local gym, Aspen Fitness. Joe told me a couple of things that I honestly didn't want to believe.

Although the details of what I was told did seem to make sense and fit into the puzzle, I did not include them here. I wanted to be careful because some of what was said was very damaging if it turned out to be true. I just kept it all in my notes for future reference and also passed it along to my attorneys. Maybe they could get to the bottom of things.

I also heard the term *spoofing*, courtesy of an expert hacker who I believe worked for the FBI. I think his name was Kevin Mitnik. Mr. Mitnik explained a few things that savvy cell phone hackers could do once they stole your identity. They could make a call from their phone but have a different number displayed as the number calling, alter your address book, change their voices while making the call, and do other devious things. I didn't know what was done. I didn't have much to go on, but I would not have been shocked if spoofing techniques were used against me.

December 2006

Nick called me on December 8 to inform me that the assistant district attorney, Weidenbaum, refused to with meet him. The prosecution misled my counsel yet again as I had predicted. I was so aggravated that we complied with them even when I told my defense not to bother. What did they care? It was four more months of my life, completely freaking wasted. What a great way to spend taxpayer's money. They were picking up the tab for this ridiculous prosecution. December 20 was the next scheduled appearance.

On about December 18 I met with my superintendent, Joanne Loewenthal. It was another nice get-together, and we discussed the usual stuff—my case, my reinstatement—and a Department of Labor hearing coming up in April. Hampton Bays was going to testify on my behalf.

"Frankie, why is it taking so long for this ridiculous case? What are your attorneys doing?"

"I don't have answers, Joanne. I wish I did."

"Tell Mom that Hampton Bays is behind you and everything is going to be okay." That made my mom smile and helped relieve pressure so she could at least try to enjoy Christmas.

On December 20, I woke up early as always and jogged six miles through the neighborhood before heading to court in Central Islip. The herd of cattle, I among them, was large. We stood in cold, windy weather, waiting to enter the unfriendly territory. All the assistant DAs were dressed in black as always, like grim reapers. They walked around like their crap didn't stink. I was not the least bit impressed by these young kids. The purpose of the court appearance was to declare that we were proceeding to trial and set a date for a Huntley hearing, when the arresting officers would be questioned regarding the arrest day and my Miranda rights. I didn't see how the prosecution could win the hearing, but Nick, Mr. Positive, said the odds were in their favor because they always get the benefit of the doubt. Of course the assistant district attorney wasn't in court, but there was a note in the file that said that the police officer couldn't appear for the hearing until the end of January 2007. The next mutually available date was February 14, 2007. Needless to say, I wasn't happy.

Walking out of the courthouse, Lori assured me that everything I had been wanting was finally about to happen. I stopped her. "That's all great, but I don't want any more promises. I just want action."

What did the officer have to do that he couldn't appear for another six weeks? There's a huge difference between how the law should work and how it does—or rather, how it doesn't work. I couldn't believe I had to wait almost another two months. I was reminded of when the district attorney's office arrested another school administrator in Long Island. After years of a prosecution, the man finally pled to a charge. The superintendent of that school said it was a shame his friend had run out of money and could no longer defend his innocence. That was such a true statement. I was not sure how I was going to pay trial fees. I had nothing officially coming in. I didn't know how people could do this to another human being. What I did know was my relatives had come to this country so that future generations could prosper in the land of opportunity, not get submarined by inept elements in the criminal justice system.

For ten months my attorneys had been literally kissing the DA's butt, trying to convince them this case was not what they thought. Now we no longer had to care what they thought. The burden of proof was on them. Now they had to produce indisputable evidence that I was guilty. The balance of power shifted when we told them we would see them at trial. They had officially bargained with something they didn't have. This was the ultimate poker game; we called the bluff. Now the prosecution and police would have to explain why a man with no legitimate proof against him had been judged guilty without a moment's glance at the so-called evidence.

I didn't wanted any of this. I wanted to be left alone and allowed to live my life. However, for reasons beyond my comprehension, the authorities named me public enemy number one. I just wanted to get back to work. I missed being around faculty and students and helping a school be as great as it could be. I was very anxious as I prepared to finally have my opportunity to rebut the charges. Hell, a monkey could rebut what was said in those lousy statements. Where was the rest of their evidence? Could I have it, please? Did any exist?

As I mulled over all I planned to do before February 14, I felt like a kid the night before Christmas. I was cautious though because I realized, just like with Christmas, you don't always get what you want. I had a strange feeling that the DA's office was far from done with punishing me for exercising my constitutional right to face my accusers. Why did I feel 2007 wasn't going to be any easier than 2006? By the way, for misdemeanor cases, the statutory right to a speedy trial is ninety days. The clock doesn't officially start to run until the defense declares trial, and the ninety days doesn't count defense motions, adjournments, and the unbelievable amount of loopholes that cause delays. The defense can't, well, shouldn't declare trial until they are given everything so they can properly prepare. Simply put—speedy trial is a myth. The way my attorneys were handling things, I would go to trial when and if they let me go to trial.

"But I have my life, I'm living it. It's twisted, exhausting, uncertain, and full of guilt, but nonetheless, there's something there."

— Banana Yoshimoto, *The Lake*

Chapter Eight
Trying to Fight Back

January 11, 2007

A brief meeting with Nick ended with "Frank, do you want me to call the DA's office to try to avoid a trial?"

"Nick, I'm innocent, and I'm not looking to avoid anything, but it seems they don't want to let me out of their grip. It doesn't have to be this way, but nobody wants to hear me out. I just want my life back, but they will not allow it."

Before I left, we discussed trial fees, and I shook his hand. I had another meeting in a few days to meet with a private investigator the law firm had recommended. I had to borrow more money to pay for those guys. I had to try everything if I wanted total vindication.

January 25, 2007

The woman who was dragged across the bar in October had a lot going for her—personality, career, attractive. She never judged me and never hesitated bringing me to her home and around her family. Unfortunately, there was a tremendous amount of pressure on me every day—and that pressure was placed on her. She had her own stress and problems. She had two young daughters to worry about, and I was unemployed and had nothing to offer but my problems. Although she never expressed concern with that, I couldn't and wouldn't add my problems to hers. We amicably parted ways. It was hard to remain positive.

February 7, 2007

I met with Nick and two private investigators. One was a retired detective and the other used to work for the FBI. I was so freaking sick of meetings. For a year it was nothing but meetings. Nothing gets accomplished at a meeting that can't be said in a memo. At work, I would always mutter, "If everyone is sitting around the table then who's doing the work?" At the meeting, I shared my insight into the case and offered witnesses and angles to investigate.

"Can you compile a list of possible witnesses?" they asked.

Were they kidding? Before that question was finished, I responded, "Here's three copies of a ten-page list of witnesses and leads."

A meeting would not be complete without me becoming completely pissed off. After discussing the background of the complainants, the PIs concluded, "The focus should be on Stephanie Veraldi and Michelle Konik."

"That's what I've been saying the whole time, right, Nick?" I also explained that Christina Impastato's complaint could help us, because she stated times and dates of calls that didn't even lead back to me.

Nick interjected, "Oh. That will help us."

I slapped myself in the forehead and covered my face, thinking, who the hell have I been talking to for the past year? I had been telling my attorneys that since February 2006, and they gave me zero validation.

The PIs also asked about the MySpace printouts, Webshots pictures, away messages, and other things, all of which my attorneys had for at least six months already. I explained that they showed a lot about the character of Michelle and Stephanie and the relationship between them. When the PI asked my attorney if they were worth looking at, Nick responded that he didn't get a chance to look at them yet. What? He had a meeting and numerous phone conversations with the ADA. He declared trial, and he didn't have a chance to look at them yet? What the hell did they discuss, her honeymoon plans? How could an attorney declare trial without checking all possible evidence that may help clear his client? It's one thing to be innocent but another thing to be able to prove the innocence. Yes, I said *prove*, because unfortunately that's how it works. I wondered if they ever planned on actually going to trial.

Next Nick mentioned a new piece of evidence that was never discussed before. Michelle recorded the conversation that she *claimed* we had on February 5, 2006, Super Bowl Sunday. The prosecution gave Nick a CD copy. Nick mentioned that there seemed to be a pause in the recording, and initially made a big stink over it, "Have you heard this? It's damaging!"

I laughed and sarcastically said, "Sure, I heard the recording. Michelle gave me a copy of it before she took it to the police. Can I please hear it now? There's no way it's damaging." I said that with a lot of confidence because I remembered that conversation and it sure was stupid and childish. However, it definitely was not incriminating.

We listened together. "That's it? Are you kidding?" What a joke. It wasn't exactly a conversation for a graduation commencement, but give me a break. It was an argument involving two people who had been emotionally involved with each other at some level. So many people have conversations like this. Almost always they remain private—unless someone like Michelle plans your demise, that is.

I began to steam and that's when I unleashed a fury of my own two cents about what I just heard and took notes on. "Did you say there was a pause, Nick? A pause means that it's paused and then it picked up right where it left off. This is recorded over. You can hear it still playing as it draws blank at intervals. The entire recording is maybe twelve minutes long, including about a twenty-second record-over in the beginning, about a minute record-over in the middle as Michelle *literally* begins to apologize, and another minute record-over before drawing blank for good. The recording clearly has her dropping f-bombs and me adamantly telling her to *stay away* from my family. And she stayed on the entire time. I ended that conversation. Does that sound like a guy who is harassing or a being harassed?

And by the way, Nick, if you checked my phone records you would have seen that the phone conversation she's referring to was actually twenty seven minutes long! Also, this recording is a CD. At the precinct, Sergeant Michael Cosgrove played a cassette for about 2 seconds. I couldn't even determine who or what was on it when he played it. Was that the same recording? Where is the full recording? Was it doctored? If so, who doctored it? Was it Michelle before handing it to the police, the police after she gave them the tape, or the DA's office after they received a copy? Is it even admissible evidence? Furthermore, how can they possibly tell when that recording was made? It could have been from four years ago for all they know. And maybe it was, since we have had quite a few arguments and it clearly isn't the twenty seven minute conversation from that day. And now that I think about it, how did they even know it was a phone conversation?

There is nothing on that CD that definitively allows one to conclude it was. There is no phone ringing, no dial tone, no hello or goodbye, nothing. And we have had a number of arguments like that in the past. For all they know it could be multiple arguments pieced together over the years, between me and Michelle live and in person, the many times she came over my house unannounced."

Nick tried to interject but I kept going. "I'm not done. Here's another question. How did they know it was me on the recording? They never spoke to me prior to dragging me out of my car and handcuffing me. So for all the police knew it could have been her and anyone else, just pretending, so they could set me up? They just took Michelle's word for it? Is that true Nick?" So one year after my arrest, and that's the only evidence thus far— my phone records from April 2005 to November 2005, and we don't know how or when they acquired them, and this CD? Nick can you please get to the bottom of things? This can't be how things work." I guess that was more than two cents.

After further review, and my input, Nick suggested, "The audio may actually help our case."

"No kidding, Nick—that recording would make the Nixon White House blush with envy!" Shades of history? Maybe if this district attorney's office had been in charge of investigating the Nixon tapes, Nixon might have remained president a little longer.

Nick should have known that CD like an old favorite song—but that wouldn't have happened unless I paid him enough money to put the rest of his cases on hold for me. It was a helpless feeling to know the case better than anyone yet still have to put my life in the hands of people who would never have that vested interest.

One last thing that bothered me about the meeting was the issue of taking a polygraph. The PI asked if I would be willing to take one.

"Well, I guess. What does it entail? Who administers it? The ADA? You?"

A couple of more questions followed, and I nodded in approval and concluded it sounded like a decent idea.

Nick didn't like my answer. "Usually people that have nothing to hide agree to a polygraph right away."

I was furious and shot back with another relentless monologue. "Maybe it's my science background or maybe it's my dwindling trust in the system or maybe a combination of the two. I just don't give answers that fly off the cuff."

I didn't know about the procedure, and I had questions. To be honest, I don't believe in polygraphs. I'll take one, but I don't think that my passing it would show I'm innocent. Anyone that agrees to anything without knowing all the facts is plain ignorant, and I'm not going have someone 'hint' my questioning means I'm hiding something. I was insulted, but I got over it quickly. People had been insulting me and telling lies about me for over a year now. I'd become an expert at experiencing humiliation.

I wasn't done. "I live off facts, and if I have a question, the person offering the test should be able to answer it. I'm willing to take a polygraph, and I made that clear, Nick. I still think the test is garbage, but I'm willing to listen to anyone that can explain how they are accurate and what good it would do. Is it even admissible in court? As a defendant, I get interrogated by everyone, even the people on my side, but whenever I question anyone or anything, it's turned back on me. God forbid I have a question or a thought of my own. I'm tired of doing a dog-and-pony show for the DA's office, anyway. I don't have to prove anything to them. They brought charges against me. Why not ask the complainants, the cops, and the prosecution to take a polygraph? You want to know who is lying, I'll show you in documents, statements, and a paper trail, and I don't need a bunch of wires to do it. I just need someone with common sense, a tiny bit of decency, and a sense of fair play to look at the damn evidence."

Nick remained quiet, sat back for a moment and nodded.

He shot back, "There's no turning back now. After this meeting the case is going to trial."

I returned his serve. "That's not true! Trials can come to an abrupt halt even in the middle of the trial. Tell me another lie! Anyway, it's a jury that I have to worry about now, not the prosecutors."

I didn't think Nick was being totally honest with me. I always felt there were things my attorneys were not telling me. Our conversations were always strange.

I wasn't finished yet. "Let them prove I did it, plain and simple. Better yet, let the complainants prove they were harassed by whatever they claim was being done to them. Lord knows their statements show know evidence of harassment." I was on a roll for a few minutes, and I felt good about it. Of course, before I left, I had to hand over about $13,000 more, and that didn't feel too good. Money is one detail that will never go unnoticed when you are caught up in the system.

February 8, 2007

The PI working with me, another Dan, said the ten-page document I gave him was very "thorough and informative." You're damn right it was. I wasn't sitting around watching Jerry Springer episodes. He was going to start making phone calls and collecting data. It was ridiculous, because they were going to uncover what I already knew, but their discoveries would be "official." The evidence these guys were gathering was the same as mine, only theirs came at a price of $150 per hour. I guess it doesn't count when proof of innocence comes from the defendant. More money has to go into the system first.

It was 4:30 p.m., exactly one year since the evil officers had cuffed me in town—one year since the beginning of a downward spiral that continued. I was thirty-five years old, out of my home, and couldn't find even menial employment in the interim. My savings was zero, my stocks were cashed out, I owed thousands of dollars, and the emotional toll this was taking on my family was immense. Many people told me it was amazing my spirit was as high as it was. I promised I would remain civil, respectful, and positive, and I would keep that promise.

February 13, 2007

Both my attorneys were supposed to meet before tomorrow's hearing to go over things—without me. Now, I didn't want to tell my defense how to do their job, because they were "the experts." By the same token, I was not a kid, and they were supposed to work for me. I expected to be kept abreast of their game plan and to be a part of it. I didn't need to know every specific detail, but they could have told me what their overall strategy was, what they were thinking, and why they were thinking that way. I never knew what was going on and that was a problem. I had a right to know what my attorneys were thinking with regard to defending my life—period, end of discussion. It was not open for debate. When I was a coach, I didn't tell my players what I was thinking at the instant the plays were being called, but we had meetings together, we went over the plays and the overall game plan, and I did get their input. The coaches called the game, but we all planned together and worked toward a common goal. I didn't respond to the athletes' questions as if they were challenging my ability. Why did I always feel like I had to apologize for asking a question?

February 14, 2007

I would've bet my life on it. In fact, I told many people, including my attorney last night, that it would happen. I received a phone call at about 10:00 a.m. today, and I knew it was bad news. Lori confirmed my hunch that there was a postponement. I was anxious to get the Huntley hearing started, but the district attorney's office had other ideas. That was so unprofessional—to cancel just before the hearing was to commence. This date had been set for almost two months now, and they waited until the last minute to cancel. When in life is anyone allowed to cancel any meeting or appointment the day of without penalty? I was informed that the prosecutor changed. You mean to tell me they found out that morning? Couldn't they have told us a little sooner? I suggested, once again, that they issue a press release and/or take a firmer stance but to no avail.

It was not like I was able to move on in life like other people with cases pending. Things could have been different, and there was not a soul on this planet who could ever convince me otherwise. I asked my attorney for the name of this new prosecutor. When he gave me the name, he asked, "Why do you want to know?"

"I have a right to know, Nick, and you should be telling me anyway without my asking!"

I was never told why the prosecutor was changed. There could have been ten different reasons, but I wanted *the* reason. Why would that young ADA, who had the case for a year with such a tight grip on the alleged facts, all of a sudden give it up? Why, after having such a rock-solid prosecution in a case with a ton of media attention, would she no longer be the prosecutor? It would have been great for her career, wouldn't it? Was it because she had no case? Were they running out of room to save face? Did they have to concede to Frank Vetro?

Maybe there was a legit excuse. Was she promoted? Maybe it was one of these reasons or maybe none of them, but I had a right to know either way. Yes, attorneys are promoted, and things happen in the normal processes of a case from beginning to adjudication, but I'll tell you for the thousandth time what the reason was: to delay. Lawyers could debate me and give me all the jargon they want, but I know. My attorneys spent over a year doing a song and a dance for some young assistant district attorney, and for what? For nothing. This convenient switch was just another loophole to my Sixth Amendment right to a speedy trial. Anything else anyone tells me is pure nonsense. They would delay again if they could, because the tactic was working. I was running out of resources to fight back, and soon I would be unable to afford a proper defense. Why would any of them care, though?

An interesting case that began during the same time period as my arrest came to a close—as did many others, I might add. It involved Yoko Ono, and I think extortion, by her driver. It further illustrates a disturbing lesson I was learning. This man was being held on something like $500,000 bail. He'd been locked up while awaiting a trial that may or may not have come anytime soon. He pled to a lesser offense, received a sentence of the time he already spent in jail, and was free to go. Why wouldn't he take that plea? He would've been in jail for God knows how much longer waiting for a trial. That's what the system does, though. Maybe he was guilty but maybe he wasn't. Maybe if he could have afforded bail, he could've fought the charges, or maybe not, but we'll never know the complete truth. The system doesn't beat you fair and square. The prosecution does everything to ensure it is always vindicated in bringing charges. I had learned an ugly truth in all of this. It's more important for police and prosecutors to send an innocent person to jail than it is for them to admit having made a mistake. As I followed stories all over this nation, that truth proved undeniable.

The court calendar for February 14, 2007, states the "defense requested adjournment." That is s u c h a l i e. We were ready to go. It was the prosecution who couldn't make it. Why did I have to suffer because they changed prosecutors? Why weren't they charged time with regard to my right to a speedy trial? The court gave me a new date of February 28 ... maybe.

February 27, 2007

I said maybe, and maybe was right. Nick called and said, "Don't kill the messenger." Yep, the day before the hearing, the DA's office put it off for another week, because the arresting officer, Wayne Heter, couldn't make it. Perhaps he was on a stakeout catching a violent superintendent who was running for the border on jaywalking charges. If it weren't my life, I would have thought it was comical. I still had to show up to court to get the next date. Nick made a stink about the adjournment and pled "ready," which meant we were present and ready to proceed, but the prosecution wasn't. Time was charged to the prosecution in the amount of six days with regard to infringement of my right to a speedy trial—six days on the record, that is. I knew damn straight it was more like six months, but not with all the loopholes the prosecution had available to them, and not with my lawyers, who were doing nothing to defend their client.

A random thought popped into my mind. Whatever happened to the fifty other charges that were coming against me? My brother-in-law Mike told me that a couple of police officers actually visited him, to ask if he wanted to press charges. They were that desperate. I couldn't get along any better with Mike. He's a great guy. And he too is not fond of incompetence. That's why he respectfully told them to get lost. And they ran out of there without even giving their names. I couldn't make this stuff up. I guess that would have made fifty-one charges. Anyone else out there want to press charges? Hey, Mom, did I ever annoy you when I was a child? If so, tell officer Heter, and he'll let you file a complaint against me to.

After the appearance, I had a half-hour conversation with Nick. He explained the upcoming hearing could easily take two days because it wasn't beginning until 2:00 p.m. Once again, that's the problem with the system. Why waste time rescheduling and delaying? Why not just get everything over with? This case was so straightforward. I'll tell you why. It was because that might be considered efficient. Instead, things get dragged out and new dates get scheduled, weeks and months go by, people make money, and the truth gets lost. It's a lesson in futility. My next court date was scheduled for March 7 ... maybe. The court calendar for February 28 read, "Case continued."

March 3, 2007

I read a *Newsday* article today concerning legal proceedings in which three young men were found guilty of robbing a couple and raping a young woman in the process. This occurred locally, in Bay Shore, New York. Two of the young men pled guilty and received sentences of about fifteen and twenty years in jail. The other pleaded not guilty and "forced" a trial—a trial that was his constitutional right. After the trial, I believe that young man was convicted of three counts, while the two who plead guilty were convicted of eight counts, including rape, and other more serious charges. Although he was found guilty of much less, he was sentenced to thirty-eight years in jail! He received double the time for half the crime! The consensus among the critics was that judges commonly punish defendants who force the court to expend time and resources on a jury trial. In other words, people are punished for asking the courts to give them a chance to face their accusers, as is their right! God forbid a prosecutor is asked to do their job. Touro Law Center professor, Richard Klein was quoted in the article. He said our courts put so much emphasis on expediency that the whole system pressures defendants to take a plea. Expediency! What planet was he from? He was way off! But he's right on regarding forced pleas.

Of course the crime was horrific. Let's be clear that I'm not defending the actions of any of them in any way, shape, or form. However, should he have been punished twice as harshly as his codefendants simply because he opted for a trial? It's something to think about.

March 7, 2007: The Huntley Hearing

Lo and behold, the Huntley Hearing began. This hearing, according to my attorney's opinion and my research, I was supposed to lose. It unfolded as I expected though. I arrived at Central Islip Court at 1:30 p.m. for the 2:00 p.m. hearing accompanied by my family. There wasn't much of a crowd in the afternoon, and of course the hearing didn't actually begin until 3:15, but that was expected. After all, anything else would mean efficiency, and we were dealing with the Suffolk County criminal justice system. As we were waiting in the desolate corridor outside courtroom 45D, I got my first glimpse of the new prosecutor. She was another extremely young ADA named Kathleen Kearon. She looked even younger than the first ADA. I was confident this would go in my favor, regardless of what my attorney thought.

I walked back outside and looked to the left, and the flashbacks began. I saw a man walking down the hallway with a crew cut and a long trench coat, carrying files. I could never forget or mistake the walk or the face. It was Officer Wayne Heter, the arresting officer who played the role of good cop on that dreaded day, February 8, 2006. He sat down in a wooden booth outside the courtroom, alone, as we all waited. He looked nervous and didn't have the guts to look me in the eye, although I tried to force a glance. Shortly after, I got the word from Nick that they were ready to go. Just before walking in, I stopped and noticed the new ADA speaking to Officer Heter outside the courtroom, and she didn't look happy.

I entered the courtroom, and Nick instructed me to sit with him at the table to take notes. I was excited. He asked, "Frank, do you have something to write with?"

Does a bear c r a p in the woods? "I've been waiting over a year for this. I'm ready." The young ADA was so nervous. If she hadn't been the one prosecuting me, I would've felt bad for her. As she spoke, her voice cracked, and her lack of experience was noticeable. Her face turned bright red, and the color radiated down her neck and chest. It was more than just red; she was breaking out in hives. Part of her opening line to Judge Lawrence Donohue almost knocked Nick, and me, right out of our seats. She conceded there was a Miranda violation! She was supposed to argue that my Miranda rights weren't violated. We were to argue they were, and the judge would make a decision as to whether the statements taken by the police were legitimate.

As I stated earlier, it was clear that I requested an attorney, yet they continued to interrogate me and secretly compile four unauthorized statements. Ms. Kearon stated she would only use one statement at trial, but if I testified, the other three would be used. We still had to debate that, but either way we had our first small victory. Her outright acknowledgment of the violation of my rights made me ponder. Was she so wet behind the ears that she didn't realize she could still try to convince the judge otherwise? Was she relying on textbook understanding, not knowing what could be done to manipulate the system? Maybe after just receiving the case she noticed things didn't add up? Maybe she was doing what an ADA is supposed to do and was upholding justice? Maybe she wanted things done the right way and didn't consider ruining someone's life unjustly an admirable thing to do? I'd have to wait and see.

As the hearing continued, she asked Officer Heter step by step what happened that day from the time he was in Hampton Bays until my final booking. Many issues no doubt were sidestepped to avoid controversial areas of the arrest day. I recall they jumped from my being handcuffed at approximately 4:30 p.m. right to 8:30 p.m. in the seventh precinct. We all mysteriously lost four hours of time. At Ms. Kearon's request, he read the four statements *he wrote*. It was obvious just off the statements that the case was stupid and not what the media had portrayed. Judge Donohue didn't even seem to be paying attention. He was looking everywhere but forward. At one point he did crack a smile and shook his head. Perhaps he realized how silly the case might be. That was basically the gist of the hearing today. We ran out of time, so my attorney didn't get his shot at Officer Heter. Heter stepped down from the witness stand and stormed out of the courtroom looking very uncomfortable. He should've been.

The acknowledgment that my rights were violated already put a small blemish on the integrity of the case. It was a decent beginning, but by no means was it a reason to start celebrating. There was a long way to go. I waited a year just to listen to the officer simply read the statements on the record? Did we really have to waste a year and an entire hearing to learn the obvious? It was right under our noses from day one.

I looked forward to Nick's cross-examination of Officer Heter. A lot of issues were avoided that needed questioning, and his answers would show just how unfair this case was from day one. I hoped Nick, with my help, would show Heter what it felt like to be grilled without mercy. The cross-examination would be the next step in proving that inept and publicity-hungry police officers railroaded me. The court calendar said the "defense requested adjournment." I didn't get it—weren't we entitled to finish the hearing? It was my right, not my request. The new date was Monday, March 19.

March 19, 2007

There was another postponement. Although the hearing wasn't going to happen, we still had to show up to court at 2:00 p.m. Lori told me she spoke to the clerk the last time in court, and he said the case didn't sound like much. That was exactly the issue. We hadn't even gone to trial yet, there were four fabricated statements read before the judge, and it was already clear that no crime was committed. The story that was created was just that: a story—which for some reason beckoned me to wonder what the hell Lori was doing for her money. Lord knows I hadn't received any PR. She said she wanted to speak with the ADA, "woman to woman." I changed the subject by saying I couldn't wait to have Michelle Konik on the stand. Nick shook my hand with slight caution, "Frank, man to man, I understand, but it's more than just Michelle Konik." He may have been right. Maybe I should have included the arresting officers, prosecution, and the Middle Country Central School District. I was the only one scheduled for court, so we sat there alone as the judge, the clerk, the stenographer, and a couple of other personnel chatted amongst themselves for a half hour. Interestingly, Nick became infuriated.

He looked at me. "Keep a poker face and follow me," and he stormed out of the room stating how he felt disrespected by what he perceived as being ignored.

It was a perfect opportunity for me to chime in. "How do you think I've felt for the past thirteen and a half months?"

He felt disrespected for a couple of minutes, and then, to him, the whole system sucked. I had my life turned inside out and got humiliated and ignored for over a year, but in that case the response was always "That's the system." Although I would never really want my next statement to actually happen, maybe lawyers, attorneys, police officers, and judges should be publicly humiliated and have their lives taken away from them for a moment. Maybe if these stakeholders in "the system" had their lives damaged by the current criminal justice system change would occur. Maybe they need to feel what it's like.

When we finally went before Judge Donohue, he said the case had to move faster. I thought, yeah, no kidding judge. Donohue followed with a brief lecture on how the prosecution would be charged time for any further delays. What did he mean for further delays? What about now, Judge Donohue? The judge also said if the defense wasn't ready, then we could forfeit my rights to a hearing. Nick immediately snapped back, "Judge, there are two people in the courtroom, and neither of those people are the prosecution." I was present, and I was ready—as I had been ready, Judge, for over a year. I was ready on February 9, 2006, I was ready today, and I would be ready any time or day after. The ADA would get charged time if not prepared, but I could lose my constitutional rights if I was not available one time in fourteen months. That's the justice system— fair as usual.

On the bright side, Joanne and a few board of education members called me. I also spoke with my union representative, Joe Kolarik. Their words were encouraging, supportive, and very reassuring. I guess that's one silver lining in this horrific tragedy. I would at least get my life back eventually. The next hearing date was set for Tuesday, March 27 ... maybe. The court calendar read, "Case continued."

March 27 and 28

We finished up the hearing in two partial days, a total of six and a half hours in which the one and only witness was Officer Wayne Heter. I met with Nick a few days prior to explain what happened the day of my arrest so he would know when the officer was misleading him. He asked me to write down notes so he could read, understand, and have them with him as he was questioning Officer Heter. On March 7 the ADA, Ms. Kearon, questioned Heter, and he was crisp. He knew every detail of the questions asked as if it had happened yesterday. Over these past two days, Nick had his crack at this "model" police officer.

Nick's cross-examination set the table for not only what really happened on February 8, 2006, but also what happened before and during the alleged investigation. A different story was put forth for the first time, describing how the officers didn't tell me what I was arrested for and how they filled in the blanks to very general, involuntary, and innocent statements. It was a story of being publicly humiliated and cuffed to the floor with nothing to eat, facing threats of having my life ruined, speaking to the media, making it rough for my family, and freezing in shorts and T-shirt during a cold February night.

The stage was set for what I thought would come if the trial ever took place. It would be a story of police officers making an unjustified arrest and attempting to build a case, after the fact, to justify their actions. As the hearing progressed I realized Nick and I could be a formidable team—key word being could. As he questioned Heter, I took diligent notes and gave him information, as he looked to me periodically. He had the know-how, and I knew the case. He realized my strength and used it. That was the recipe for success, and I was feeling real good to be a part of it.

I didn't expect Heter to remember every detail of an arrest he made fourteen months ago, but Nick caught him in so many lies and contradictions. I found no sympathy for the man whose forehead began to fill with beads of sweat. Heter was disassembled, and I was very confident we could systematically destroy this case step by step if given the opportunity. Leaving court, Nick said, "Frank, we have begun to plow away." Yes, but could we sustain the momentum?

What I vaguely recall about the hearing was a delay regarding exculpatory evidence and probable cause. There was some discussion regarding the prosecuting attorney refusing to turn over certain documents after being warned by Judge Donohue that she could win the case and it could be for nothing if she withheld certain evidence. She said she understood but adamantly refused to turn over certain documents in her possession. What the hell? Turn it over! I smelled a rat. The court calendar said, "Defense requested adjournment." That was not true. Nicholas was ready to finish with oral arguments on the spot. The ADA refused. The new date was May 10 … maybe. Another month and a half!

Chapter Nine
Abandoned

Joanne and I decided to meet for lunch soon to discuss my reinstatement and the results of my April 11 unemployment hearing, at which Hampton Bays testified as promised. They did so by phone. This day ended on a happy note for individuals I had never met and didn't even know I existed. Since March 2006, I watched and read about their case with great interest. Today the rape charges brought against three young men from Duke University were officially dropped. Like me, they were put through hell because of an investigation and allegations with no basis. The authorities and much of the public convicted them from the onset.

I watched the press conference and could see the sense of relief. It was a feeling that I had not yet achieved although my lousy misdemeanor case had been going on longer than their felony case. I was happy for them and hoped they could counter all the injustice thrust upon them. If that couldn't happen, then that was the true crime. One of the accused said it best, stating if they didn't have access to a lot of money for a defense, they would be in a lot of trouble. Exactly! But they did, and their attorneys worked diligently because finances dictated it. I didn't have that same luxury. District Attorney Mike Nifong, was taken off the case, and it was put in the hands of Attorney General Roy Cooper from North Carolina. There were key findings in Mr. Cooper's investigation that led to the dropped charges.

1. The identification procedures used in the DA's probe were unreliable.
2. There were many contradictions in the complainant's story.
3. There were many inconsistencies between the accuser's statements and the evidence.

These same findings, along with many others, also existed in my case. I believe Mike Nifong was brought up on charges, resigned, and maybe even disbarred. If only "the system" were based more on truth and justice instead of money, maybe my case would have been resolved too. I wrote a letter and wanted to send it to the chief prosecutor in Suffolk County, Thomas Spota. Nick emphatically told me not to send it. Why not? It was very respectful and complimentary. What was he so afraid of? Why wasn't somebody saying something to defend me and my life? Why was I being told to hush by the courts and my own defense?

April 13, 2007

Diane, my superintendent's secretary, called to tell me someone sent Michelle's superintendent at Middle Country Central School District an anonymous letter and also sent a copy to Hampton Bays Schools. The letter mentioned, among other things, her relationships with Jim and me. It was a scathing letter that attacked her character using some racy, descriptive words and was written by someone who seemed to know about Michelle's history and her current work-related issues. Unfortunately, the person didn't put his or her name to the letter, and that detracted from it.

April 20, 2007

I had lunch with my superintendent today. It was another communication and reassurance that, to be honest, I needed at this time in my life. With a smile on her face, Joanne asked, "Frankie, did you write that anonymous letter?"

I laughed hard. "No way. When I have my say it will be no secret that it came from me, and the audience will be larger than two school districts. Plus, the letter mentions her current work issues which I'm unfamiliar with. I'd love to learn more about them though."

Joanne nodded her head in understanding. She faxed a copy of the letter to Michelle's superintendent, Roberta Gerold, and also spoke to her at a luncheon. Joanne told me that Ms. Gerold said Michelle's current principal, Gordon Brosdal, was a single man and that there wasn't much she could do about their relationship. Nonsense. According to that letter, her relationship with her principal was not all you could take away. It also mentioned things regarding inappropriate relationships with her students, manipulating and using them, committing other crimes, and other things. It was quite detailed.

Interestingly, the letter mentioned a club that Michelle was involved with, Students against Relationship Abuse (SARA). It was associated with a larger group, Suffolk County Coalition against Domestic Violence. Ironically, two of the organization's honorary board members were Richard Dormer, the police commissioner in Suffolk County who held a press conference, and Thomas Spota, the District Attorney. The two men at the top of the criminal justice food chain were forever linked at some level to Michelle Konik.

As an administrator, I received a few anonymous letters. I thought they were crap and didn't pay attention to them. If someone has something to say and/or feels strongly about something, then he or she should put his or her name to it. Only cowards and gutless wonders go the anonymous route, and that's why they went in the garbage. However, this instance was a little different. That letter spoke about a teacher with a history of work-related and personal problems who was once again involved in questionable activity and litigation and referenced her as a threat to students given her known history of inappropriateness. My cousin Ron, who had daughters in public school, said it best. He said if an anonymous letter was written or phone call was made regarding a bomb threat, the school would react, because if it were true, the safety of the staff and students would be at risk. It was a point well taken, as this anonymous letter clearly pointed out the *potential* danger that Michelle posed to students and staff *if* it were true. It deserved looking into to see if there was any truth to the letter's claims. I wanted to know more!

May 2007

After my May 10 court appearance, I felt that going against the DA was like gambling at a casino. They use house rules and stack the odds so much in their favor that it is near impossible to beat them. They used every trick in the book to delay and ensure I couldn't fight them to full capacity. The appearance was to submit a motion about suppressing statements based on Officer Heter's testimony a month and a half ago. The problem was that after I shelled out $1,235 for the transcripts, borrowed money, we still didn't receive the court reporters work. How could my defense submit a motion without having the relevant data to do so?

Nick asked me, "Why do you show up to court even though your appearance is waived?"

"I have to show up every time so I can be reminded of how much the court disrespects and treats me like a third-rate human being."

They spoke about me like I wasn't even there and referred to me as "the defendant." I was trying to remain positive and civil, to let them see I'm not the enemy. It was difficult to not develop a hatred for everyone. In today's society the presumption of innocence until proven guilty has been overshadowed by the presumption of guilty until proven wealthy. The court calendar read, "Case continued"—continued to push me around. My next court appearance was June 8 ... maybe.

Meanwhile Diane Albano told me Joanne was testing the waters regarding my eventual return to the district and I should be expecting a phone call. And, like clockwork, on May 12 at around 3:26 p.m., I received a phone call from Hampton Bays Central Office. It was sixty-five minutes in length as we discussed in great detail my return to the district. Joanne said she recently spoke with Andy, the teacher's union president, and he assured her my return would be just fine with the union. I spoke to Andy three hours prior to Joanne's call, and he confirmed all she said. To be honest my return had nothing to do with any support I had. I was entitled to be reinstated as soon as I was cleared by the state education department. But it was nice to be supported.

June 2007

Two and a half months after the conclusion of the hearing, Nick finally received the transcripts. That's the good news. The bad news is he received them just before today's court appearance. Both he and I wanted to make sure we didn't put together a half-assed document just for the sake of submitting one. We wanted to do a quality job and break everything down properly before putting any claims in writing. After all, police officers and ADAs would make sure they had all their ducks in order before making any claims, wouldn't they? Surely they wouldn't rush something just for the sake of getting it done. No way, never. That means yet another "adjournment requested by the defense."

There's a sign outside the courtroom that reads Cases Will Be Called to Order at 9:30 a.m. Judge Donohue entered the room at 9:45 a.m. today. I couldn't tell you when court actually began on time, because it never did—taxpayer's money being thrown away little by little. I heard a few attorneys jokingly comment to a particular ADA about getting rid of some cases because there were way too many on the calendar. Her response: "Today is a light day." There are bound to be so many when you have ridiculous cases taking well over a year and a half to conclude. That was the real crime—what they were wasting taxpayers' money on. The minutes, which cost me $1,250, really annoyed me. How did the DA's office pay for them? They used the taxpayer's money. Meanwhile I used personal finances. Last I heard I was a taxpayer, right? In a perverse sense, I paid for the minutes to my own hearing twice. I guess since I was unable to work, thanks to a system playing dirty pool, they no longer considered me a taxpayer. Wait, don't tell me—that's the system.

Judge Donohue gave us more time to look over the minutes and hand in our memorandum of law. He gave us a new date of ... July 20, four months after the hearing was completed. We still wouldn't have a decision until sometime after that, because the judge would need time to review everything. Needless to say, when we left the courtroom, Nick and I had an argument. This one was actually initiated by him after he saw the look on my face and anticipated I was going to fire at him. It was the same old argument but with a different conclusion. Nick, who never gave me a clue about how he personally felt about the case, let loose.

"Frank, there have been quite a few delays and maybe a couple of things that could've been done differently." I respected that. Bad judgment calls happen—nobody is perfect. I guess it was standard knowledge that the longer a case takes, the better it is for the defense. But I always thought that was if you wanted a plea deal. I was trying to get to a trial.

I replied, "The delays will eventually hurt more than help."

Nick sat me down in a wooden booth outside of the courtroom in the abandoned hallway. Nick said he was playing devil's advocate, because all criminal attorneys have to. As the case was unfolding, either way, guilty or not, he felt what was being done was overkill and unjust. After learning about the case and me as a person, he thought it was total crap—hearsay at best.

I had nothing to say except, "What now? Let's get a trial going already."

I didn't like his body language. The court calendar read, "Defense requested adjournment." The court could shove it.

I had lunch with Joanne in Westhampton Beach on June 20. We spoke again about the same stuff, different administrative positions in Hampton

Bays, a possible restructuring, and the possibility of my taking a central office position. I expressed that it was difficult being unemployed. She responded that there was nothing that could be done to speed up the clearance process, the criminal matter had to be completely resolved. My union representative also reassured me that things would work out in the long run.

July 2007

On July 18 a young lady in Colorado named Joy reached out to me. She was one of my students at William Floyd High School and thought I was a good teacher. She heard about my arrest, wished me luck, and suggested I explore another avenue on MySpace. I did and found posts by Newfield students critiquing Michelle Konik and that club Students against Relationship Abuse. Stephanie chimed in at a completely inappropriate level, bashing everyone who didn't share her opinion of Ms. Konik and inviting anyone with a problem to meet her personally so she could shut them up. She also referenced what a crazy man Jim was. She never even met the man. I wonder who fed her that information—the same person who fed her lies about me? Anyway, I was honored to be remembered by one of my first students. Her assistance from across the United States was appreciated.

Jim called the same day to give an interesting and intuitive perspective on how Michelle operated. Michelle magnified a small bit of our character, how people perceived us, and turned it into uncontrollable personality traits that made us menaces to society. He was always perceived as an intense athletic figure, volatile at times—not in a bad way, just excitable and passionate about his particular sport and his job. She created the perception of a man who couldn't control himself and was extremely violent and dangerous. People always perceived me as being around women, flirtatious and dating a lot. That wasn't necessarily a bad thing as long as I was respectful and conscientious. Michelle took that perception and spun a story of a man who couldn't control himself or his urges. With both of us she spent years creating a problem that never existed, and when her plan came to fruition we were left playing catch-up.

He also said someone heard about his affair with Michelle from years ago and questioned him about it. He wondered how that story leaked to another state and how much longer he would have to answer questions about the one personal mistake he made. That was why I was trying to endure the nightmare. It had to stop with me. Neither Jim nor I should ever have to answer for our personal mistake again. The focus had to shift away from us and toward the real problem.

July 20, 2007

Another month went by and another court appearance approached. That courthouse was so damn depressing. Some four months after the completion of the Huntley hearing, we finally were able to hand in and receive the prosecution's memorandum of law regarding the withholding of statements. What's the rush Suffolk County? Why not wait another four months? Four damn months just to exchange documents that were literally a few pages in length, and we still had to wait for a decision! I didn't even give a damn if they used the statements doctored up in my name. They didn't say much anyway. When Nick and I left the courtroom we had our ritual debriefing in one of the wooden booths. He handed me a copy of his memorandum, five or six pages of detailed information, case law, and his argument that the prosecution shouldn't be allowed to use the statements. The prosecution's memorandum, on the other hand, was a joke.

It was a page and a half of garbage. Nick said it was baseless and said nothing. My response: "Of course—their entire case is baseless." I'm not an expert on the law, but I know a piece of junk document when I read one. Their opening line read, "On or about August 7th 2005 at approximately 1600 hours, the defendant was charged with seven counts of Aggravated Harassment...." That's way off. When the hell were they ever going to get anything right? That wasn't just a misplaced word or number. It wasn't like they wrote Wednesday but meant Thursday. That was the wrong time, wrong day, wrong month, and wrong freaking year! They didn't know a damn thing about this case. A mistake here or there would perhaps have been understandable, but it seemed every document and statement they made was inaccurate. The Suffolk County District Attorney's Office wasn't even close to accurate. I prayed my case was the exception, not the rule, with regard to how criminal matters were handled.

When I arrived home I received a ton of calls. The pattern was, before a court appearance, I would receive "Good luck!" calls, and afterward I would receive "How did it go?" calls. I explained my day in court, and I knew what their response would be: "That's the system." It was as if everyone knew the system always was and always will be broken. So why is it that not one person anywhere in the world wants to change the system? Is everyone okay with the fact that it doesn't function efficiently? Everyone accepts the way things are while those at the top of the criminal justice food chain reap the benefits. As an administrator I was aware of problems in education, but at least I tried to improve conditions and streamline procedures.

The next court date would be mailed to my attorney along with the judge's decision. I didn't anticipate it would be any time soon. I noticed on the DA's website that the incident date for my arrest was listed as March 13, 2005. What the hell were they talking about? Their bogus evidence didn't even begin until April 19, 2005. Who the hell was running things in Suffolk County? The court calendar read, "Motion submitted." How about a motion to dismiss the case—or would that be too logical?

August 2007

Gordon Brosdal left Newfield High School to take a job in another school district, William Floyd School District, my old stomping grounds. I believe they were in the headlines for years, rocked with financial scandal and also prosecuted by the DA's office. Michelle got engaged to the retirement-aged school administrator. Stephanie posted away messages about planning the wedding and being a maid of honor. I couldn't make this stuff up. Michelle has an older sister, Doreen, I believe she's a doctor. In fact, I always thought Michelle's breeding business, Doriann Bichons, was named after her sister. Yet Stephanie was her Maid of Honor? Why did I even bother to ask anymore?

Away Message

Stephanie (August 3): In the city buying my Maid of honor dress!!!

My Cell Phone Account Notes

My attorney subpoenaed my phone records for the past few years, not just the seven months the district attorney's office gave us. More importantly, AT&T Wireless sent us the "notes," a detailed record of every change made to my phone account, including actual dialogue exchanged with their representatives. Here's what the notes referenced. On or about;

- April 19, 2005, a new online account was added at about 3:46 p.m. (The prosecution's evidence begins on this date.)
- May 25, 2005, the e-mail address where my phone records were being sent was changed at about 8:48 p.m. to sassynsweete@aol.com.
- May 29, 2005, at about 11:21 a.m., the e-mail address was changed from sassynsweete@aol.com to hootie@msn.net, and the account password was changed.
- May 29, 2005, the e-mail address was changed from hootie@msn.net to hootie@aol.com.
- September 18, 2005, the mobile e-mail address was changed from sassynsweete@aol.com to tjohns@hotmail.com at about 5:07 p.m.
- September 18, 2005, the primary e-mail was changed from hootie@aol.com to tjohns@hotmail.com.
- September 22, 2005, after the online account was brought to my attention, I spoke to a representative, Ken Daughty. The notes state, in summation, Frank says that somebody has been getting his bill online.... Change bill to paper only. Customer didn't recognize E-mail address so we removed it.... I apologize for any inconvenience this caused.
- December 17, 2005, I changed my cell phone number at about 2:42 p.m.
- February 14, 2006, after my arrest, I spoke with representative, Chris Knipp, and learned my records were still being sent to a strange e-mail address. The notes state, in summation; Web address isn't allowing him access. Updated email address. Customer stated that the email address in there was not his. I had to unregister him so he could regain access. It was asking for a security code that he did not know. My password and e-mail address were finally correctly changed by about 9:14 p.m.
- February 27, 2006, I called them at about 9:58 p.m. In summation, they said although I made a claim that my identity was stolen and an account was set up without my knowledge, there was nothing they could do about it. I had to contact the local police.
- July 19, 2007, I called at about 3:15 p.m. because my account was compromised again.

I wasn't making this stuff up. Someone did steal my identity. They didn't just hack into an existing account. They literally set up an account in my name, and had my phone records sent to various email addresses, which were periodically changed. Could somebody, maybe my PI's, anybody, figure out precisely who did it? Could we get to the bottom of anything?

September 2007

I didn't openly complain or show signs that I was struggling. Maybe I shouldn't have been so positive and upbeat. Perhaps my wanting to remain better than them was hurting me and assisting in my demise. I tried not to let anyone in on what was really happening. I didn't enjoy bringing misery to others and didn't think they wanted to hear it anyway. In fact I know for a fact that some of my "friends" didn't want to hear it. I was out of my house. My losses were accumulating at an exponential rate. My financial status was on life support, and I couldn't afford another dime for my defense. Yes, I claimed I could hustle and make money on my own, and that was true. I'm a worker, and I'd do anything to earn a buck. However, pressed with the circumstances, it was impossible. In the internet age there are no secrets. It was becoming harder and harder to even acquire gas money for the week, not to mention my other menial expenses. Any money I "earned" went to my debt. My family offered me money numerous times, but I come from a modest background and couldn't ask them to acquire debt on my behalf. I knew they would—they did already. Plus my older brother and sister had kids of their own to worry about and I would rather their well-being come before mine. The delays were working. My defense was going to be compromised.

I was watching one of those court shows on cable television the other night. They were bragging about a prosecutor who was undefeated. In fact, the win percentage of the DA's office in Long Island is something around the upper ninetieth percentile. All I can say to that is: big deal. When the playing field is level, then we can talk about wins and losses. I know every case is unique, but there were many cases that began after mine and finished already, trial included. It was over nineteen months. I was resisting every temptation to absolutely despise everyone involved with my misfortune. A person can wait just so long, lose so much money, and see his or her life paused for just so much time before anger sets in.

Like my friend Marc said, "Frankie, now I understand why so many people take a plea." Yeah, me too. In fact, whenever I see or hear about someone taking a plea, I doubt that person's guilt. I may be wrong to take that approach, but how else am I supposed to feel? It's tough to fight city hall. What if I had kids? I would've been forced to take a plea and move on. My family would have needed to eat. In that respect, I thank God I was single. I'll tell you what else I was: I was innocent. No matter what happened, I was innocent, and I would know in my heart that I gave it my best shot.

My next court appearance was scheduled for October 3. Judge Donohue ruled in favor of the prosecution with regard to the memorandum of law that was submitted. I expected that; it really wasn't a big deal. That meant the ADA conceded that my rights were violated but she could use the unauthorized statements if I took the stand. I already explained that what the officers wrote down was not what I said. Either way I would take the stand and I would tell the truth. The problem I did have was having a hearing a year after my arrest and then waiting another five months to get a simple decision. There was absolutely no logic to it. We wasted a year and a half waiting for the judge to officially say my Miranda rights had been violated. It took me all of three minutes to realize that just by reading the police documents after my arrest. It was all a game. How was the document the ADA handed in given any merit at all? The facts that she opened with were not even close to being true. Shouldn't a memorandum of law be precise? The individuals involved were anything but precise. The title of this book should have been Court Jesters.

Nick explained that October 3 would be a pretrial conference and that trial dates would be given to us. There was a zero percent chance of that happening, because they needed to save face, and I knew better than to think the Suffolk County DA's office would carry out its duties in any way resembling fairness. I didn't know what would happen, and didn't expect to find out until that day since I was never kept in the loop. But I knew I would be ready as always.

October 2007

I was in court on October 3, in enemy territory, flanked by my family. We were very talkative and upbeat considering the circumstances and excited to be receiving trial dates. It was crowded, and I couldn't find my attorneys. I opened the door to the courtroom and noticed the ADA wasn't there.

Another bad feeling rushed over me. When Nick arrived, he greeted me and went to find the ADA Kathleen Kearon. Minutes later he walked out of the courtroom.

"Don't kill the messenger. Kathleen Kearon is no longer the ADA on the case."

Our smiles quickly turned to anger. "Nick, this is ridiculous! They don't tell us sooner? What's the reason?"

He didn't have answers, or at least he didn't give them to me. "The new ADA is Michael Manning," he said, and he walked back into the courtroom. I followed. Mr. Manning was also very young, had short dark hair, and, yes, was dressed in black, like all the ADA's. He glanced at me every once in a while in the courtroom. Mr. Manning may have put on an air of confidence, but I was not fooled. He was just another puppet working in the massive DA's office.

Nick spoke with Judge Donohue and voiced his displeasure, haggling back and forth. Judge Donohue gave a new date of October 26, "Maybe you'll get an acceptable offer." As I sat twenty-five feet from the bench, I felt like strangling someone. *Either try my case or dismiss it already!* I thought. Everything that happened so far had been predicted. Although I was very frustrated with Nick's approach, I was trying to be open-minded and see the big picture—trying. I suppose I could've initially retained a different attorney. That onus was on me, but who knew the case would unfold like this? Every legitimate plan should include a plan B. Every war general, every soldier, every coach has a plan he or she believes in, but when things don't go accordingly, each one would regroup. The prosecution was forcing us into a different kind of fight. At some point we had to fight back. We had to adapt in this war, and I didn't think that was too much for me to ask. He was supposed to protect his client. I didn't have any money or I would have changed a long time ago.

In the interim, Nick set up a meeting with the new ADA, Mr. Manning. He still didn't know the details of my case, and he was meeting with a prosecutor just picking up the case after twenty months who obviously didn't know it either. What was the point? What the hell were they going to chat about? The only person who knew the case was me. How could they punish an individual and prosecute him for this much time without ever having a conversation with him? Where was the damn logic? I have a voice, a brain. Speak to me, guys! I was not expecting anything except another disappointment come October 26. The court calendar didn't even acknowledge October 3, 2007, as a court appearance. My checkbook said I was there.

On October 26, just before leaving for court, I received a phone call from my brother Sal. He and his wife Inma were obviously pissed about my case, so they sent a letter to Congressman Tim Bishop's office. They hoped maybe something could be done to get the case moving. He told me Congressman Bishop's office sent the letter to the chief district attorney in Suffolk County, Thomas Spota. He didn't want me involved but figured he'd give me a heads up in case the letter was mentioned. I personally didn't give a damn who received a letter. I wanted everyone in the world to know how bad I was being screwed over. I was not going to be angry because my older brother and his wife wanted to do something. After that phone call I made a few more, sent a few e-mails, and received my share of text messages. Many people were pulling for me to have some good luck. I told everyone I would be getting trial dates and also predicted I would be offered a plea bargain. I was reading this case as if the prosecution was sitting on the other side of the table in Vegas. The problem was that I would soon have to fold a winning hand, and I didn't feel good about it.

The court appearance was crap as usual. Of course Judge Donohue didn't begin his day until close to 9:50 a.m. instead of 9:30 a.m. That was another twenty minutes when something could've and should've been done. The waste of time and money—taxpayers' money—was so immense. Nick had a few words with the judge before requesting a November trial. The judge wouldn't listen and set a date for January 8, 2008, exactly twenty-three months after my arrest. I was just happy to get a trial date. If the trial didn't happen, then the case would be over for me. Actually it was over for me already. I predicted the day they cuffed me that they would never go to trial. I wasn't wrong yet, and didn't think my streak would end.

In fact, I had predicted plea bargain, and I was right. A year ago, the first prosecutor, Adina Weidenbaum, wanted to throw the book at me. I was a sicko, I needed therapy, and they were going to give me a gratuitous deal of a criminal record and sixty days in jail. The tone had dramatically changed since the sham began. Michael Manning had an off-the-record discussion with Nick. He made a new offer, which would result in no jail time, no criminal record, and the records sealed. I pretended I would consider the offer, but Nick knew I wasn't going to. I wanted Michelle on the witness stand bad. Now I was the one bluffing since I knew I couldn't outlast them.

Michael Manning told my attorney this case wasn't one that he would rush to trial for. Really? What a surprise! He knew about the issues with the complainants, and although the charges were no big deal, a big deal was made of them, so he was pretty much handcuffed. How come a year ago it was the crime of the century, and now, after a third prosecutor looked at the same files and read the same exact facts, it was no big deal? It was a big deal when the police commissioner took the podium for the news cameras. I always thought those scoundrels knew a long time ago that I was railroaded, yet they were all happy to sit back and watch my life crumble. Of course, I must reiterate that I was never around for these discussions, but this was what Nick conveyed to me about his "man-to-man" chat. The prosecution could and probably would deny it all, but I would challenge them the way I was challenged. Let's all take a polygraph and see who's really telling the truth.

A few community members from Hampton Bays gave me some advice: "Vetro, you proved your point. It's over. We believe you're innocent, so how much longer are you going to torture yourself?" Another said, "Just take the plea and get back to work." Another community member said many people in the district wanted me back and I should give up already and get back to work. Two others told me it was taking its toll on everyone and they were becoming worried. Despite their kind words and sound advice, I decided to forge ahead with the trial although it was against all odds that I would last that long. The court calendar read, "Case continued (adjourned)." The calendar left out the part about the court refusing to be honest and refusing to give us a trial date as promised.

January 2008

January 7 finally arrived. I was ready to respectfully turn down the prosecution's offer and proceed to jury selection and trial. The dates were set over two months ago, so everyone should've been ready, right? I didn't think either of those scenarios would happen, because Nick attempted to contact the ADA the prior week and never received a return call. I also knew from an inside source that the complainants were not yet prepped for this trial. Why would they go to trial with a case they weren't confident with if my defense was allowing them to delay?

I hated the fact that I was always right about this damn case. My attorneys met with the judge and Michael Manning to discuss things, in chambers, "off the record." It did not go well. Nick said he wouldn't be well received by his peers if it was found out what the judge said. I didn't give a shit about his peers. Their unwritten rule was not mine. Once again, all they have to do is deny, but I know the truth. Maybe my attorneys were lying. Maybe they were trying to scare me out of a trial. They weren't exactly pushing for it. And as far as plea bargains go, yes, they have their place, an important place in the system, but not when they are forced. Nick said the ADA didn't say one word, just sat there, and the judge was livid.

Nick said that Judge Donohue thought the offer was generous and felt if there were eight charges, I must have done something. He said if I refused the offer and forced a trial, the judge would make sure I was thrown in jail if convicted of even one of the counts.

"Nick, the judge doesn't even know me or the case yet, and he's completely biased in favor of the prosecution? He intends to spend thousands more in taxpayers' money on locking a guy up for alleged prank calls?" I still can't believe this case is about alleged prank calls!

Nick and Lori got serious. They said the judge could maneuver around the rules of evidence so that the jury would not be able to contemplate key facts supporting our defense. That could ensure I was found guilty of at least one count, and he could throw me in jail. They said they couldn't shop around for judges because then everybody would go to their favorite judge.

I shot back, "Guys, I beg to differ. I've heard of attorneys requesting a judge step aside and even judges deciding on their own to recuse themselves."

Nick stated there's no way I was going to get a fair trial, and I should strongly consider the plea.

I shouted, "It would be fair if he was being watched—a higher authority or the media! Say something, do something, fight!" I sat down. I felt dizzy. I began to sweat profusely. The hallway was spinning and felt like an incinerator as my heart began to race. Everything I was going through caught up with me at once. I had to sit alone, quietly, and regroup. After a few deep breaths I was back in action. I refused to be threatened.

We went back into the very crowded courtroom to face the judge. I made a strong play at my winning hand. We respectfully declined the offer and stated we were ready for trial and immediate jury selection as discussed on October 26, 2007, about two and a half months ago. Judge Donohue wasn't happy and said he already scheduled a trial for the upcoming week.

Nick reminded him, "Judge you are the one who scheduled this date for trial." Judge Donohue didn't want to hear it and gave us a new date of February 22, 2008, for yet another conference and then trial to follow. I felt like a kid who had just had his candy taken from him. They never had any desire to begin the trial. That was why the prosecutor sat quietly during the conference. That was why the complainants weren't called, and that was why the judge had already scheduled another trial.

When we left the courthouse, my attorneys told me the prosecution was aware that I had reached out to the media. "Why did you invite certain people and organizations and the media to be at the trial?"

"What's the difference, and what are they worried about?" I asked. "Why do they care who's in the courtroom? I don't care if Hampton Bays School District is there, the state education department, Newfield High School, the media, or whoever else wants to show up. I want everybody to know what's going on."

Why would the judge, prosecutor, or complainants care? Hell, the media was invited to the party when the theme was "destroy Frank Vetro's life" in 2006, so why not now? I was so aggravated that we continued to bow down to these guys. Where did playing nice get us? It was not like any respect was reciprocated in the past two years. The court calendar read, "Case continued." It should have read, "We are all cowards and liars, we refuse to take any responsibility for destroying this man's reputation, we will continue to show no regard for his life, and we will continue to ignore the real issues."

How much longer can one unemployed man make it through life while taking on city hall? Next month I would be losing my car, my health insurance, my cell phone, and everything else. The delays would continue, and I simply couldn't afford to fight the battle anymore. I predicted this day would come, but it fell on deaf ears. I was very confused about certain things, and perhaps some of my words in this story hint at my confusion. It was hard to keep track of and make sense out of all that continued to occur. My attorneys seemed to be willing participants in this crap.

No person in his or her right mind could honestly believe the DA's office would go to trial in February. There was absolutely zero evidence to suggest they would. There are four people who had any say regarding whether there would be a trial. The prosecution pretended to be ready for trial until the time came and some lame excuse surfaced. Judge Donohue vehemently voiced his displeasure in clogging the courtroom for weeks over a misdemeanor case. Lord knows Nick's law firm did not want him at trial for weeks. That would mean one of their attorneys, who made about $350 per hour, would be tied up without taking in any more money. Hell, they stood to lose in the neighborhood of $50,000 dollars if this went to trial. That's three out of four people who would rather not have a trial. I was the fourth, and I know how I felt. I had a feeling from day one that I was the only one who actually planned on going to trial.

Lori, my other attorney, or whatever she was to me, separated herself from my case because I had no more money. What she and her firm did, I truly believe, was unethical and unjustifiable. Two years of empty promises—$41,000 thrown in the garbage. My brother Sal came with me to speak with the firm in person. I asked, as per the client's bill of rights, for her firm to explain their billing and services for two years. It was a simple question: what did they do for the $41,000? They never answered.

The money I spent on Nick's private investigators was another $15,000 or more for nothing—literally, because at the end of the day that was what they accomplished. It was just me and Nick, who was pissed because he wasn't getting paid and wanted out of this case in the worst way. My friends and family all offered words of wisdom. They knew how tragic my life had become. Well, not quite how tragic, but they knew it was bad. Their comments struck a nerve, which was their point. My situation affected a lot of people. My parents had enough and were thrilled I could have a conclusion without jail time or a criminal record. I felt bad for my friends Jon and Lesley, who put up the $17,500 bail. They needed that money but never once mentioned it—never once. I won't go into the enormous number of people, including the town of Hampton Bays, affected because of seven coldhearted complainants, incompetent police officers, and a DA's office that covered for the ineptitude. I could plaster the walls with e-mails and cards I received.

Speaking of Hampton Bays, I would not try to suggest the entire town was one hundred percent behind me. In fact, I could give you the names of parents, administrators, and teachers who would rather I not return. I also didn't have this desperate personal need to be in Hampton Bays. To be honest, as much as I loved working there, I didn't want to go back. I am prideful, and I wanted to show I could move on. I was very confident that wherever I wound up, I would work hard, make my rise to the top, and endear myself to the people in the same way. That was just not happening, and not going to happen with the negative stigma surrounding me.

I wondered if the cheerleaders who wanted me to continue fighting really gave a damn. So many people rooted for me from the sidelines but weren't behind me in battle. There was support for me, yes, but with the exception of maybe a handful of people, maybe, nobody did a thing. And there sure were a few people who could have done something to help. Everyone went back to their family, got married, got promoted, had kids, and celebrated life while I rotted in hell. They were not the ones losing their car, home, and personal belongings and risking jail. Although I was not happy, the bottom line was that the criminal charges were being vacated. I was facing eight misdemeanors and up to eight years in jail, and I could walk away with nothing. That's how the imperfect system works, like it or not. I did my best, but I'm not a millionaire. If those people insisted I keep fighting with what was at stake and what was being offered, were they ever on my side?

Imagine your child or loved one was publicly raked over the coals and humiliated for years. If he or she was threatened with jail time and a criminal record but could walk away free to pursue a chosen career with just a small fine, no convictions to crimes, and a clean fingerprint record, would you push him or her to go to trial? Would you risk his or her solid case and put the decision in the hands of an angry judge and a jury, or would you open your checkbook and pay a fine of a few hundred dollars? There are innocent people in jail, and there isn't one parent, caring parent, that could convince me he or she would roll the dice and make their kids risk jail time. I saw the big picture—well, I was trying to, at least—but others in this world did not. I thought maybe I should take the offer and get back to work.

The Sixth Amendment

I'd like to think the right to a speedy trial was designed, in part, to help people in my exact situation. Perhaps if my arrest wasn't advertised to the world I would have been able to lead a somewhat normal life while the proceedings were going on. However, while the prosecution and possibly my own defense continued to skirt my Sixth Amendment rights, I was stuck, spiraling downward, awaiting the conclusion. The prosecution would never be ready and certainly never be willing to go to trial. They did a good job of covering the fact they were denying me a speedy trial. As early as April 2006, in every document, the prosecution made it clear that they were ready for trial. Nick, a former ADA himself, told me that was standard procedure. The problem was that I didn't receive any evidence until seven months after my arrest and another piece about four months after that. That evidence was nothing more than my phone records—and not even the complete record, just April 19, 2005, to about November 23, 2005—and what at least I knew was a doctored recording. My attorney made numerous discovery demands requesting important disclosures and items crucial to prepare a defense, but I still didn't receive those answers. They cherry-picked the information they released. In March 2007 I recall they refused to turn over documents. We were on the eve of trial, and I still didn't see key paperwork leading to my arrest.

On top of that the police officer was so busy fighting rampant crime in the suburbs of Suffolk County that it was months before he could break free to testify at a hearing. On another note, if I was a new prosecutor just out of law school, I would immediately request to be assigned to Frank Vetro's case. It was a sure way to be promoted in a short period of time without doing any work, or at the very least not have to learn the facts of a case and still get paid. The prosecution's motives were obvious. They didn't want a trial to take place, and if one did, they didn't want my defense to be fully prepared. Because of their delay tactics, my right to due process was substantially prejudiced while my good name, reputation, and well-being continued to suffer. That's the system, though, and that's how prosecutors force a plea. Makes you wonder how many poor people are in New York jails, doesn't it? Makes you wonder how many others are forced into criminal records.

It should be mandatory that every single piece of notes or evidence be given to the defendant at the very first court appearance. Every single piece of paper in their possession. If someone is arrested, then there must have been a reason. Absolutely nothing should be held back. There shouldn't be a need to ask or make motions. Turn everything over—or else. What's the reason for waiting to hand things over? Just do it and fight fair. If you can't, then don't make the arrest. Neither the prosecution nor the defense should be able to use tricks to delay. You make an arrest and then lay all your cards on the table from day one and give a reasonable amount of time to mount a defense and/or discuss a plea. The delays to the system are unjustified, dilute the truth, and waste taxpayers' money. Speaking from experience, the delays also ruin lives.

The police were liars, the complainants were liars, and no one was interested in finding out the truth before a man's life was ruined. Nick said the ADA would twist statements and ask questions to manipulate and steer the facts. My attorneys would do the same thing. Jesus—wasn't anyone going to tell the truth? Why did we even need the ADA or my personal attorneys? Why couldn't they tell their story and I tell mine? I didn't have to twist anything. Trials are about anything but the truth. The whole process was a lesson in futility. I didn't know what the outcome was going to be, but I wondered—if I got cleared, would it be because I was innocent or because I accessed a hundred thousand dollars for defense/survival fees and had the fortitude to withstand the delays and public scrutiny? The bureaucracy of the legal system couldn't be worse. What if I'd had a family? What does it say to people who are penniless? Would they rot in jail because they couldn't afford to have the truth be known? Would I still be in jail if I wasn't able to post bail? The question deserves to be asked. How many people are rotting in jail for crimes they didn't commit?

February 2008

I had lunch with Joanne on February 19, in Westhampton Beach. The same old conversation took place and it was simply another reassurance that, if and when I was cleared for employment by the state education department, I would return to Hampton Bays.

I met with Nick on February 21. He suggested if I didn't accept the offer it might be "legal suicide". He had a phone conversation with ADA Michael Manning. As I figured Mr. Manning was under a lot of pressure and couldn't make everything disappear, people were leaning on him. When I asked who, Nick said he believed him. He said he too began his career as a young prosecutor, and when the DA's office pressures you as a new guy with a long career ahead, you don't have much say.

Prosecutors don't go to trial to lose cases. They stack the odds in their favor, but in this case that high chance of winning was not there and it was never going to be there. Nick lightheartedly stated a term he used for situations like mine is legal fiction. Translation: if I took the offer, I would be admitting to a minor infraction that wasn't factual. I hope everybody is learning a very important lesson. When you read about an alleged criminal taking a plea deal, don't jump to conclusions. Acceptance of an offer does not necessarily mean guilt.

I didn't understand why Nick didn't fight harder. I distinctly remember shaking his hand in 2006 and securing his word that he would fight to the death. It was not happening, and it never happened. I wanted to believe he was one of many good attorneys, good people, working in a broken system fueled by finances and politics, with strange and unjust rules. I strongly disagreed with his approach, and things that he did and did not do. There was a part of me that felt he threw me under the bus. I was going to court soon to give a decision on the offer. Having been given very sound advice by numerous individuals and hearing them all suggest I take the offer, I was forced to do some soul searching. For Christ's sake, if I wanted to take a deal, I wouldn't have shelled out six-figure sums for defense fees. I would've just paid Nick his money and played the waiting game until a deal came across. Who needed private investigators or a female attorney who did nothing for me?

The fact that I loved my chances at trial was a moot point. How many misdemeanor cases actually go to trial? The answer is not many at all. The prosecution made it clear that they would rather not go to trial, and as of today, February 21, the complainants still had not been prepped for a trial that should be starting. Therefore, they were not going to go this time or any other. It was not a matter of backing down. It was a matter of not being allowed to follow through. They were never going to put Nick in front of a jury. It was such a shame, because the Suffolk County DA's office was currently being scrutinized for how they had handled the widely notarized case of Martin Tankleff. A young man who grew up a few miles away from me who was convicted of murdering his parents as a teenager. He served about seventeen or so years in jail. The conviction was overturned after new evidence surfaced. The Duke Lacrosse scandal also touched some nerves, given that one of the accused players was from Long Island. Also, on January 13 there was an article in the Sunday *Newsday*, "Justice Perverted." It was a great account of Suffolk County's long history of misconduct by police [and] prosecutors. I wanted to publicly clear my name, especially since my arrest was still one of the small television segments for a Channel 12 News commercial.

I couldn't sleep and finally got out of bed at 4:00 a.m. I sat for what seemed like an eternity, holding my hot coffee like a safety blanket as it snowed furiously outside on this February 22 morning. I thought about and carefully considered everyone's advice one last time, took a shower, put my suit on, and headed out to court early—*to decline the offer*. I had to give it one last shot. The traffic and roads were terrible, and just my luck, I got into an accident. It actually happened well within a quarter of a mile from Michelle's house. I guess that would be another violation according to the keystone cops on my case. Luckily, I only hit the guardrail, and no other cars were involved. I got out in the snow to gather the significant pieces, somehow avoided being killed, and continued on my way. I had to make sure I made it to court so the judge wouldn't think I was skipping out. I was certain he would have loved to throw me in jail for anything at that point.

When I arrived, I was dirty and soaking wet but happily surprised to see my friend Dan Nolan at the courthouse. He drove in the downpour of snow to show his support. "Asshole Island" sure was right back in the day. Dan is a good man, to say the least. Other than that my day didn't get any better: Judge Donohue was not in. The clerk of the court said he didn't show up to work. Even better, Nick said Donohue had already scheduled another trial. That was the second time he did that. I thought he scheduled mine already. Nick said if anyone deserved to have their luck turn for the better, it was me. That was the understatement of the year. Needless to say, I didn't tell him I was going to turn the offer down. There was no point. That was the final nail. They were forcing the offer down my throat.

The day became much worse as a close family friend died. It was a reminder of our mortality. When my dad came to America from Italy, John was the man who met him when he got off the boat. They remained friends ever since. He was another individual with a past that I'm not too sure I would brag about. Nonetheless, he was good to me and wanted to see me vindicated. He died knowing a person he cared about was being destroyed with no end in sight. I wanted to someday be able to give him good news. That would not happen. The next court date was March 5 ... maybe. The court calendar read, "Case continued (adjourned)."

Three Special Supporters

I was invited to attend the Hampton Bays varsity girls' basketball game on February 23. It was a big playoff game, I believe they were on their way to the Long Island Championship. I stayed away from events in Hampton Bays for the past two years because I didn't want to be a circus sideshow, but I couldn't stay away from this one. I went to see three young ladies who were eighth graders when I first began in HB and were now seniors. Two of the girls were playing in the game, and I knew the other would be in the audience since they were all close friends. As an administrator I supported all of the students, but for one reason or another Sami, Genna, and Kenzi seemed to appreciate my efforts more than most.

I nervously walked into the crowded gymnasium. I wasn't sure how I would be received and immediately heard people whisper my name. Head held high, I walked over to the side bleachers, where there were very few spectators. Regardless of my reception, I was there to say hi to those girls and support the team. It turned out I was well received, and people slowly and steadily came to say hi. My superintendent, Joanne, gave me a hug and thanked me for always supporting the kids. She said she would call me to talk some things over. That agenda was on the back burner. Some people came right up to me. Others were more reserved, and that was okay—I really did understand. But the two young ladies on the team didn't think twice as they gave me a big wave hello and smile from the basketball court as they warmed up. After they won the game, all three gave me a warm hug, smiling ear to ear. They were thrilled I attended and asked if I could also attend the next game. Damn right I could.

It reminded me of what was printed in the media two years ago as they wrongfully stated one of the "alleged" victims was a former student. Say what you want about me, but don't say I would do harm to a student. I would give my life for all of them. I'm not sure why I decided to write about the game. I suppose just being there reminded me of the students. I missed them, because although many do, I never forgot I was in education for them. Many, actually most students supported me, and I thank them all. However, I feel obligated to give a special thanks to those three special girls. I wish I had been there to support them the whole way through.

I received an e-mail on February 26—and unfortunately have many more like this, illustrating what some of my "friends" did. It was from Anthony DeBlasio, a man I hired in Hampton Bays and influenced to become an administrator. This e-mail is one example of an individual who I had helped professionally and also socialized with prior to February 2006, an individual who had cut off all communications with me. I was no longer of any use to him. This was his first communication with me in about a year. It would be his last.

Frank,

It was good to see and talk with you. I was hesitant initially to come over and say hello. Over time I know our friendship has faded, and I was not sure on how you would welcome my hello. I know I have not been the best of friends or as supportive as I could have been, getting this certification and this job has seemed to have taken over my life. When I looked over and saw you at the game and then looked back to who I was sitting with I was hit with a wave of emotion. I very quickly remembered back to all the fun times we had in the hallways, at the class nights, at the dances, always with the best interest of the kids in mind and doing great things for the school. Now things at school are very different. I very much valued your friendship, work ethic and was inspired through many of our conversations to go in this direction with my career. I truly hope the best for you regarding this case and apologize sincerely in not being more supportive. You are a good person and a great friend, I wish you the best of luck in the next couple of weeks. It was good to see you and I will see you at the next game. Take care.

March 2008

March 5, was Frank Vetro's last stand. I went to court with the intention of telling my attorney to turn the offer down, but it didn't matter, because the prosecution delayed again. It's just unfathomable. Once again I felt compelled to call bullshit on every prosecutor involved and the entire justice system. I didn't have words to describe the nonsense anymore. I was amazed at the leverage I should have had, yet somehow they were tossing me around like a rag doll. Before this waste of time ended, I had to sign new temporary orders of protection. They are only good for a year. The courts, ever so aware of details, had the OP's signed today, although the old ones were expired for about three weeks already. I guess I was not too much of a threat. To top it off, they only had me sign six of them. I guess they felt Stephanie Veraldi's life was not as important as the others'. She didn't have to be protected from the violent madman named Vetro. I was so disheartened at the continued lack of attention to detail. The new court date was March 26. The court calendar read, "Case continued (adjourned)." It should have read, "shove it Frank Vetro, you're screwed".

As if I didn't have enough problems—I was subpoenaed to be a witness for a discrimination lawsuit against Hampton Bays. On about March 9, Joanne Loewenthal called me, I believe it was to prevent me from appearing as a witness and, if so, I didn't appreciate her attempts to circumvent due process. If an individual was going to be fired, as the teacher in that case was, then they should be entitled to a fair hearing, to have all of their witnesses take the witness stand. Perhaps I was a little sensitive because of what I was going through. I honestly didn't know who was right or wrong in the discrimination case, but that wasn't the point. This is the United States of America. Earlier I said that I had an innate need in me to fight the good fight and I considered it a curse. This was just the latest example of why I felt that way. I couldn't afford to have Hampton Bays angry with me but I couldn't ignore this either. Regardless, when I asked Nick what I should do even he said he couldn't ethically tell me not to appear.

Therefore, on about March 11, I did appear to testify. I didn't actually take the witness stand though, because they ran out of time. I asked Steve Lerner, one of the representatives in the case, why I was subpoenaed. He explained and it confirmed my suspicion. My testimony likely would not have been favorable to Hampton Bays. That teacher's attorney said she was going to request the case be reopened because she felt I had to be questioned. Hopefully I didn't screw myself over and get Hampton Bays pissed. I really had no choice but to appear. I was subpoenaed. I was a neutral party.

On March 11 I also had another debate with Nick. It would be our last. He completely leveled me, and I realized that I never had a chance of being completely exonerated, at least not with him as counsel. I only felt the way I did right then one other time in my life: when I lost my temper as a kid and my mother helplessly said she didn't like the person I was becoming. Once again I felt like I was hit by a Mack truck. Nick hit me with a major-league dose of harsh reality, and I'm certain he will deny all of this. I know the truth.

He began by stressing that what he was about to say—any other attorney would feel the same way but just wouldn't admit to it. After a moment of silence, he asked, "Would you like to change attorneys?" I was floored, because he knew I was tapped out of money.

He said for him to do everything I asked would take much more time and would mean knocking heads with many people. He described the multitude of layers that existed in the Suffolk County DA's office and the endless resources they had at their disposal. He looked me dead in the eye and said I didn't have the resources to take them on the way I wanted.

It got better.

There were eight crimes charged against me. With their "deal," I would have zero. On the surface, that was a win for me, and I should have been happy about that. From the perspective of the DA's office, they would save face, because I would have made a deal. From the perspective of my attorney, he could say his client was facing eight crimes and none of them stuck. They considered it a win all around, and in their eyes there was no use continuing, especially when I couldn't give any more money to the system. For all of them, the case, the game, was over.

Nick said he would make enemies. He said he understood if I were upset, but that's how it works, and its times like this that he questioned the system he worked in.

There was nothing more to say. My instincts were correct from day one. I was the only one who ever intended to go to trial. Everyone else was just wondering how far I would go. I went as far as my money took me, and I wish I could have gone further. Perhaps when you're fighting a good-old-boy's network, you need to acquire attorneys outside of the jurisdiction so that they don't care about future dealings. Either way, I could no longer fight the layers that were carved throughout the DA's office. I will say one thing in Nick's defense—only one. I paid him $30,000. I think he commanded about $350 per hour, and therefore one hundred hours would have cost me $35,000. He probably put in more than that. They just weren't all worthwhile hours. I wish he focused elsewhere. I wish he listened to me. At least he didn't completely abandon me like my other attorney, but at the end of the day I felt betrayed.

Chapter Ten
Blood in the Water

I was up all night reflecting on how I was railroaded. On March 26, 2008, six of the eight misdemeanors were be dismissed. Included in those six counts was the alleged order of protection violation that was separate, not even a part of the trial, and, I might add, total nonsense. The prosecution requested that, of the remaining two, either Michelle Konik's or Stephanie Veraldi's had to remain. That was because they were the only two who gave a damn about this case. The others were just weak-minded soldiers who blindly carried out their will. The two charges that were going to linger for a while were Michelle Konik's initial charge from February 2006 and Michelle Rogak's charge from December 2005. Those charges would be vacated after an additional court appearance in a year when I would withdraw my plea for a lesser one. There was no rhyme or reason for why those particular charges were chosen. Pick a card, any card—accept this illusion was with my life instead of a deck of cards. As far as the one-year interim period was concerned, there were no requirements on my part—no community service, no therapy, no drug tests, nothing. It was nothing more than further hush tactics so the authorities could save face.

It didn't have to be this way. For two years I listened to acquaintances that could have come forward: "Frank I was going to do this, but...." "I was going to do that but.... " Yeah, but you didn't. Believe me, I appreciated the ton of moral support I received, but if the few who could have spoken out actually did, including my own attorneys, then the case would have unfolded differently. I really believed that. I guess everyone has their own problems in life.

I swear, I would never allow someone to get screwed if I knew I could help or at least speak out. I was never one to take the path of least resistance if it meant someone would suffer because of it. I'm not just saying that because of what happened to me; I have proved it throughout my life, time and again. It was going to be a long day. I felt worse than the day I was cuffed. I never expected to convince everyone of my innocence, and I never once asked anyone to tell me I was innocent. All I ever asked was for people not to presume I was guilty based on what they read in the poisoned media. I tried to fight. I did my best. I hoped people didn't feel they were wrong to believe in my innocence.

I had a cup of coffee with Nick in the courthouse cafeteria. "Who is Salvatore Vetro?" he asked. "He wrote a letter to Michelle's superintendent requesting a meeting."

"I'm not mad because my brother tried to do something," I said.

He said that Michelle found out and so did the prosecution, and it was somehow seen as third-party contact.

"Michelle's name is never even mentioned in that letter. He never even accused or implied guilt but suggested that evidence warranted a look. Why would the school district automatically assume the teacher was Michelle Konik? There were three other teachers that were involved from that district. Plus, how was that third-party contact? I didn't say or do anything. I can't control other adults."

I continued, "Nick, did it ever occur to the prosecution that they should ask Michelle what she's worried about? Of course not, because she's being protected by the courts, police, and her school district. Don't worry, Nick— her superintendent, Roberta Gerold, personally called my brother to deny him a meeting. Michelle can breathe easier."

After that frustrating conversation we walked to the courtroom. The proceedings didn't begin on time, but why would they have? Eventually Nick approached the bench. He was there for a while, haggling with a judge, who wasn't happy with me—another person who didn't even know me but because of Michelle's lies, despised me. Finally I was called to the bench. I felt like I was going to the electric chair. The ADA Michael Manning began the proceedings by saying based upon his extensive conferences with defense counsel and "your honor", as well as people's investigations into the facts and circumstances, as well as the availability of the witnesses, the people were offering a deal. What did he mean, "Availability of witnesses"? I didn't give a damn about the witnesses or their calendar, schedule, or desire to take the stand! Let me translate Mr. Manning's opening line : "After the prosecution quickly realized there was no investigation into the facts and circumstances and the witnesses and arresting officers weren't credible, the DA's office never wanted to go to trial and thus needed to somehow save face." I am sure that was what Michael Manning really meant to say. I never admitted to anything specific, just the general statute, responding yes when asked. For the record, I never denied calling, arguing with, or yelling empty threats at Michelle Konik. We both exchanged similar dialogue on many occasions, and that's a fact. I do deny what I was accused of in this case and question their recorded evidence. I also had to admit to calling Michelle Rogak "with no legitimate purpose of communication." I also never denied calling Michelle Rogak, as we both called each other. We both said explicit sexual things to each other, and we both did even more explicit sexual things to each other. I just couldn't tell you the last time any of it happened, because I didn't give a crap about her, and I left her behind when I left Newfield High School. With regard to "no legitimate purpose of communicating," I would like to say that for the past two years, "the system" was communicating with me with no legitimate purpose, and it, as a whole, should have been up on charges.

The judge followed with a little warning about not violating probation. What probation? There were no restrictions to violate. It was all imaginary. Finally he warned me about writing or saying anything to anybody that would indicate, because the charges were being dismissed, I was taking advantage of the courts. If I said anything that embarrassed the police or courts, then the misdemeanors would stick, because that would be considered denying my admission and violating terms. The problem was that there was nothing I could say about anyone involved that wouldn't embarrass them. I was coerced to stay quiet for two years prior to this, but it was never officially stated on the record like it was that day in court. What better way to ensure that than to hold it over my head for another year and then threaten me with more consequences? My words should have been of no concern to them and no jeopardy to me. Unless they were trying to hide something or cover up for something. I walked out of that courthouse baffled once again.

When I returned home, Nick called to discuss, in depth, the fact that I should stay quiet. He didn't want to listen and said I could argue my right to free speech all I wanted but I better lay low and not say anything. Yeah, why question anything? Why stand up for your client? How was I ever supposed to fight back? The cascade of events that took place was immense. I really felt everyone was protecting Michelle, because once she went down, their case would crumble. What extremes would they take to cover up for a botched murder rap if all this was taking place over lousy alleged prank calls? God, it doesn't matter how many times I say it, it sounds ridiculous every time. This entire case is about *alleged* prank freaking calls!

This might sound out of place, in bad taste, and perhaps conceited, but I always had to work extremely hard for anything and everything I accomplished in life. Nothing ever came easy to me. However, finding female companionship was the one thing I never had to work for. I never even had to initiate a relationship. Yet somehow the one thing that came easy for me was perversely mutated into a story of me having an uncontrollable problem.

April 2008

Judge Donohue warned me to keep my mouth closed, but that didn't stop the district attorney's office from running their mouths on April 2 and 3. A press release was published in both Newsday and the Southampton Press. My mouth was duct-taped shut and then damaging, one-sided statements were released that I couldn't defend. Judge Donohue should have made sure nothing was released, but that would have been fair, wouldn't it have? They wanted to sink me further in the court of public opinion.

The headlines read, in big bold letters, "Ex-principal pleads to harassment" and "Vetro Enters Guilty Plea". But what was behind those grabbing headlines? When you pay a speeding ticket, you plead guilty. It didn't matter, because the message was sent that I was guilty. They grabbed everybody. I could happily report that I officially reached the level of local celebrity. In sports we have Jordan, Tiger, Gretzky, and Babe. In entertainment, we have Oprah, Elvis, and Madonna, and Beyonce. In the business world we have Trump, Forbes, and Rockefeller. I go by one name: Vetro, the man who was crucified by the system but lived to tell about it.

The spokesman for the DA's office, Robert Clifford, referenced that the plea was negotiated to spare the victims from testifying in open court. He was so ignorant to the facts, and there were no victims. They didn't want to testify because most of them didn't give a damn, never did, and would've looked like total losers on the stand if they had testified. Mr. Clifford was in business to make the DA's office look good, though, not to make a wrongfully accused defendant sound like a decent human being. There was a reference to one of the victims saying she was glad it was over and another stating the victims didn't want to testify. No kidding! I'd been saying that for two years. That was why they ran me into the ground instead of apologizing. That's why the ADA himself made reference to the unavailability of the complainants. Nobody wanted to be a part of the nonsense. I'd bet my life that if the complainants could do it over again they would tell Michelle and Stephanie to shove it where the sun doesnlt shine. Mr. Clifford didn't know one thing about my case. Who the hell was he, anyway, and why did the prosecution have to waste taxpayer money on him instead of speaking for themselves?

All this crap prompted phone calls from people wanting to give one hundred percent credibility to what they read. There are still people who don't understand there's always a slant of some sort in what the courts release to the press. I no longer had the patience to explain things to people who only checked in after reading or hearing news about me. I invited people to court every single time. The media had access to the court calendar and could've at least once called to ask me. Why didn't they bother? Why didn't anybody get the story as it was unfolding? Instead, they had it relayed from a spokesman who knew nothing about my case. The result, once again, was a telephone game, a story printed with a complete misrepresentation of the truth.

The Southampton Press was at least kind enough to get one quote right when Nick told them the case involved adult women who I had long standing intimate relationships with, not students or underage children, or anything more offensive. Nick also said they were mature though. I'm not sure I agree with that description. Meanwhile, my brother Sal once again wrote a letter to the editor in response to the press releases. *Newsday* didn't bother to print it.

My superintendent, Joanne Loewenthal, met with me on April 15 at Ruby Tuesday's in Sayville, Long Island. Same old discussion. Unfortunately she said she couldn't reinstate me yet because if I was cleared for employment by the state education department, it wouldn't be until the final disposition. That was one year away.

My brother Sal called on April 29 to tell me that an investigator for the state education department, Matthew Couch, called him, following up on yet another letter he wrote. My brother told him we had information regarding Michelle that should be looked into. He also said we were not allowed to release it thanks to the gag that was placed on me, and the incident with Michelle's school district regarding warnings of third-party contact. It was up to Mr. Couch to take it from there. He didn't.

The First Amendment

What happened to the days of a few news channels and newspapers? There must be over a dozen news stations running nonstop, simultaneously, on cable alone, combined with local and national news on your basic channels. The print media is just as saturated, with so many local, national, and global papers. Throw in the internet and social media, and the news comes in literally by the second. I guess it's nice to be so aware of events that, if needed, you could find important information, but the key word is important*. Today's media breeds its own inconsistencies and failures. Every nonsensical thing is put in the tabloids, the newspapers and on television and social websites. Half of the stuff is personal information and no one's business. Because of the multitude of news outlets, real news gets lost in the sizzle that every station, channel, and blog wants to have the world see and hear.*

The internet is an amazing tool for society, but it needs more regulation. It's a bastion of anonymity for cowards who want to say malicious or cruel things about people without having to suffer consequences or have their words personally challenged. If a person were to Google my name these past years, they would find many sites and blogs where the general population posted their opinions and so-called facts about me, a man they never met. The lies told about me were over the top, flat-out defamatory, and helped destroy my reputation. I received more than my fair share of vile accusations from ignorant and anonymous cowards shrouded in the obscurity of the internet.

The media is also way too involved with arrests and criminal cases. It's not their fault. If they're allowed, why not be there for the story? But much of the information shouldn't leak out to them. News outlets should only include what can be concretely verified. The media relies on "sources" and/ or people who would rather remain "confidential." Let me translate those words to cowards*. Then, if/when the authorities are asked a question, they say "no comment" because of pending litigation. Well, there I was, guys—no spokesman or attorney on my behalf, no anonymous source, and no request to remain confidential. I would have loved a public debate with everyone outside of the safety net known as court motions, objections, and criminal procedure laws. Nobody ever bothered to ask me though.*

Whatever happened to investigative reporting? When did reporters stop asking questions when someone gave them a story? From day one, if a reporter just asked the police, the prosecution, or me a couple of key questions, one of two things would have happened. They would've been lied to, or they would've received a very suspect answer, which would've led to two more questions, which in turn would've led to two more, etc. There was never once a moment of free thought. All the media did was write down what the authorities told them. Maybe people didn't care either way if what they printed was true anymore.

Yes, there are excellent journalists and reporters that uphold the truth, research stories, and relay news with integrity. However, there are too many news outlets that hold little or no regard for truth. I have paid extra close attention to the media since my unfortunate occurrence, and there seems to be very little factual stuff being reported. They all have "expert opinions" and fill the column or time slot with words like if *and* maybe. *The word* spin *is now such an accepted part of our culture that we pick specific media outlets that tell us the news the way we want to hear or read it, truth be damned. Maybe if the news left out opinions and just reported absolute facts, the public could make their own decisions without being influenced by ifs and maybes. The facts become an afterthought, especially when ratings are in need of an increase. We don't need reporters to self-promote and be the stars of the story. We need reporters to act like referees at a sporting event. They should not even be noticed. They should not bring attention to themselves. They should report the factual news and that's it.*

Without all the hype, though, you wouldn't have high ratings. After all, what makes cases interesting are their controversial components. I was a young, "good-looking" principal, there were seven "victims," and one was a "former student." The allegations were laced with "sexual" overtones and "violence." It was all crap, of course, but that didn't matter. News should not be entertaining. It should be cut-and-dry. It is what it is: a current event. I am reminded again of the Duke Lacrosse scandal. Network hosts toasted those kids for months. What those kids went through was because of a DA who wanted his face on the news every night and media that were happy to oblige. I watched a news anchor go into a diatribe about how the book should be thrown at them and then say, tongue in cheek, "If they are guilty, of course." In a way, those kids and I share a unique bond. We did nothing wrong except live in a place and time where someone in authority needed to solidify their reputations. Those Duke players were used for ratings. I was used for ratings. I wonder if I was eligible for an Emmy.

The names of victims are always left out of a story because they are

165

"potential" victims. If they are "potential" victims, then the accused is merely a "potential" criminal. Isn't it only fair not to ruin someone's name until it's definite that a crime was committed and the individual accused was indeed the culprit? Prosecutors use the media as a tool to put pressure on the accused. Their lives become so miserable that they can't possibly sustain the months and possibly years of financial and personal ruin. Shortly after my arrest, a man named Gary Feinberg, was arrested for some very embarrassing, reputation destroying acts. That case, also on Long Island, included a press conference too, and Mr. Feinberg was a deer in headlights. If I remember correctly, he committed suicide. After being through it myself, I can tell you that many people cannot handle the humiliation. I'm not saying whether the man was innocent or guilty. We'll never know the complete *truth. One side of that story will never be heard.*

I could write a book about people being tried and convicted in the media about whom no one knows the truth. That's because certain media in America rather report the scandal than the complete story. They'd rather run wall-to-wall stories that cover Britney Spears shaving her head in the midst of a mental breakdown. Weren't there bigger concerns in the world? I took abuse while my name and picture were plastered throughout numerous newspapers and TV stations. A person's status in life, socioeconomic background, accomplishments, physical appearance, or ethnicity should have nothing to do with justice being served. The law is not supposed to be prejudiced with regard to hindering or helping the accused. I wonder now if the blindfold on Lady Liberty is a representation of justice being blind to prejudice or blind to the truth. Maybe that sculpture's creator was screwed by the system. I lived with these inequities since February 9, 2006, so forgive me if I deign myself an expert on the subject. I always kept a watchful eye on the news and I've seen and read enough to know that nothing in this world deserves our explicit trust. My position on the topic has been solidified.

Similar to our criminal justice system, the media realm needs overhauling. Yes, our First Amendment right to free speech and press are very important. That doesn't mean we can't revisit and adapt the amendment to better serve justice in today's society. So much of the media has become nothing more than gossip at best. Through their rush for headlines and juicy stories, lives are ruined. Even after innocence is proven (proven!), individuals are many times still guilty socially. Actually they are never innocent, they are declared not guilty. There is a difference. Once the words are said or written, it's done. You cannot un-ring the bell. The media has to be held more accountable. Do you really think the creators of our First Amendment knew these modern day media outlets would exist? When will our leaders decide that enough time has passed to review the policies by which they govern? As an educator I reviewed policies every year and made appropriate adjustments. That's how you refine and bring your profession to the top of its game. Let's start raising the bar.

June 2008

I went to the DA's website on June 24 and printed out a new copy of the court calendar. The calendar entry for March 26, 2008, read "pled guilty, pre-sent investigation." Please—the sentence was already handed down. I had it in front of me. The calendar fast-forwarded a year to March 26, 2009, and read "probation review." There was nothing to review, because there was nothing for me to violate! They just didn't stop. They had to maintain that negative stigma surrounding me. It wasn't bad enough they destroyed my life for two years. They wanted to ensure I never got it back. I was eating breakfast that morning at my brother Sal's house. It was one of many places I resided since my arrest because I wanted to keep moving so certain individuals would not know where I lived. I was chatting with my brother and his wife, Inma, about a case in the media that was also taking forever to reach closure. My niece Gabriella overheard and asked, "Why don't they just go back immediately and get the story? This way they can just find out the truth the right way. They won't forget, and they can solve the problem right away." That's exactly the point—and it was illustrated by a twelve-year-old. When did the adults of the world lose sight of such an elementary concept? When did we allow the jargon and technical crap to get in the way of truth?

August 2008

They just wouldn't leave me alone. I interviewed for a school administrative position in another state. I was a finalist. However, the system back in my township of "Crookhaven" was not done robbing me of every right I had. I was told I couldn't accept the job anyway. You would think Long Island would want me to move on and get out of their hair. Nope—they wanted total destruction. I called Nick to ask/tell him to do something about it. He said he was surprised and could not believe they would prevent me from obtaining employment. It was one thing to have this charade where they fooled the public and told stories to the media to justify their ridiculous case. It was another to take my manhood away and force me to rely on others for financial support. When I told my brother Rocky this news he said I could have any money he had—anything I wanted. It was a caring, loving gesture, but he's my younger brother. I should have been asking him if he needed anything.

I heard more bad news on August 12—well, what I thought could be bad news. I was told by insiders that the superintendent and board of education in Hampton Bays were not happy with me because I appeared as a witness last March for that discrimination case. Because I appeared, that case was going to be reopened so I could be questioned. I was told Hampton Bays thought I aligned myself with the enemy. Jesus—I simply responded to a legal subpoena. I didn't even know the facts of the case. I just knew how justice should be served and felt this young woman should have been given a fair hearing, guilty or not. When will I ever learn to stop worrying about everybody else? It's hard for me to sit back, though, when things are not done in a fair and just manner. I don't allow injustice to happen if there is something I can do. Maybe I was just being paranoid.

October 2008

I just wanted to jot down a quick note that my friend Robert Clifford of the DA's office had some fresh comments for the media. He insisted one of the complainants in my case was indeed a former student of mine. His ignorance was amazing. Or was it just maliciousness?

March 2009

On March 8 I went with my friends Jon and Craig to a couple of bars in Port Jefferson called Tara's and JK's. While at JK's I saw Stephanie Veraldi and decided to leave. As we were walking down Main Street, who should walk past and stop in front of us? You guessed it—Stephanie, the "victim." She left the bar and her friends and by herself ran down the street to confront me. Sarcastically, loudly, and with a mischievous grin, she shouted my name over and over and ask how I was doing, then walked away. Harassment? Harassment! I couldn't believe my life had spiraled downhill because of these people.

A year went by and on March 26 was my final appearance. I entered court flanked by my close family. I was so nervous too because I was hoping that my "probation" had gone okay and I hadn't done anything to violate the terms. Oh, yeah—what terms? There really was no probation, and it was never an issue! Judge Donohue no longer presided in the courtroom. The new judge, Patricia M. Filiberto, was so confused and took forever. It was understandable, I suppose she was trying to make sense out of three years of complete ridiculousness. The ADA, Michael Manning, took his sweet time getting to the courtroom, and that didn't help. I believe the section numbers on the disposition were incorrect. They also tried to force me to admit to something that wasn't agreed upon last year. Hey, at least they were consistent throughout—consistently inaccurate. I actually s t o r m e d out of the courtroom. All bets were off. The judge was stating the wrong terms on the record and I wasn't having it. Nick chased after me and caught me in the hallway. He assured me of what would ultimately happen as he verified, in writing, ten months prior. Thus I went back in and put the baby to bed.

The judge wished me luck and said my attorney did a good job for me. Perhaps on the surface it seemed that way with all eight crimes gone. Nick walked my family and me to the window so my mom could pay the fine; I was broke. He was very defensive. He must have had a bit of guilty conscience. He must have. I immediately mailed out envelopes to the State Education Department with a few things concerning possible misconduct involving Michelle Konik with students. As an educator with experience in these matters, I could tell you that there was enough to warrant an investigation. Whenever students are involved, at any level, you have to at least ask the questions.

April 2009

Because of the witnesses that came forward, and what the evidence I acquired suggested, I sent two letters to the office of Chief District Attorney Thomas Spota. I thought perhaps if he had any sense of justice he could at least have his office look into some things. I also received the decision regarding the State Education Department's investigation into my license. The commissioner of education's office concluded that there was no moral character issue or misconduct on my part and I was cleared, without penalty. I was fully cleared to work. Thank god—finally! As Joanne, my union representative, the board of education, and I had planned since

June 2006 I would return to work. And there were two administrative positions that opened up, one of them was that central office position that I was interested in. Finally I could get my life back on track. Finally, things would go in my direction.

Part III
AND I WAS LEFT FOR DEAD

"If we are going to be kind, let it be out of simple generosity, not because we fear guilt or retribution."

— J.M. Coetzee, *Disgrace*

Chapter Eleven
Finish Him Already

Not so fast. Joanne did a complete 180 on me and decided I would not be returning! I sent a letter to the Hampton Bays Board of Education but received no response. The state administrators association refused to listen to me, as did the head of the Hampton Bays Administrative Association, Joseph Kolarik. They sent me letters filled with complete nonsense. Mr. Kolarik was one of the Hampton Bays power brokers who communicated with me before and after my separation. He knew the truth. Thinking perhaps they had simply forgotten I offered to show them all documentation, but they refused to acknowledge me. The responsibility of a union is to make sure that members are treated within the rules of the state and the collective bargaining agreement. To ensure that a superintendent does not do whatever he or she wants without, at the very least, being questioned. All I asked Joe Kolarik to do was meet with me and review my documents before deciding not to take a stance. I never said he had to save my job. He did nothing. Why take on the burden and the title of union president if you're not going to perform the duties? Or if you're going to mislead the person you represent.

My friend Marc Meyer, a veteran and tenured administrator in Hampton Bays, also stopped speaking to me. This man was not *like* a brother—he *was* a brother to me. I thought he might quietly and respectfully take a stand for me. God knows I would have for him, at all costs. I never asked him to fight for my job either. He could have pressed Kolarik, a man he was very close with, to do what he was supposed to do, and at least meet with me. Instead he stopped speaking to me. I knew Marc better than anybody, and I know why he bailed out on me. I know why Marcus. However, I'll keep that reason to myself at this time.

So there was yet another wave of "friends"—friends from Hampton Bays who could have attempted to do something but chose not to. They ran for the hills. If the union wasn't going to do something and my friends from the district weren't going to take a stand, then why would the others with no real connection to me offer help? They probably assumed there was no battle to fight, and so I was on my own. Thank you, Hampton Bays, the courts, the police, the DA, and all those who refused to help, for stripping me of every ounce of freedom. Is this what Hampton Bays taught their students? To run in the face of controversy? To believe everything we read and hear? To follow the heard like blind sheep? Aren't we supposed to teach our kids to stand up for what's right regardless of the controversy? I taught students to fight for what they believed in, to stay strong in the midst of adversity, and be their own person. Judging by the e-mails I received, the students responded to my situation much more maturely than their leaders in Hampton Bays. Why was Hampton Bays doing this? I was cleared for employment. I lived up to my end of the agreement. The violations I was forced to plead to weren't even an issue with regard to employment, legally speaking. I was forced to take on another battle.

June 2009

Last month I sent a third letter to Thomas Spota's office and hand-delivered a fourth. I also sent two letters to County Executive Steve Levy. I didn't even receive a general, boilerplate response from either office. As far as finding employment, I had over a thousand applications for education jobs, and jobs outside of the education field sent everywhere. Not to brag, but if you saw my résumé, you would notice it was pretty impressive. It was impossible to secure employment. Thank God I happened to know a pretty influential woman with a lot of pull in education. She was a political figure in the town of Brookhaven, and I'd known her since I was seven years old. I grew up with her son and was a member of his wedding party. She used to lightheartedly call me her son. Surely she could do or say something to help me get my foot back in the door. When I begged her for help, she called me to say she spoke with her attorneys, and they said it would not be in her best interest given the circumstances. She followed with "How's Mom doing?"

My friend Wendy Olsen tried her hardest to help me and introduced me to a friend of hers who I believe was a headhunter. She too was unsuccessful and even apologized for not being able to help me. Of course it wasn't her fault. So I decided to write a letter to some educational leaders from the Western Suffolk Board of Cooperative Educational Services (BOCES). A regional agency that provides educational programs for local school districts. Thomas Reilly and Joseph Meyers responded and invited me to meet with them. When I explained my situation they said they were already aware because "education is a small world." They said there was a job as a part-time teacher, paid hourly, with no benefits.

They also said the issues were very political, and nobody wanted to be on the front page of the news with me. One of them said he was in a similar position as a young administrator, but unlike me, he went home to his wife on a Friday night. He said I had a meteoric rise [he stole that from the headlines], and needed to be careful. He ended by advising me to stay out of bars.

I was so pissed. Don't want to be in the news? God forbid they were in the news for doing the right thing, knowing the truth, giving a good administrator and human being a chance, and helping to save a life. As embarrassing as it would have been, I would have accepted that hourly position. That was how bad things were for me. When I inquired further they didn't respond. They didn't expect me to be interested. The meeting was a complete waste of time.

On or about June 11, I received a letter that stated the commissioner of labor requested to reopen the misconduct hearing from 2007 because he discovered I paid a fine for two violations. Even worse, Hampton Bays also took a stance against me. I was shocked and thought they did that for two reasons: first, in retaliation, because I obeyed that subpoena, and second, to justify not reinstating me if they could prove I committed misconduct. The department of labor wanted me to pay back the money I received from unemployment. I didn't have a nickel to my name, never mind an extra $26,000. They really wanted to wipe me out completely. It was ridiculous. The State Education Department already ruled that I did not commit misconduct, nor did I have a moral character issue. I was officially back in the legal mess, this time civilly. And this time alone. Actually I always was alone. What I wondered was, how did the commissioner of labor know I paid a fine for two violations?

August 2009

Joanne Loewenthal was absolutely heartless. Not only did I feel she turned her back on me, but she also wanted to take away my manhood. She "allowed" me to interview for two of those open positions within the Hampton Bays School District. I was supposed to be reinstated, not interview for positions of a lower level. I immediately wondered why they were interviewing me when they were trying to claim I committed misconduct. Something wasn't adding up.

Given my situation I couldn't turn the interviews down so with my tail between my legs, and with hopes of earning a dollar and moving on with my life, I went on the interviews. I tried to take one for the team yet again. The interviews were for a chemistry teacher position and middle school assistant principal position. It was well documented how well I already performed in both jobs. Joanne herself labeled me a "dream team" administrator.

Richard Gostic, the science chairperson, and Christopher Richardt interviewed me for the chemistry position. I had more experience than the teachers who applied. I think ten individuals were interviewed, and I didn't even make the second round.

The assistant principal position was also entry-level for the administrative level. Dan Nolan, Grace Mcguire (my former secretary), and Lars Clemensen were among the members of the committee. Not one of the eighteen candidates had my experience. I should have been applying for superintendent jobs at that stage of my career. Again I didn't even make the second round. It was so humiliating to interview in front of people who, at one time, worked under me. Honestly, I would rather not go into details and instead forget about these interviews. I'll say this much. Nobody knew the answers to the interview questions better than me. Nobody, anywhere, is more qualified than me for that particular job. I did way too much for that school district, actually for the entire community. I didn't deserve to be treated that way. The members of the interview committee, including my one-time friend, ally, and secretary, Grace McGuire, hung me out to dry. I actually called Gracie afterword. She was cold and abruptly hung up on me. However, she admitted she eliminated six of eighteen job candidates prior to their interview even taking place. A secretary eliminated candidates prior to their interview?

Instead of reinstating me, one board of education member interrogated me by asking why I plead guilty, and why didn't I just have everything [the charges] completely cleared. She followed that up with a summative order to stay away from Steve and Andy, the representatives in that discrimination case I was subpoenaed for. So they were pissed that I obeyed the subpoena. That, in my eyes, is retaliation and in violation of the law. I was just obeying a subpoena!

My one last inside source on the committee was Dan Nolan, "Frankie, she had an agreement to bring you back. Obviously it's okay for you to return, so why did she interview you anyway. Why didn't she just bring you back?" After he spoke with Joanne Loewenthal, he said, "Joanne had agreed you were by far the best person for the position." Joanne told him the reason I wasn't reinstated was *because of my guilty plea to violations.* New York state law prohibits discrimination based on convictions unless they are directly related to the employment sought. The state education department had already concluded I was fine. There was no relation to employment.

I was banging my head against the wall. What was this crap about my pleading guilty to two violations? My plea was not supposed to be an issue.

October 2009

I received notification last month from Deborah Marriot, the supervisor for OSPRA (the Office of School Personnel Review and Accountability), the state education office that investigated me. They decided not to question Michelle's student, Michelle, or anybody with any information whatsoever. I thought it was a big mistake, and it made me wonder more about any possible cover-up. How could they refuse to even ask a question or look at documents that showed a student may have been mistreated by a teacher?

On October 18, I turned thirty-eight years old. Prime years continued to be taken from me. I don't know how people could stare at themselves in the mirror. Nick Dyno, my former boss and one-time friend, was now an assistant superintendent in the Southampton School District. He had a picture of me on his Facebook account with a caption reading, "my good friend Frankie, miss working with him." There were two job openings in his district, and as the directions read, I sent my résumé to him. He never even communicated with me or returned e-mails when I reached out to him. Of course I didn't get an interview. I suppose posting that picture and caption for the world to see helped this man sleep at night. The world saw a loyal friend. Was he? I was trying to secure any menial employment. That included jobs earning minimum wage. I even applied to be a paper boy. I never even received a phone call for any of them.

Everybody needs a break in life. Couldn't somebody throw me a life preserver? I read all the time about people being given second chances. The man who shot the pope was given a second chance, wasn't he? Individuals with criminal records find work. Felons are employed somewhere. Hell, there are individuals with prominent careers (athletes, politicians, actors, and educators, etc.) who were arrested, convicted of crimes, and, after paying their dues, were given more than a second chance. What about me? When would enough be enough? I wasn't even guilty as charged. Was I supposed to live in the woods? Walk into Penn Station, sleep on the steps? Die? One of the many great things about the United States of America is that its citizens love to give people second chances. Yes, society likes to watch a train wreck, but it is also very willing to build the person back up. If you own up to your mistakes and take the steps to apologize, make amends, and pay back society, you'll be forgiven, not destroyed. Believe me, I would've gladly apologized from day one. I can't apologize for something I did not do. I swear I didn't harass these freaking women!

I didn't have a clue where to go or how to get my life back on track. I went from a promising young leader making a "meteoric rise" to a man who continued to free-fall. I'd fallen from my position as a member of an "administrative dream team" to a man that nobody wanted to go near. I was a forgotten man, an outcast of the very world that once embraced me as a quality leader. Once constantly surrounded by "friends" and strangers alike, enjoying a productive and exciting life, I was reduced to a lone man with nothing left but close family members and maybe a few childhood friends. I could have been anything I wanted to be in life, anything. I chose education and gave my life to it. In return education left me to die. I was disappointed in many people. I would've responded differently. In fact, one reason my criminal and employment situations were playing out this way was because I tried to protect and help others. And what did it get me? A one-way ticket to hell. Nobody gave a damn about me.

My 38th birthday, and somehow still smiling.

Know Who Your Friends Are

Sometimes our minds and hearts play tricks on us. We inherently want to be liked and to have friends—many of them. We often refer to or introduce people as our friends. The truth is the word friend *might be the most misused and/ or overused word in any language. I attended Longwood High School. It had somewhat of a tough element to it, if you couldn't handle the diverse population and socioeconomic backgrounds. I didn't associate with a particular group. I always fit in with every group. In my neighborhood I hung around with kids who indulged in a lot of drugs, always found trouble, and didn't do well academically. My personality exhibited a strong will, so I was never pressured by them, nor did I do anything out of character. We lived near each other, and I had a good time with them. Therefore, as a stupid youth, I genuinely considered them my friends. I hung out with another group of guys more routinely, though, because we had more in common. We would play football, softball, or any other sport at Tanglewood Park just about every Sunday afternoon. I sure remember those twelve hour days playing handball and basketball with my buddies, Mike and Marcus Jefferson. Some of the best times ever.*

One particular Sunday, about ten of us were hitting the ball and clowning around, having a good time. My friend Jamie Nussbaum mentioned some stupid argument he had with a girl who was dating one of the "druggies." Just as the discussion was taking place, the park was taken over by six or seven cars that sped in to a screeching halt. Thirty people must have unloaded with bats, chains, two-by-fours and pipes, and they headed right for us. Holy cow it was a scary sight. Luckily I recognized many of them as my "friends" from the neighborhood and immediately tried to diffuse the situation.

"Frank, we're here for Jamie—just a one-on-one fight." I didn't even get a chance to respond as their "guy" bull-rushed him. Jamie did not want to fight, but in self-defense, he proceeded to beat up on the guy pretty good. Jamie was a big kid, strong, fast, and athletic, and there was no way this one guy was going to beat him. Of course, they didn't come with thirty guys and weapons just to watch. They jumped in and proceeded to beat the daylights out of Jamie and anyone who tried to stop them. We were outnumbered at least three to one, and somehow they wound up with our only bat! It was a slaughter—all because of a shouting match? These guys were my friends?

There was no way we could win this massacre, so we began to scramble. They could never catch me, as nimble as I was at the time, and I got away by dodging, weaving, and then scaling the ten-foot homerun fence in leftfield. Jamie didn't have the same luck as most of them honed in on him. I looked back to see the mob kicking, punching, and hitting him with pipes and bats. Jesus, I couldn't abandon my friend and still look myself in the mirror, so I hurried back. It was useless—there were too many, and I couldn't initiate an effective offense. I took a few shots but nothing even noticeable, as I somehow avoided direct hits. Plus the animals quickly scattered before the police arrived. I felt bad that I didn't get beat up worse since they did a real number on my friend. My real pain was in having considered those assholes my friends, and, just as discouraging, very few of the ten softball players I was with even tried to help. I stared some of them right in the eyes as they sat on the bench while we tried to fend off the attackers.

Know who your true friends are. The catch is that something extremely unfortunate has to happen before you make this realization, and that happens very rarely if at all. Most people go through life without ever having to show true friendship. Everyone is your friend when things are rolling along, but who's there when things go bad? Who's there against all odds? Who's there because it's the right thing to do, not because it's the popular or easy thing to do? The answer is not heartwarming. The answer is not many at all, if any. I needed a friend.

No, I didn't expect everyone who was behind me to call every day, and I didn't need to be coddled like a little kid. I didn't even expect that from my own blood. Like many Italian families, my extended family is very large. With Italians it seems everyone you know is a relative, even if they're not blood related. We were all very close, and I have fond memories of my cousins as we grew up together. Over time we naturally grew apart. That's what life does to people and families. You get pulled in so many different directions that it's easy to find yourself not keeping in touch as you did years before. I am not so self-absorbed that I expected everyone to put their own lives, their own problems, on the back burner for mine. They were all behind me, I knew they were. They're my cousins, my blood, and we will always be there for each other. My cousins Ron Capalbi and Salvatore Ceravolo have solidified my view. They made an effort to stay in touch with me and their unwavering support has been tremendous.

But I will not forget those who said they were busy and used other lame excuses. The word is not busy; it's fair-weather. I considered the positives when contemplating losing what I thought were friends. The fake people who only associated with me because of my position, because I could help them in some way, or because of some other cheap thrill they could get in their otherwise stale lives were gone. I would still be there for them if they ever needed me. I could guarantee that. Other than under those circumstances, those people will never occupy my time or thoughts again, ever.

They say when people get locked up they become worse while fraternizing with other inmates. I don't know enough to seriously make that claim, but in February 2006 I did witness a disturbing transformation while "on the inside". As a guest of the Central Islip Courthouse, I heard a soft, scared voice from the corner of my holding cell call out, "Vetro." He was a skinny little kid with an innocent look, frightened and out of place. He was also a graduate of Newfield High School. I didn't know him—he was never my student—but he remembered me. He asked if I could stay close, so I did and tried to reassure him. I didn't initiate conversation with him, but whenever he needed someone to talk to I listened. We were separated when I went for my arraignment, but I saw him again in the holding cell as we both waited for bail. He stayed next to me once again, but this time around he wasn't too afraid to chat with others. He also sat with me on the ride to Riverhead jail. At Riverhead we were split up, and I didn't see him for a while.

After checking in, we were reunited in a holding cell, where he was acting a little boisterous, like many of the other guys. I don't know if his true colors were showing or if he was just trying to survive, but I know he had a different look on his face. When I was finally bailed out, I saw him again, and I didn't like what I saw. The scared, innocent kid was acting as if he had been there a dozen times. He looked at me and turned away with no acknowledgment. They say spending time in jail can make a man worse. Maybe there's truth to that saying ... maybe. I hope that young man didn't fall victim to the anarchy of jail.

After dredging through what I'd been suffering, I could see how a person may commit another crime or become plain bitter. The system publicly breaks down the accused and destroys those who are convicted, but what does it do with them after they served their time? What exactly does it do besides chew them up and spit them out with no regard for their future or society's future? Thank god I had my family. And thank God I didn't have a family of my own to care for. I'm not sure what I would've done. Commit a crime just to get by? I couldn't say either way but that's probably what my foes wanted so they could justify my arrest and prosecution.

I'm not justifying repeat offenders or people who do bad things after an arrest. I'm saying that it's very hard to get by after being publicly labeled. A person can become hardened, desperate, and do anything to survive. I wonder how many people go through the system who aren't terrible people, but because of the events surrounding their arrest, prosecution, and lockup, they fall deeper into the dark side. Is it the person or the system that creates repeat offenders and career criminals? I don't know the answer, but I do know that if I wasn't strong willed I could've been in a lot of trouble the last four years. I read a news article about the growth of gangs on Long Island. I guess that was the next stop for people like me—the individuals who had been through the system, been broken down, and had society turn its back on them. I'm certain a gang would have accepted me and been my new inner circle. Now I know why some young men and women take that plunge.

Chapter Twelve
Too Young to Die

December 2009

Quite a few witnesses came forward, and all of their stories seemed to line up. I also acquired documents that confirmed what they said. I was convinced there was foul play regarding my arrest and my employment. I was convinced there was evidence that would prove I was torpedoed, and the real criminal was still at large. I was determined to uncover it all, and I filed claims against everyone who adversely affected my life. I was flat broke so I acted as my own attorney against political and powerful agencies with endless, publicly funded resources. Perhaps their biggest mistake was not thoroughly investigating Frank Vetro, the man. If they did, they would've learned I was a fighter from a township infamously known as "Crookhaven" and I would never quit. I spent my days at the Riverhead and Central Islip Law Libraries, learning procedure, laws, etc. I prodded, interrogated, and searched for any clues. I became a modern-day Count of Monte Cristo.

A sneaking suspicion came over me, so I went to the Central Islip Courthouse to rummage through my files. I discovered a sworn statement I never saw before. It was made by Michelle Konik, to the police, on December 19, 2005, about a month and a half prior to my arrest. In the statement she admitted to unauthorized access to my cell phone, contacting a woman I went on dates with, and using my Social Security number to access my phone records online. She's the one who set up the AT&T e-mail accounts and accessed my records! She should've been arrested months before me! This document was her own sworn admission. There was no debating it. She confessed! My now former attorney, Nick Marino, verified via email that the statement was never turned over to us.

HI FRANK –

WE RETRIEVED YOUR FILES & BOTH MYSELF & MY SECRETARY, SEPARATELY, CAREFULLY WENT THROUGH THE ENTIRE FILES. IT APPEARS FRANK YOU ARE RIGHT!! WE DID NOT FIND A STATEMENT FROM MICHELLE KONIK DATED 12/19/05!! WE CERTAINLY REQUESTED/DEMANDED ALL STATEMENTS ETC., & YES, FILED AN OMNIBUS MOTION SEEKING ALL BRADY MATERIAL, AMONGST OTHER THINGS. FEEL FREE TO CALL ME TO DISCUSS THIS.

TAKE CARE, & HAPPY NEW YEAR, NICK ....

Because of this new found statement, on about December 17, 2009 I tried to file a report for ID theft at the sixth precinct at 11:30 a.m. After looking at my paperwork, Officer Lindfers said the entire case seemed strange and respectfully referred me to the seventh precinct. So, on or about December 23, 2009, my brother Sal and I went to seventh precinct. Officer John Klein, who was also very nice, took a report, which stated that my claims were founded. His supervising officer referred me to the DA's office. He told us if the DA was willing to prosecute Michelle Konik-Brosdal, they would take action. On about December 28, 2009, I filed reports with the New York FBI office, Federal Trade Commission, and Social Security Administration. Johanna Esposito of the New York FBI called me. She advised that I had to take action at the local level. I also sent another letter to County Executive Steve Levy and Attorney General Andrew Cuomo.

January 2010

I wanted to re-open an investigation into my criminal case. It couldn't have been legitimate to hold back that sworn statement I discovered last month. However, I was unemployed, flat broke, and barely staying alive. I also had absolutely no understanding of how to do it, or if it could even be done. I tried to find an attorney but none of them wanted to take on this battle pro-bono. I was concerned that if there was a way to reopen the case, it would be a long time before I could come up with the money to retain an attorney.

I also sent yet another letter to Andrew Cuomo and again did not receive a response. Maybe these individuals weren't receiving the letters I was sending? Maybe the letters were opened by some low man on the totem pole and never reached the intended recipients? I didn't know, but someone should have responded with at least a boiler plate response.

Unable to secure employment, any employment, since June 2006, a random thought popped into my head that my constitutional rights were violated. The fourteenth amendment states, "Nor shall any state deprive any person of life, liberty, or property, without due process of law; nor deny to any person within its jurisdiction the equal protection of the laws." It seemed to me, as a layman, that my liberty interest right under the fourteenth amendment was violated. Because the events that separated me from employment were so public, because I wasn't reinstated as promised and agreed upon, and because I was not allowed to pursue employment in my chosen field for some time, my rights were violated. It has been legally shown that if the results of a forced separation from employment cause such a terrible scar on an educator's reputation that it limits him or her from being rehired in his chosen field, then the educator is entitled to due process prior to being separated. In my mind I was stripped of every single right, criminally and constitutionally.

February-September 2010

Over the next seven months or so, I pressed hard to learn how to navigate my way through the civil court system. When I had a minute to catch my breath I tried to gather any and all evidence to support those cases. Somehow, someway I also found time to keep digging into my criminal matter.

The hearing at the Department of Labor, regarding the new misconduct claims against me, took place in February. I appeared with evidence, sworn statements, a live witness, and proof from the state education department that I did not commit misconduct. The Hampton Bays attorney, Kelly Spina, of Miranda, Sambursky, Slone, Sklarin, Verveniotis, LLP and the commissioner of labor's representative—I believe his name was Mr. Poretta—appeared against me. They had no witnesses, nobody from

Hampton Bays, no sworn affidavits, and no new evidence. They just said I pled guilty to two violations and that was it. The initial hearing was already ruled in my favor in 2007, so to overrule it after all these years, the parties should've needed indisputable and overwhelming evidence. Nope, not when it was about destroying Frank Vetro. The administrative law judge, Craig Fishkin, the man who initially ruled in my favor, overturned his own decision. I was shocked and filed for an appeal.

At some point I went back to the Central Islip courthouse. I figured I would look through the files again to see if I missed something the first time around. Would you believe I made another discovery? My case wasn't sealed! Of course I researched the differences between cases being sealed versus not being sealed. I did not like my findings. The legal ramifications were tragic. Nick never discussed those ramifications with me because he emphatically stated that my case would be sealed. Actually the entire disposition of my case was different than what Nick assured me would ultimately happen. Either he didn't even know the correct disposition of my case, as evidenced by his own, official letter—or he flat out lied to me. I would have never taken the plea if I thought it wasn't being sealed. That's one reason I walked out of court at my final plea, and that's why Nick followed me into the hallway and reassured me of what he stated in his letter. What the hell did he do to me, and why? I used to have a picture of myself standing in the main office of Hampton Bays, holding a globe over my head. I did so much that it was often said I was taking on the world. That joke became a harsh reality.

After finding Michelle's sworn statement at the courthouse, and learning what the real disposition of my case was, I continued my search for documents. The prosecution's response to Nick's questions in 2006, regarding the arrest procedures, were in Nick's files. He received some, not all of the answers to his questions. The police claimed my voice was identified by the victims. So Nick asked, what type of identification procedure did the police use? Their response was, there were no police arranged identification procedures. So how was I identified?

The police never heard my voice until after they already arrested me, and according to the evidence they turned over, they didn't have my Feb 5, 2006 phone records. Neither Michelle nor I made a reference to the day the conversation took place in that freaking doctored up recording. So they couldn't have possibly verified my voice or that the recording was from the day, or even year, Michelle Konik claimed. Accept for Michelle and her student, none of the "victims" even claimed to recognize my voice nor did they accuse me. Did the police simply rely on a doctored audio of a man and Michelle, with Michelle continually calling the man Frank? If so, how hard would it have been to pick out Frank?

The Huntley Hearing Revisited

Nick's file also contained documents that he acquired from the 2007 Huntley hearing. I did what he should have done and broke down each document. First were the transcripts of Officer Heter's testimony at the hearing.

Heter testified that they didn't arrest me at the school on February 8, 2006, to avoid embarrassing me. What a freaking clown. It was 4:30 p.m. on a cold day in the dead of winter when the school was desolate, a ghost town. They arrested me in town in front throngs of community members, instead of at my home, which was one minute from the precinct, and held press conferences. Their exact goal was to humiliate me. Heter also said he stopped questioning me after I requested an attorney. Later he admitted to asking some questions after my request. The veteran NYS police officer also testified that he never heard of videotaping or audiotaping an interrogation and that he didn't know the full scope of the Miranda law. I sure had the right police officer in control of my life.

Nick asked Heter if he kept a memo book regarding his thorough investigation. Heter said no. Nick persisted by asking how he performed a "thorough" investigation without writing notes. Heter was caught and handed over some, not all, of his papers. And, as I thought I recalled in March 2007, the judge did warn the prosecutor, Kathleen Kearon. He told her that she could win the case and it could all be for nothing if she withheld documents I was entitled to. She said she understood and still refused to turn documents over. In my eyes it was official, I never received the sworn statement of Michelle Konik from December 2005 where she admitted to stealing my identity. That is no doubt something I was entitled to. *They were in violation*! Ms. Kearon also defended to the death that she didn't have to turn over a fax cover sheet, among other things. This made me wonder—if it was only a fax cover sheet, why not turn it over? What was the big deal? There had to be more.

Reading the transcripts I also learned that Nick cost me the opportunity to question whether or not the police had probable cause to arrest me. At the hearing Judge Donohue actually overruled himself regarding that issue.

At first he said Nick could address the issue of probable cause, but after the prosecutor adamantly opposed, Donohue changed his mind, because Nick never made an official request for a hearing on probable cause. Nick thought he could argue that issue at the Huntley Hearing. Thanks, Nick. Nice job, buddy. How was I supposed to know that there even was such a hearing? I was pissed because I seriously questioned whether or not they had probable cause to arrest me.

Some other documents that the prosecution turned over to Nick included a picture of me at Disney. Half of the picture, the half that was Michelle Konik standing next to me, was taken out. That was because it wouldn't look good for the prosecution to have a picture of Michelle with me at Disney, four months after she stole my identity. Michelle being with me at the time some of these alleged calls were made would have put questions marks on their rock-solid case, wouldn't it? No doubt it would have made Michelle look crazy knowing that she vacationed with someone she thought was dangerous. Or maybe it would have made her look like the criminal? If they wanted a picture of me at Disney, I have a much better one of both Michelle and me in the bedroom. A jury would have found the more risqué picture more entertaining as Michelle, unclothed, smiled ear to ear while taking the picture. She sure had a peculiar way of spending time with crazy men who harassed women. (See page 247-248, which shows the picture the prosecution turned over and the full, unaltered picture)

Officer Heter's Investigative Notes

There was a reason the prosecution did not want to turn the notes over. Alas, I got to see what my tax money was funding. I got to read Officer Heter's own words, expert analysis, and crime-stopping wizardry. It seemed Heter and company decided an investigation wasn't necessary. After all, they had Deputies Michelle Konik and Stephanie Veraldi to do the investigating for them. Heter's notes state, on or about;

December 8, 2005, at 3:30 p.m., the case was officially assigned to officer Heter.

December 10, 2005, at 10:30 a.m., Michelle Rogak responded to the precinct with phone records. She stated that other teachers had been getting phone calls, as did a former student. She gave a statement and left.

December 15, 2005, at 5:00 p.m., the interviewing officer called Michelle Rogak and asked her to call him back. She never did.

December 17, 2005, at 4:30 p.m., Stephanie Veraldi responded to the precinct with a copy of phone records. Michelle Konik was also present and was interviewed separately. Konik stated that another teacher, Allison Engstrom, was also getting phone calls. The interviewing officer left a message on Allison's phone to call him back. The complainant stated that women in the store had been getting calls. The interviewing officer spoke with the store manager, who stated they had been getting sexually harassing phone calls. The complainant stated that other women had also been getting phone calls (no names given). Stephanie's parents, Rocco Veraldi and Nancy Maletta, were listed, along with their phone numbers.

December 17, 2005, at 7:50 p.m., an officer called Michelle Rogak once again and left a message to call back. Again he stated she never did.

December 19, 2005, at 7:00 p.m., Allison Engstrom responded to the precinct and gave a statement. An officer received Allison's phone number from Michelle Konik and called her, and she called back.

December 19, 2005, at 7:30 p.m., Michelle Rogak responded to drop off phone records.

December 19, 2005, at 8:30 p.m., Michelle Konik responded to the precinct with phone records and was interviewed about the situation again by Officer Heter and Sergeant Cosgrove. Michelle stated that we started dating in 2001. She claimed that in 2004 she was in Las Vegas with me, and she took my cell phone while I was in the shower. She saw an unfamiliar phone number and called it when she got back to New York because she thought I was cheating on her. The time and date of phone calls were recorded and referenced on phone bill. The statement was taken, and phone records were taken and reviewed.

January 1, 2006, at 5:05 p.m., a request for my phone records was faxed to the DA's office.

January 1, 2006, at 9:00 p.m., an officer called and left a message for Christina to call him back.

January 3, 2006, at 7:15 p.m., an officer called Christina's job and left another message.

January 9, 2006 (no time listed), after Stephanie said she saw my phone records, she gave the officer a lead on other potential victims. The officer looked into at least six other potential victims and left a business card for them to call *if they decided* they were indeed harassed.

January 9, 2006, at 10:45 a.m., an officer called Christina on her cell phone and left a third message for her to call back. He then called her job and finally contacted her and convinced her to make a statement.

January 11, 2006, at 1:45 p.m., Christina responded to the precinct and made a statement.

January 14, 2006, at 5:00 p.m., Christina called the officer and claimed she'd received another harassing call from the suspect on January 13, 2006, at 8:58 p.m., and there was a successful trace with the phone company.

January 30, 2006, at 4:30 p.m., phone records were received for February through April 2005.

February 7, 2006, at 9:00 a.m., Michelle Konik called to complain about receiving a threatening phone call.

February 7, 2006, at 2:50 p.m., Michelle Konik responded to the precinct, gave a statement, and left a tape of the threats.

February 8, 2006, after arresting me, the authorities filled out other paperwork.

- The surveillance notes state that two officers drove to Hampton Bays at 9:30 a.m. They saw my car and went back to the precinct. That afternoon, a team of officers went back to the school and set up surveillance with an entire team on the suspect's vehicle.

- The prisoner activity log stated I waived my right to an attorney and phone call. Heter also testified that I never requested a call to an attorney, meanwhile the log shows I called an attorney. The activity log also stated that I never claimed pain or discomfort— although I clearly said the cuffs were too tight and I was freezing.
- The booking data sheet clearly indicates they lied and falsified arrest records. The police claimed there was "a crime in progress". But Heter admitted under oath, at the hearing, that there was no crime in progress. I immediately thought that's how they avoided any probable cause requirement. If there was a crime in progress, a surveillance team to catch the alleged terrorist in the middle of committing an act of terrorism was warranted. Following the arrest, the witch hunt continued. Numerous other women were questioned.

On or about May 29, 2006, at 9:30 p.m., two others were questioned about harassing calls. The officer left his card just in case females or employees heard differently.

On or about May 30, 2006, at 8:30 p.m., seven other women were referenced in regard to possibly receiving harassing calls. The notes were highlighted with the officer's own words, saying, "All persons did not want to press charges and did not call PD in past about phone calls."

On a personal note I would like to add, no kidding! Stop listening to Michelle Konik and her student/friend! In 2006, the prosecution bluffed my attorneys into thinking there were fifty more complaints on the way. After listening to those two idiots, the police went on a wild goose chase and learned they were both full of it. They failed to secure more "victims" to build their case. That's why, after they came up empty on May 30, 2006, Michelle Konik claimed I violated that order of protection. What better way to boost the case than to have the crazy man arrested again on June 1—the very next day?

Based on documents in Nick's file, the complainants themselves referenced the possibility of Michelle Konik stealing my identity and accessing my cell phone when they filed complaints in 2005. A week later Michelle Konik, who I now thought was the real criminal, went to Heter and sergeant Cosgrove with her student and literally admitted to stealing my identity and taking my phone as early as 2004. I guess the seventh precinct was too busy debating whether or not Michelle's breasts were real to worry about enforcing the law. All they had to do was ask me—they're fake! Next, Sherlock Holmes, aka officer Heter, followed Michelle and Stephanie's leads and initiated multiple calls to Allison Engstrom, Christina Impastato, and others to pressure and convince them that they were harassed. He was the one guilty of harassment! Heter used phrases like "decided" and "just in case." Either they were victims or they weren't. They couldn't flip a coin a year later.

After being coerced to file a complaint, a successful phone trace was claimed to take place. Of course that number, that important piece of evidence, was never turned over either, because it didn't lead back to me! Heter attempted to secure dozens of other complaints. Two officers had the nerve to approach my brother-in- law Mike to ask him to press charges. Out of those "fifty" complaints they secured only seven, all related to Michelle Konik. One would think after such a canvas of possible victims they would notice the obvious pattern surrounding Michelle.

Also, did the police really need a "surveillance team" to apprehend a principal for alleged phone calls? I could see the practicality of a wiretap, maybe, but surveillance team? I suppose having the report state that hours were spent in surveillance helped bolster their story, their lie, that the police, after extensive and thorough investigating, made an arrest. They hid the fact that harassment complaints came six months, and perhaps a year, after they allegedly happened. They falsified the arrest documents by claiming a "crime in progress" had produced the arrest rather than the criminal mind of Michelle Konik. I finally realized why Konik's complaint against me in 2006 said she was involved with an ongoing investigation with Officer Heter. She was the entire investigation.

Heter's notes also mentioned that the complainants' handed the officers phone records. However his notes did not decipher whose phone records were turned over? Were they Michelle's and the other complainants? As a principal I didn't want community members to know my phone number when I called their homes. Therefore my number was blocked and would not have appeared on the complainants' records even *if* I called them. Were they my phone records? Heter's notes do not reference him having my phone records, they reference subpoena requests after statements were already taken. But Michelle admitted to the police that she had illegal access to my records. Did they use her as an agent to access them prior to having probable cause to obtain a subpoena? How did the authorities verify that calls were being made by me prior to charging me with the crimes? Did they even have supporting evidence or probable cause to arrest me? I seriously started to believe that regardless of how many statements they had against me, there simply was no probable cause to arrest me. There were just too many questions and inconsistencies, and there seemed to be no evidence.

There were also other notes written by Heter titled "Vetro Notes." In sum they stated I started hanging out with Michelle around five years prior to the arrest, but not exclusively. Michelle Konik was jealous of me talking with various other women, including Newfield employees. His notes reference Michelle Konik setting up an online Cingular Wireless account in my name and listed the women that he mentioned during his interrogation of me. There was even a mention of a Reunion.com account set up in my name, and letters that defamed me being left on cars. All of that is what actually happened and Heter was aware. His own notes helped explain everything surrounding the charges against me yet he ignored them and went after me!

The last document that I noticed the prosecution turned over was a clean FBI criminal background check. That's it. That's all I saw of their slam dunk case against me. Maybe Michelle batted her eyes at the cops and made them salivate over not only talking with her, but also having a chance to have something exciting happen on an otherwise boring day. Michelle seemed to have a history of using every means possible to keep men close so I wouldn't be surprised if something surfaced regarding her liaison with the police. After all, a case that didn't warrant an arrest let alone years of personal angst occurred because of what seemed like corruption, ineptness, and perhaps even something Michelle did to make these officers pursue a school principal on made up charges.

Oh, and Nick came through again. I stumbled upon the original retainer I signed with him in February 2006. The first line states that the retainer included his representation of me regarding my job status with Hampton Bays School District. So why was I alone, unemployed for years, and without representation? It was impossible to keep up with everything over the years. Attorneys are retained to take care of all the legal stuff and protect the interests of their client. I had a right to rely on his expertise. I shouldn't have had to spend months and years researching things on my own. I shouldn't have been uncovering things after the fact. I had a right to trust him. That's why attorneys get paid a lot of money.

> *Police Officer Paul Failla was a guest speaker for my criminal justice class when I was a high school senior. He was a real character, funny and animated, and had a good message for students. He played the telephone game with us, where a person tells someone a message. That message gets passed along numerous times, eventually distorting the original statement. Officer Failla explained it was precisely why we should never wholeheartedly believe one person's version of a story. Many times, without bad intention, facts become distorted by way of human error, if nothing else. We must be careful before passing judgment. Officer Failla's closing statement was very elementary but maybe the most important lesson of all. Standing at the chalkboard, he stared us down, leaned closer, squinted, and said, "Treat people with respect, the way you would like to be treated."*

I never forgot that presentation and did my best to treat all people with equal respect no matter what their status—because they were human, not because they could help me in some way. Why couldn't the people that affected my life live by such a standard? About fifteen years later I lobbied for Officer Failla to do a presentation for the student body of Hampton Bays. His message, although simple, was that important.

Four years passed by and I was at a loss. I wanted a steady relationship, kids of my own. I wanted to work, and to live life. Was that too much to ask? My right to earn a living, to earn a dollar, was taken from me and nobody cared. An embarrassing admission is that I went to Social Services for assistance. I'm a proud person so I never told anyone about that day, the new worst day of my life. They turned me down too. I was turned down by welfare. It was all gone: money, livelihood, and any means for me to work my way back—all gone.

The only reason I still had my car, and a few other possessions, was because my brother Sal, and his wife Inma, refinanced their home and gave me money. I didn't ask for it, but I suppose it was an older brother's instinct. I wasn't even going to show up for Christmas because I didn't have money to buy gifts. I gave my family some stupid excuse as to why I couldn't be around. My brother saw through it, yelled at me, and literally threw money at me. This was all done "on the DL," so nobody was supposed to know. Oops.

I couldn't calculate what my parents sacrificed. I looked at a picture of them taken around the time I was arrested. They suddenly aged. I was sorry that my life brought my mom the worry she went through each and every day. My parents worked so hard all of their lives, and they should not have had to spend their retirement years like that. They seemed to be on the brink of financial hardship and I was certain that was in part because of my life. That was not why my ancestors came to the land of opportunity. Many days I'd spend extended time at a local gym (the membership was a gift). I would take showers there, put on a shirt and tie from my days as principal and go off to pretend I was doing something to earn money. I spent a large majority of my days in my car, twelve-fifteen- eighteen hours, just so my family wouldn't have to see me suffer more than they already did. So my mom could at least have hope for her son. It's cold in the New York winter. I was poor.

I found myself speaking about my life in the past tense, telling stories from years ago, as if my life was over, as if I were about to die. There was just nothing new to speak about on a daily basis. It was the same negative stuff every day. It had been years since I could bring something new to a conversation. Unlike everyone else, I wasn't promoted at work, no one would even hire me. I didn't get engaged or married. I wasn't lucky enough to have children and brag about their firsts. I didn't buy a new gadget to show everyone and compare. I didn't go on vacation and take pictures to share with everyone. Nothing happened for me to share with anybody. I had nothing in the present and nothing to look forward to in the future. New York State had collectively beat me to the ground, took away what little I had left, and were trying to completely erase me from existence. That was my life—slowly and surely, I was dying. Fade to black?

Chapter Thirteen
The Fight Continues

Screw that! I never quit. I don't stop, ever. And I sure wasn't attempting to solicit pity. The previous paragraphs were simply the cold hard facts of a story involving painful admissions. The fact is, if you didn't already know about my situation, you wouldn't have known about my situation. I'm sure my family and friends are going to be very surprised, and pissed, to read how bad my life had become. That's because I did what I do best: I stood tall every day, remained positive, and crawled and scratched to try to move forward. I smiled ear to ear. I smiled because those heartless animals would never break me. Those heartless animals *could never* break me. I kept fighting, fierce as ever, and as proud as ever. I had to find out precisely what triggered my arrest. Although I just about lost my faith in humanity, I never lost faith in myself.

Perhaps their one mistake in their quest to destroy me was failing to finish the job. Perhaps their one mistake was thinking they *could* finish the job. I had to consider these next words carefully. I come from a family with a deep religious background. I have a faith and would like to believe there's more, but I would not consider myself very religious, by most standards. Therefore I didn't want to sound like a hypocrite by mentioning religion or thanking God. Having said that, when the entire world left me for dead, one man reached out: Father Frank Pizzarelli. The same priest who called me to offer support following my arrest in 2006. I scheduled an appointment with him, and he met me at Hope House Ministries. I was just looking to talk, vent, and perhaps gain some perspective on why my life had become what it was. He greeted me with a handshake and warm, genuine smile. "How are things, Frank?"

Father had ties to the Hampton Bays community, and he knew my personal and professional background. I explained exactly how my life had turned out, and he listened and voiced his opinion. Out of respect for him, I will keep his opinion confidential. I'll just say he thought I deserved better. That's a safe statement to make.

He appreciated my accomplishments and abilities and felt they were wasting away. I wasn't even aware that he had a school, but he offered me a position to help me regain my life and simply survive.

"Frank, it isn't the money you should be making, but hopefully it will help get you out of your car, and give you something to build on."

The academy he hired me for was founded in the spirit of Saint Louis De Montfort, who had a commitment to the poor and the courage to do what no one else had the courage to do. That's my kind of human being. The school's mission:

> Provide compassionate, comprehensive and competent care for the poor, the marginal and the wounded among us. This commitment is woven in the Gospel vision that all life is sacred and every human person is unique and has the right to be respected and protected. Specifically, we are committed to young people and families in crisis, pregnant women and mothers and babies in crisis, and all other wounded people, in our society, who are seen as abandoned and neglected. Thus, we seek to be men and women of hope in a world of shattered dreams.

The academy educates young men, who often come from low socioeconomic backgrounds, have been arrested, thrown out of school, and maybe have stayed at numerous other facilities. Many have been given up on, and many of them have given up. They need help, and they need somebody to care and give them a break. Father thought, "With your professional background, approach to education, and your experience these past years, who better to help these kids?"

The youths reside with us, and we work very close with the courts and their public school. It's quite ironic that in a sense I started working with the court and public education systems. The systems that were involved in my own demise.

They realize the benefits of our program and work with us, in an effort to give youths another chance at life. For that I commend them, and thank them. They allow us to acclimate a young man back into society after a mistake was made. It's a safer transition for the youth, helps reduce the risk of recidivism, and is less burdensome on the school district. And it's what I do. It's what I have always done. I help people.

I could never do Father Frank justice with just a brief description. He has done so much for individuals and communities on Long Island. When the world turned its back on me, he stepped closer. I am forever grateful to Father for what he did for my life. He may have saved it.

My new position gave me a parachute but I was still falling and would need much more to move on in life. Hopefully it would be a start. It did allow me to, very slowly, save money to retain an attorney for my criminal matter. My debt did not make saving easy.

October 2010

With regard to my lawsuit against Hampton Bays, I learned that my superintendent, Joanne Loewenthal, was the one who actually reported me to the State Education Department in 2006. She created the entire premise to remove me from employment. For years we spoke, e-mailed, met for lunch, etc. She smiled to my face and didn't even tell me she was the reason they investigated me, and I was prevented from working. I also acquired paperwork proving I never had a chance at the positions I interviewed for in summer 2009. The interview was just a front. Communications between the school district's spokesman, Michael Conte, and Joanne Loewenthal emphatically state that they were never going to hire me, regardless of my credentials or the fact that I was the best candidate. Their reasons focused on my plea to violations and nothing more. There are laws in New York regarding such discrimination and I believed they did just that, discriminated.

With regard to my lawsuit against Middle Country Central School District, you couldn't make up what I discovered. A retired teacher from Newfield told me that during the school districts 2001 investigation, Michelle began to play the victim when she was questioned about her affair with Jim. He said when the administrator asked if she knew he had the numerous letters she wrote to Jim, she immediately stopped crying and went from victim to a look of "Oh, no."

"Frank, it's too bad those letters aren't around anymore, they must be very revealing." Guess again.

Over the years, Michelle gave me scores of letters and cards laced with sexual overtones and statements professing how much she loved me. Not only did I not give her one card in return, but I also discarded most of the cards she gave me, save a few personal notes she wrote inside books. Jim managed to save a decent amount because he gave copies to Middle Country Central School District for their investigation in 2001. He was good enough to mail them to me. The documents span about two years, give or take, and the pattern was obvious.

My hair stood on end as I read them. I could have used Wite-Out on Jim's name and replaced it with mine. Some words she used were the same as in her cards to me, and even the away messages posted under her screen name. The tone, the emotions, and the sense of urgency was identical. It was a similar template—the same pattern but with a different story line. Michelle sealed his fate months before his arrest. Like me, Jim never saw it coming. It's something very few people could understand or make sense of. When you were caught in Michelle's web, you couldn't walk away. The following paragraphs, based on those letters, illustrate this woman's nature and mindset.

As Jim's personal life began to fall apart, Michelle was there to convince him that everyone except her was his enemy. Each letter was filled with her convincing style, using love, explicit sex, loyalty, and friendship to keep him around. She suggested; she was his true friend, he will always be her true love, she would take care of him forever, she wanted to give him all the love, devotion, and peace he deserved, they had something that would never die, she was the luckiest girl to have a friend and hero all in one, Jim was the best friend she had, she was his biggest fan, he would always be her soul mate, she looked up to him, she wanted to listen to him and be protected by him, he was everything she ever wanted, she would give up everything to spend forever with him, she would always hold a place in her heart for him, he could trust her.

She also addressed cards to him as her sexy, hot, gorgeous man and filled them with sexual desires of ripping his clothes off with her teeth and descriptions of how much she wanted him naked so she could use her tongue. He, like I, had no clue it was her causing the problems.

The letters clearly illustrate Jim's realization that he made a terrible mistake and his desire to withdraw from her. She suggested; She knew he was trying to push her away, she missed him, she didn't think she could ever find a guy like him, it was sickening that she couldn't be with him, it killed her inside when Jim said he had to cut her off, being without him was hell, she hated being without him, he didn't want her in his life and she missed him terribly.

His attempts to rid himself of Michelle failed and his life spiraled out of control. Michelle seemed to become irrational in her thoughts and words. Her handwriting started out neat and legible but slowly morphed into extremely large, illegible, and incoherent text by the time the letters ended. She fell into desperation mode, suggesting; he's stuck with her, she must have him, she was miserable without him, she had to alter her mind, she was either amazingly high or devastatingly low, she couldn't take it, her mind was a mess, she drove all over Long Island and drove by places they've been, she pretended she was going to see him, she couldn't live without him, she was never saying good-bye to him, she would do anything in this world to be sure that he didn't leave, if all she could ever be is his girl and not his wife she would treasure it, she would die for him, her heart is broken, she didn't know how to get him out of her mind, she was going insane, she couldn't pull herself away from him, it killed her, she couldn't deal with it, she will never be able to control herself, she was not saying goodbye to him, she didn't like to face painful things, she would never let go of their relationship, she was going to have to get hypnotherapy, and she thought Jim should know that she was not okay with the situation.

Shortly after her last letter Jim was arrested and his days at Newfield High School were over. Who was the victim? Michelle was right when she suggested she couldn't say good-bye to him. Instead, like she did with me, she made it so she didn't have to say good-bye. She recruited others to do her dirty work while she claimed to be a victim to them and a friend to him.

Besides those letters, Jim also sent me copies of two police reports he filed against Michelle more than a year before she had him arrested. In August of 2000 he filed a report for aggravated harassment that claimed Michelle was making threatening phone calls to his house six or seven times daily. These were the exact allegations that destroyed my life! He filed another report on August 31, 2000, when Michelle had a couple of gentlemen approach him at Newfield High School. Jesus, someone associated with her approached me at work too! Even worse, the documents regarding Middle Country's 2001 investigation mentioned that a student became involved. Michelle also involved a student with my arrest.

So a woman with a history of having past lovers arrested and inappropriately befriending students, and who also had unauthorized access to my cell phone and cell phone records, was reported for allegedly making harassing and threatening phone calls? The same allegations that I was arrested for? Why were none of Jim's reports investigated but when Michelle filed report over a year later, he was automatically arrested? Why was Michelle allowed to continue to teach yet Jim was forced from the building? How is it that my police reports in 2002 were never investigated yet the police immediately acted on the bogus reports against me?

Since 2006 I wondered where the hell Michelle thought up the idea of telling the police that I said I had thirty seven letters that could ruin her. Maybe she figured those letters she gave Jim would come back into play? Perhaps she saw me talking with Jim in Las Vegas the same time she saw me there, then made up a story to have me nailed a second time? That woman truly was ten steps ahead.

November 2010

After acquiring all the new evidence, I decided again, as a mandated reporter, to notify the proper agencies. I didn't want to risk my license if it became known that I should have reported what I knew. I didn't want to jeopardize my new job, because lord knows it probably would have been my last. So I reached out to the state education department. I sent the letter to Matthew Couch, the man who investigated me when Joanne Loewenthal reported me. I also contacted the district attorney's online crime victim's page because of Michelle's identity theft admission, among other things. Jeremy Scileppi of the DA's office immediately returned my e-mail, called me, and left a number for me to call him. I returned his call and left a message. I called one other time, e-mailed him the information he had requested, and eagerly awaited his response. Obviously he was interested.

December 2010

After learning the details such as my name and her name, and the entire scandal, Mr. Scileppi stopped communicating with me. I called his office many times. Each time the secretary asked my name, and I was put on hold before being told he was in a meeting. I sent one last e-mail, which was not returned. On December 23 the Unemployment Insurance Appeal Board upheld Administrative Law Judge Craig Fishkin's ruling that I had committed misconduct while employed at Hampton Bays. On that decision was Leonard D. Polletta and Michael T. Greason. They didn't put forth any reason for their decision. It seemed as if all my evidence and the law were ignored. The opposing sides never even put forth any evidence in opposition. I decided to appeal to the next level.

March 2011

I was in complete shock as a school administrator and a human being. The student who was mentioned in the documents regarding the 2001 investigation into Michelle and Jim's affair came forward. This student was never questioned as part of their investigation. There are no excuses for not questioning this student. None! And I will never be convinced otherwise. If Middle Country Central School District had done its job and questioned this student, they would've been told disturbing details, and given other avenues to investigate. Perhaps the real problem would have been dealt with, and Jim and I would've been spared. Based on this student's sworn affidavit, from 1999–2001 Michelle Konik;

1. Developed close relationships with students/cheerleaders who were sixteen years old;
2. Drove them around in her car;
3. Picked them up from their summer activities, not related to school;
4. Took them to her house to see her dogs;
5. Spoke to them about her sexual affair with Jim, who was this student's teacher;
6. Went to lunch with them;
7. Explained to them how she ran bathwater over her private parts to have really good orgasms and suggested they try it;
8. Told them that she had laser surgery to remove her pubic hair and it was the best thing she ever did.

Does any of this behavior with a student sound familiar, as in this wasn't the only time she was so close with a student? That young lady couldn't have made up those details out of thin air. I know personally, for a fact, that Michelle Konik did both seven and eight. When in a student-teacher relationship did the conversation change from school-related topics to having good orgasms and removing your pubic hair? This was the teacher involved with Students against Relationship Abuse? The student told me she was just a kid/student during those years, but as an adult, she

205

knew better, and both Jim and I were teachers she respected. As an adult she realized the inappropriateness. For a former student to come forward some ten years later said a lot about how strongly she felt about how her teacher behaved with her. She shouldn't have been ignored.

September 29, 2011

One of my lawsuits was against AT&T Wireless, for wrongfully compromising my records. The federal magistrate presiding over the case was the Honorable Judge William D. Wall. He confirmed everything about Michelle stealing my identity in his twenty page decision. The multibillion-dollar company completely disregarded my well-being. Through their lax security, they allowed Michelle Konik-Brosdal an easy avenue to steal my identity. Even after I warned them that the account was illegally set up and they promised they would take action, they still did nothing to prevent it. Unfortunately, according to the decision, AT&T could not be held liable.

Although AT&T had a policy to protect their customers and go after individuals who compromised their security systems, they would not take action against Michelle. Their attorney, Frank Velocci, said he had to defend his client with great zeal. Yeah, but what about his client protecting their customers, with great zeal, from known threats?

I did learn some important pieces of information though. Mr. Velocci gave me a zip file that Michelle gave him. It contained my résumés, work from administrative classes, documents dating back to 2001, and even my transcript from Queens College! That transcript contained my student ID number, which was my social security number. That was the key. That's how she obtained my social security number. I had no idea how she had any of the documents though. I didn't have a computer back then and I certainly did not have a lot of that stuff stored on a computer file. As far as my resumes and class work, some of that stuff was on my brother's computer, but he was living with my parents at the time. She even had content from my brother's personal files.

AT&T also deposed Michelle. While under oath, she referenced use of a calling card and being in my home when I wasn't around.

Mr. Velocci also gave me three subpoenas that the authorities sent to AT&T back in 2006, to legally request my phone records. Alas, I finally realized perhaps why, at the March 2007 Huntley hearing, the prosecution didn't want to turn over documents and even refused to turn over simple fax cover sheets. The fax cover sheets I received, along with Michelle's sworn admission in December 2005 that she stole my identity, may have proven my prior thoughts that the police did not have probable cause to arrest me. Follow this:

There were two separate types of complaints filed against me. There were complaints that referenced someone saying inappropriate things and/or simply hanging up without saying anything. However, those complainants never even accused me, identified my voice, or said I did it. Also, although I didn't harass them, my phone number was blocked and would have never appeared on those complainants phone records even if I did. Therefore my arrest could not have been based on their phone records, their identification of me, or on their statements in general. So what was it based on?

The police claimed the statements against me were based on phone records. However, according to the dates on their subpoenas, the requests for my phone records were made *after* already securing statements against me. What records were they talking about? When Michelle was deposed by AT&T, she also admitted to printing out my phone records for the police after they asked her to do it. So that ended that debate. She did hand the police my records. Asking a civilian to print out my phone records *after* she admitted to stealing my identity to gain illegal access? The police still used her as an agent to acquire them illegally? That could not possibly be legitimate.

The police knew they had no probable cause. So first they acquired complaints against me. Then they illegally acquired phone records and pretended that they had them legally the entire time by saying that the statements were based on phone records. Then they used those statements as justification to subpoena my phone records. For Christ's sake, the probable cause standard to obtain a subpoena is such a low standard, and they didn't even have that. That's when they tried to cover for their procedural flaws. The fax cover sheets from the DA's office to AT&T prove the panic they were in. They stated "please rush" and "urgent", because they wanted to make it look as if they had my records the entire time. However, they got a huge bite in the rear. That's because according to the subpoena responses, AT&T *never* turned over my phone records from April 2005 through November 2005. Therefore their evidence against me was never, ever, legally acquired. Their plan completely backfired.

Compounding one error with another, the police also said those complaints were based on phone traces. But there were no phone traces, just the identity theft. In fact, according to officer Heter's notes, the only trace that existed didn't lead back to me.

Either way, those complaints were made prior to them having even the illegally accessed phone records, so they couldn't possibly be based on them as the police claimed. They had those complaints, those "victims", including what they claimed was a former student, months before my arrest, and still did nothing. They still let me be around students. The reason they didn't arrest me was because they knew they had no probable cause or evidence to support the claims.

The only remaining possibility for my arrest in February 2006 was because Michelle Konik accused me of threatening her over the phone. Did that give the police the probable cause they were desperately looking for? If not, is that why they falsified documents by claiming there was a crime in progress when they arrested me? Was that their last resort after securing not one piece of solid evidence against me? I had to find the answers.

October and November 2011

In light of all the information I learned in the AT&T case, I e-mailed Mr. Scileppi of the District Attorney's office again, to see what he'd come up with or whether he had done anything at all regarding my initial correspondence. Mr. Scileppi responded and I returned his e-mail. Mr. Scileppi responded again but this time with some force. He included criminal statutes and suggested that I didn't have a valid complaint. Not so fast, sir. I responded in depth with my own references to statutes regarding Michelle Konik-Brosdal's actions. I also wrote another letter to the State Education Department. I never received a response.

December 14, 2011

After numerous individuals came forward with sworn affidavits regarding Michelle's conduct, I went with my brother Sal and spoke at a Middle Country Central School District board of education meeting. As I was speaking and respecting confidentiality by not naming names at the public meeting, the board of education president, Ms. Lessler, became concerned. I believe she was on the board of education in 2001. I didn't expect her to remember every detail regarding the massive 2001 investigation, but what I was saying should have at least rang a bell. It was a very serious investigation. The kind that does not normally take place during a board of education member's tenure. Ms. Lessler cut me off to suggest I meet privately with the board and its attorney to discuss the *potentially* very serious matter. That sounded great. I would've been more than happy to meet, and put the issue to rest once and for all. If my evidence was baseless, and the witnesses were lying, I would have never said another word.

The community was taken aback but they were glad I had the guts to speak about the serious topic. When I was done they approached me and offered supporting words. Like I told my superintendent, Joanne Loewenthal, at one of our lunches, when I had something to say, it would not be via a cowardly anonymous letter. Before leaving the meeting a local reporter for the Times Beacon Record Newspapers gave me her card so she could speak to me about it. Yeah right, I knew better. That small circulation covered the school district and would never print anything that scathing about the hand that fed them. I gave her my contact info and she gave me her card, Susan Risoli. I didn't hold my breath.

January 2012

Another year gone by. On January 4, because of my e-mails to Jeremy Scileppi, Detective Daryl Burger of the DA's office in Hauppauge Long Island called me to schedule a meeting. I met with him the very next day. He was with another detective whose name I somehow forgot. He said, even if Michelle had done something wrong the statutes were up, and referred me back to seventh precinct. On the same day in my civil case against the Suffolk County police and district attorney, it was confirmed to me, through discovery, that the recording used as evidence was indeed doctored. At least according to what they turned over, a full twenty-seven minute recording did not exist. They also turned over even more documents regarding my arrest that I never saw before. I went back to the same old question. Was my arrest and prosecution really based on a recording that was not admissible in court? Or was there more?

On January 8 I sent a follow-up letter to Detective Burger, and, on January 11, I e-mailed Mr. Scileppi again. Scileppi forwarded my e-mail to Detective Burger. In this live version of the game hot potato, I was passed along from office to office. Detective Burger referred me to the seventh precinct again. So I called the seventh precinct and spoke with Officer

Ryan. She was very nice and honest, and said my initial complaint against Michelle back in 2009 was never investigated. She referred me back to the DA's office. On January 13, Detective Burger called me back. He was very cordial, as he was since his initial phone call to me. He just wanted to clarify some things that I wrote in my follow-up letter to him. Sure, no problem. On January 17, Detective Burger communicated with me again, and again he referred me back to the seventh precinct.

Being persistent, I did reach out to the seventh precinct. I spoke with Detective Hughes, who after speaking with me asked why Michelle wasn't arrested. That was the million dollar question. Hughes transferred me to another officer who referred me to Detective Gabriel from the seventh precinct ID theft unit. Detective Gabriel called me at about 1:30 p.m. I returned his call the next day, January 18, at about 12:25 p.m. He too was very nice, they all were, but he simply did not have any answers. He didn't know why no action was taken years ago and could not piece the puzzle together. He also said the statutes were up and that any felony charges should have gone to the FBI. I did go to the FBI, and they sent me back to local authorities.

I wanted to believe that the authorities I spoke with this month had no clue about the mess that was created dating back to 2005. In fact I did believe that. It's a lot to grasp in one brief phone call. Each time I spoke with an officer or detective they were very cordial, and seemed to want to understand the situation. The way they sounded and spoke with me, they seemed to realize something was wrong. However, everybody kept telling me the statutes were up. The problem I had wasn't with the detectives and officers I spoke with, it was with the fact that the statutes were up. They weren't up when I first complained. Certainly they weren't up in 2005 when Michelle admitted to what she did to a police officer from the seventh precinct. It was not my fault that I got the runaround. How about consequences for the individuals who failed to act when they were made aware of the situation, and maybe could have prevented my arrest?

Actually, one official whom I will not name, did say something that was a little troublesome. He said nothing was stolen, so there was nothing I could do anyway. I mentioned a few identity theft cases to him, including the one involving the politician Sarah Palin a few years back where an individual hacked into her e-mail account. He wound up guilty of federal charges for simply hacking into an existing e-mail. That's nowhere near what Michelle did to me. She used my social security number and literally set up accounts in my name, so my personal records could be sent to her, amongst numerous other fraudulent activities. The official responded that I was not Sarah Palin or famous, so it didn't matter that my identity had been stolen. If he was right about that then add it to the list of things that needed to be changed. I could understand that such a crime may be taken more serious if committed against a government official due to national security. But to say that it doesn't matter if a civilian's identity is stolen is simply not right. Laws should protect everyone.

I also received a letter from the attorney general's office that stated an investigation into what happened was not warranted. Total bullcrap. How did they know? The attorney general's office never even spoke with me or any of the witnesses or looked at the evidence in my possession. My head was spinning from the runaround this month—actually, the past few years. Now I'm going to sound like an infomercial, though. Wait—there's more!

I never heard from the Middle Country board president or that reporter, of course. So, on January 18, my brother and I quietly attended the next Middle Country Central School District public board meeting. We hid in the back so no one would see us. I couldn't believe what I heard. The Board President, Ms. Lessler said my claims were unsupported and unfounded! There was no way I was letting her get away with that. I immediately approached the podium, to their surprise, and addressed the community. I tried to explain that she could not draw that conclusion because there was no investigation. Among many other things, at least seven witnesses (including former students) were never contacted, and my documentation was never reviewed. Plus, if they investigated already, then why was Karen Lessler so surprised at my comments at the last meeting, and why did she want to meet with me? I said I *tried* to explain, because the superintendent, Roberta Gerold, cut me off and emphatically referenced a well-documented investigation. Investigation? Ms. Gerold personally called my brother to deny him a meeting! How could she claim there was an investigation? I was determined to blow the lid off of what I thought was shaping up to be a massive cover up.

Chapter Fourteen
I Win! Hey! Is Anybody Out There?
Does Anybody Hear Me?

March 2012

I finally saved enough money to retain an attorney to try and reopen my criminal investigation. The criminal procedure laws in New York allow this under certain situations. I didn't have just one legitimate reason. I had a ton. I, with my brother Sal, met with Nick Marino first. I figured it would be the easiest thing to do because I wouldn't have to explain the background too much. Nick wasn't too thrilled with my idea. Why would he want to admit to being an ineffective counselor, which was one of my reasons? Nick knew damn well I was strapped for cash, so he said he would meet a second time but at the "I don't want to do it" price of $400 per hour. Yeah, sure. He should have done it for free. Scratch him off the list. Why did I even bother? What a dumb idea.

I reached out to a dozen or so other attorneys, and, on March 7 I met with Mr. Phillip Jusino at his law firm of Phillip J. Jusino & Associates. Right off the bat he suited my personality much better than Nick. No tension. Naturally Mr. Jusino played devil's advocate, and grilled me for a while. That's par for the course though, I understood it had to be done. I liked how he went about it though. He never spoke down to me or showed any sort of superior or condescending attitude. And he didn't mind me asking him questions and me voicing my opinion. When our meeting ended he seemed very sincere when he said, "I hate injustice." It felt right so I retained him, gave him a ton of evidence, and we went to work immediately. Yes, we! I was allowed to participate in putting the argument together. Mr. Jusino kept me

213

in the loop. He realized the value of my knowledge and input. Thankfully he was going to be flexible with the billing because he was sensitive to my predicament. That was a huge reason why I was able to even attempt the monumental task.

I was certain the courts were going to claim that all bets were off because I took a plea and they had to preserve the finality of court proceedings. That would be bullshit. If that were the case, then there wouldn't be any type of regulation allowing this type of request in the first place. This wasn't your standard case where I simply decided to take the plea. I fought for a trial tooth and nail, and things could have been different if the district attorney didn't knowingly withhold evidence and my other attorney didn't do just about everything wrong, including telling me the wrong disposition. Not to mention, I was broke and had to come up with the money, and I just received fresh evidence to support my argument. It's not like I waited too long to file my request.

April 2012

On April 19, the Appellate Division, Third Department, sustained the misconduct decision. I think they may have mistakenly overlooked   public policy, witness testimony, and a plethora of other evidence that I put forth. In fact, unless I am mistaken, numerous prior decisions stated the courts always deferred to the commissioner of education's office regarding situations like mine. I'll say it again, like a broken record, that office fully cleared me! There was no reason given for the decision. I'm not sure there was a justifiable reason. With all due respect, I just wasn't sure that my papers were given fair consideration.

May 2012

On or about May 18, 2012, I had a conversation with Bart Zabin of the New York State Education Department. He was the man who, in a letter, stated there was a hold on my education license back in 2006. That's the hold that resulted from Joanne Loewenthal reporting me without my knowledge, and the hold that prevented me from working as an educator. That was also the office that refused to investigate Michelle Konik. When I asked him the tough questions, he ended the conversation.

July 2012
The Hampton Bays Depositions

My brothers and sister kindly gave me money so I could personally depose Superintendent Joanne Loewenthal and the board of education, George Leeman, Christopher Catz, Jennifer Boyer, Marie Mulcahy, and Craig Tufano. They were difficult to prepare for as a lay person. Questions had to be posed a certain way, and even when I did use the right form, I thought the opposing attorney, Kelly Spina, would object just to throw me off my game. Believe me that's all it was for everyone: a game of how to best hide the truth and keep it from being discovered. My friend Craig had been advising me throughout the civil proceedings and he prepped me on how to approach the depositions. I was as ready as an individual acting as his own attorney could be. When I was stumped during the depositions I excused myself and called Craig to ask his advice. Besides my own discoveries, I also had some inside sources who supplied me with information.

Tom Maloney, a community member in Hampton Bays, was very close with board members and the superintendent. He stayed in touch with me over the years, was sympathetic to my cause, and kept me current on important information. Once again my friend Dan Nolan was there for me. He continued to work in Hampton Bays after my sudden departure and had a lot of information that he submitted in a sworn affidavit. Another individual who helped prepare me was Steve Lerner, a leader for the Hampton Bays teachers union for many years—not my union who turned their backs on me. He battled with Joanne Loewenthal many times and took the time to offer areas of insight, and supply important and relevant documents for my case. He too gave me a sworn affidavit.

Diane Albano, Joanne's former secretary, knew the truth about what happened to me, and her friendship was amazing. When everyone in Hampton Bays, including my own secretary and friends, distanced themselves, Diane not only stayed close but actually grew closer to me. To think she was Joanne's secretary, her right hand, working just steps away from her. Unlike the other cowards, she had no fear of the superintendent's wrath and wanted to do what she knew was the right thing to do. She also gave me a sworn affidavit and even appeared as a witness on my behalf. The world needs more people like her. The woman is a saint.

I can't go over every question and answer, but the moral of the story is what I predicted. Before the board of education decides on anything they must be given *all* relevant information. Joanne Loewenthal's duty as superintendent was to supply the board with *all* relevant information. These duties are as per education regulations. But according to the sworn testimony, it was impossible for the board to make an informed decision regarding my separation or my reinstatement to employment. Joanne Loewenthal *did not* give them the information they were supposed to receive and wanted to receive. Board members even stated under oath that they would have voted on my employment differently *if* they knew the truth. Ms. Loewenthal had premeditated thoughts to do the wrong thing from the start, and my separation from employment was not legitimate. Here's just one example, of many;

Joanne Loewenthal testified that under education law, she was not allowed to accept a resignation letter from an employee with a moral character issue. Ms. Loewenthal was the one who filed a Moral Character complaint against me in 2006. In spite of that, she drafted a resignation letter and played it off as if I handed it to her! She also created letters for the community that said I resigned before I even spoke with her in June 2006! I had no intentions of willfully walking away and did not willfully walk away from employment.

I also discovered that while I was wrongfully separated from employment and living almost an hour from Hampton Bays, they decided to treat other employees much differently then they treated me. Other educators working for Hampton Bays were never wrongfully separated or reported to the state education department after being arrested or committing far more egregious acts of misconduct directly linked to students, employees, and school property.

1. A non-tenured teacher was caught on video using physical intimidation and verbal threats to abuse, humiliate, and make her minority students cry. The video was confiscated from the minority student. It was so disturbing that the teacher's union representative requested he *not* have to watch the entire footage. The teacher was awarded tenure and the district later stated that no such video existed.

2. A non-tenured teacher was arrested for DWI. She was awarded tenure.

3. A board of education member was arrested on charges that also received negative publicity. He pled guilty to felony charges in

2008. The state qualifications make school board members ineligible to serve if they are convicted of a felony. He maintained his position until he was sentenced in August 2008 because his case was still pending until the final sentencing. Why was I forced from Hampton Bays while my case was still pending?

4. A non-tenured teacher admitted in a sworn affidavit that she was driven home from a bar by a student when she was intoxicated. She swore that she knew it was wrong but did it anyway. According to Joanne Loewenthal's own words, that alone was reason to be fired. No action was taken, and the teacher received tenure. In fact, at a hearing in 2008, Judge Vespoli questioned Ms. Loewnthal's inaction. Her response was that she didn't know about it (I don't believe that). She didn't do anything after it was brought to her attention either.

5. Another teacher was arrested multiple times and never fired.

6. An administrator who was married with children was spoken to on multiple occasions because of his affair with a non-tenured teacher in the same building. She also was married with kids. Obviously a serious conflict of interest, abuse of authority, and violation of moral standards. No action was taken after they disregarded the warnings and continued the affair. That teacher, of course, received tenure.

7. A single non-tenured educator had a well-known affair with another educator in the same building who was married with a child. He received tenure and was promoted to the administrative level.

8. Another teacher allegedly chewed tobacco and cursed in front of students, left notes for them that asked for money as loans, and offered rides to them. That teacher remained employed.

9. A substitute teacher/coach was arrested on felony rape charges. He was afforded due process and simply relieved of duties "pending" the outcome of the investigation.

My goal was never to judge these aforementioned individuals or bring harm to them. That's one reason they remained nameless. If they received proper due process then God bless them. But what about me? Why was I treated so differently? The allegations surrounding me were not in any way connected to work. Education regulations apply to all educators in New

217

York. They were not allowed to treat me differently because of my status as a principal.

As one former student said, she was in shock and ashamed of Hampton Bays because of what they did to me. Another sent an e-mail stating;

> You were the best principal HB had. Myself and a group of friends think it was a shame you were forced to give up a job you worked so hard to earn. I hope Hampton Bays realizes that they lost a great principal and that more people should've spoken up.... There are worse scandals in Hampton Bays such as [name withheld] openly cheating on her husband yet nothing is done about that.

Those were just two of the tons I received. Of course Hampton Bays did not want anyone to learn of its practices. That's why video footage no longer exists, and that's why when I requested information regarding my interview process in 2009 they told me the interview files were stolen. Ha! Stolen! Yeah, I'm sure those files were a hot commodity. When I was their administrator, I always filed police reports when a piece of paper was misplaced. God forbid the stapler was missing—I would have called in the Navy SEAL's.

The fact of the matter, and bottom line is, to this day the only concrete reason I received for why my employment ended in Hampton Bays was because it was alleged that I violated an order of protection in 2006. That's also why the hold was placed on my license. That's what was put forth on official letterhead. The order of protection violation never happened, the hold was removed, and I was fully cleared by the state education department.

There was so much more that was discovered but the moral of the story is that Joanne Loewenthal kept important individuals from communicating with me and for years reassured me with false promises. In the end, she, and Hampton Bays played a major role in taking away my career and my livelihood. Why? I gave my life to that district, that town, and made her look as good as possible every day. Joanne knew the type of person I was and the type of family I came from. She had the documentation surrounding my arrest. She knew the truth.

Here's one other, new piece, of information I learned from the depositions. With regard to the misconduct hearing that was reopened at

218

the department of labor, every single person I deposed from Hampton Bays testified that they never stated I committed misconduct! Joanne Loewenthal even testified that it was up to the state education department to make that decision. That's what I said—and that department fully cleared me! Even more disturbing, Hampton Bays representatives testified that they were unaware a misconduct hearing even took place. Their attorney never once spoke to them regarding their own misconduct appeal? For over three years their attorney made representations that I committed misconduct, and accepted compensation to litigate a three-year appeal that their client didn't agree with or even have knowledge of! That's what happens when your client has a bottomless pit of money—also known as taxpayer money. Just keep billing the district and they will blindly pay without questioning.

That appeal should have never even taken place! There's no way the commissioner of labor had my paperwork sitting on his desk for over two years waiting for my criminal matter to end. There's no way he was aware that I plead guilty to two violations. I would bet my life that he received a phone call because someone else wanted to reopen the hearing. It seemed no matter which way I turned there was foul play.

The commissioner of labor, and Hampton Bays (without their knowledge), were allowed to reopen that hearing over two years after a decision was ruled in my favor. That was because it was claimed that there was newly acquired evidence. That new evidence was literally one piece of paper that was completely inconclusive. Subsequently I attempted on numerous occasions to have it reopened because of my newly acquired evidence which included piles of legal documents and numerous witnesses. I thought it was only fair that I get the same opportunity that they were afforded. But I was continually ignored and denied the same due process. Isn't the objective of a legal proceeding to get the decision right? Not when it's Frank Vetro's life. Nobody seemed to care about the truth. I wasn't done trying.

Michelle Konik-Brosdal Deposition

On July 19, 2012, I deposed Michelle. She was there with her 178-year-old husband, Gordon Brosdal. Okay, so he's a little younger than that—a little. When Michelle entered the room I thought she looked like she aged, I mean more than she had actually aged, of course.

Michelle was flanked by her attorney, Kelly Spina, of Miranda, Sambursky, Slone, Sklarin, Verveniotis, LLP. Coincidentally, the same law firm that was defending Hampton Bays was also defending Middle Country Central School District. She played dumb—tried to play dumb, at least—to a lot of things, by stating she didn't recall. A textbook response from a witness prepped by her attorney. If she thought that would let her off the hook, she was mistaken. I did recall, and I had her prior sworn statements and other documents. A funny moment was when I questioned her on the letters she sent to Jim. Her husband, who she claimed was her best friend, began to read them. When Michelle noticed what he was reading she shouted for him to stop. I of course encouraged him to continue, with antennas up. I thought the pattern was clear. Jim was her best friend, I was her best friend, and now he was her best friend. I suggested, "Things happen in threes, Mr. Brosdal". Unfortunately, he stopped reading at Michelle's command.

I caught Michelle in some lies, but she did admit to a couple of things worth mentioning. First, she admitted she was issued a disciplinary memo following the infamous 2001 investigation. Second, she admitted she was never questioned by Middle Country Central School District with regard to her conduct with Stephanie Veraldi. Yet Middle Country had the nerve to publicly say my claims were unfounded.

I couldn't wait to be done deposing her. I didn't ever want to see her again unless she was on a witness stand. I couldn't believe she actually admitted to receiving a disciplinary memo after the 2001 investigation. Very rarely would a court allow a plaintiff access to a teacher's personnel records. I had to try though and that was my next step. I thought that disciplinary memo would reveal a cover-up. I also had to focus on deposing Michelle's "friend", and now former student, Stephanie Veraldi.

August 2012

On August 30 the Appellate Division, Third Judicial Department denied my request to reargue or renew my appeal of the misconduct decision in spite of all my newly acquired evidence. I just didn't think it was fair. I didn't think they were giving me the time of day. On the decision were the names of pretty much the same judges. They referred me back to the unemployment appeal board. I wish they would have at least given me a reason, this way I could see if there was something I was missing.

October 2012

It took seven months because there was so much, but on October 19, my request to have my criminal matter reviewed was delivered to the Central Islip Courthouse. Most requests like this are based on one reason. My request had clear evidence of just about every reason that existed to make such a request. I had ineffective counsel, my plea was not made knowingly and voluntarily, the prosecution knowingly withheld evidence that was favorable to my defense, I was denied due process, and everything else discovered *after* the prosecution of my case.

On October 20 I sent a complaint against the NYS Department of Labor with a ton of supporting documents. It was sent to the US Department of Labor, Civil Rights Center.

December 2012

On December 19, the US Department of Labor, Civil Rights Center responded. They said I did not fit into any of the protected classes they covered. No matter who or where I complained, I always slipped through the cracks. I just wanted to be heard.

February 2013

The assistant district attorney opposing my newest argument was Edward Bannon. Like he really knew my case, sure he did. He opposed my motion, didn't even address three-quarters of the issues I presented, and even said I received the deal of the century. I'm not kidding. And that Judas, Nick Marino, actually gave him a letter to support his opposition! No matter— the letter didn't help or prove anything except my points, because nobody understood this case, including the guy who was supposed to defend me, Nick Marino. Either way though, why couldn't Nick just mind his own business? He knew of the difficult time I was having in life. It wasn't like I was going after him. Why couldn't he just butt out? Was it about his ego? Did he refuse to even consider that perhaps he may have made a mistake? What kind of defense attorney writes a letter against his client, to the opposing side? On February 8 our final papers were delivered to the Central Islip Court.

Stephanie Veraldi Deposition

On February 12, I deposed Stephanie Veraldi. Her uncle, Domenik Veraldi, was her attorney. He also appeared against me as an opposing attorney when I deposed Michelle. It was a dog fight to get Stephanie to the deposition because Mr. Veraldi submitted a motion to the court to quash the subpoena I sent her. I didn't understand, if someone questioned a teacher regarding inappropriate behavior with one of my nieces, I would not be objecting to any question that teacher was asked. Nor would I argue against my niece being questioned. I would want the truth, would be happy to let it happen, and just make sure my niece was treated fairly and respectfully while being questioned.

The Honorable Judge William B. Rebolini read his argument, and he actually read my opposition papers too. It showed in his detailed decision. It wasn't a simple one sentence denial that I was used to receiving as a decision. The result was what would happen if/when someone would give my papers the proper time. Judge Rebolini agreed with my points and ordered that Stephanie be deposed.

Regarding Stephanie's deposition, nothing new could be said. Simply put, Stephanie confirmed, under oath, her inappropriate relationship with Michelle. Michelle established the relationship and Stephanie did much of the legwork to have me arrested. Nobody could ever convince me otherwise. The documents, along with the pictures, and comments that were posted by Stephanie in the past only solidify her testimony. Stephanie also admitted that she was never questioned by Middle Country Central School District. Why did the school district state that my claims were unfounded at a board of education meeting? How could they? If there was nothing to hide, why ignore the witnesses and evidence?

There was even more to this Jerry Springer episode. I unexpectedly received an e-mail from a family member of Michelle and her husband/former principal. We actually exchanged a few e-mails and spoke on the phone a couple of times. We even met up in the parking lot of a Ford dealership in Port Jefferson Station. On February 18 I received a call from this person and what I was told was quite disturbing. The allegations were very serious. So disturbing that I did not think it would be right to include the details in this forum. I actually hoped what I was hearing wasn't true. I have the information, and the communications are very well documented. I will keep it all in my possession so it can be reviewed. I will say, if it were true, it may help explain a lot of what has occurred. Why would their family member reach out to me, a stranger, and relay such serious information?

On February 19, I received the decision on my latest criminal motion. Now, assuming the judge put his entire caseload aside when he received my papers, it took him all of about three business days to decide on my five-hundred-page motion of detailed facts, laws, and exhibits. It took my attorney, Mr. Jusino, a former prosecutor and defense attorney for over twenty years, months to learn those facts. This judge had zero prior knowledge. That explained the brief and, in my opinion, inaccurate half-page reason that he denied me. With all due respect, I don't believe the judge really considered our papers at all.

Total anarchy. The police could pick a man off the street and wrongfully arrest, defame, and destroy him. And the prosecutors could perform equal misconduct without their actions ever being questioned? Perhaps I should have used the twenty four hour rule before putting my thoughts into words. Perhaps I should have let my emotions settle first. I apologize, I didn't, and I hope everyone can excuse me and understand the emotion that's vested in this matter. I'm not trying to be disrespectful to the courts. Of course I decided to file an appeal.

Justice to the Highest Bidder

The criminal system is a disaster, and I was learning the civil system is as well. I am not referring to the personnel, I am referring to the systems. Something that shouldn't be so difficult is really, really confusing. The paperwork is immense, time-consuming, and needless. That's the legal monopoly that attorneys have. The system is designed to force us to rely on attorneys. It's all built into an end product packaged as justice.

Every joke has some truth to it, and those attorney jokes we've heard throughout the years have their share. I'm sure people will debate this segment with me, and maybe even take offense to it. It's hard to argue with a man caught up in the system, who took diligent notes every day for years. I corresponded with many attorneys on a regular basis for quite a while. I observed both criminal and civil attorneys as well as the systems they work in. I listened to them gather at the courthouse as if it were a fraternity. I heard their conversations and the way many of them spoke to clients. They were salesmen who needed to show their worth, whether warranted or not, in a twisted system.

I know it must be tough. Clients probably lie all the time and I'm sure attorneys have to pull teeth to get paid at times. They should remember, though, they made a choice in life. They chose to be attorneys, and many of them have made a good living doing that. Even with all the nonsense, they still should treat people as people, not inanimate objects. Attorneys should look in the mirror and ask themselves why they're in the profession. If it's to make money or for political aspirations, then God bless, I hope they make millions, but just think of the people who have retained you once in a while. I understand attorneys cannot become emotionally caught up in their clients' cases. When you start thinking and acting with only your heart, you become clouded to important aspects of a case and miss the big picture. That doesn't mean an attorney can't show some type of compassion. The day a person loses their sense of humanity is the day they should change professions.

Back in 2007 an attorney not in any way associated with my criminal case once commented about all the work my attorney was doing for me. Was he kidding? That attorney was talking to the wrong person. So many motions are standard boilerplate format adjusted to suit individual cases. I know that because while acting as my own attorney, I took forms that were given to me, added case law that I researched, and made changes to suit my particular needs. Showing up to court maybe once a month and having a few meetings was not my idea of doing a lot of work. For Christ's sake, I'm not dumb. The court appearances are scheduled conveniently so that an attorney can address multiple tasks the same day. If only they knew what I did as a school administrator. I guess I should've made at least $20 million per year. Maybe not everyone works as hard as I do, but doing hardly anything, including studying and knowing my case, is not my idea of work. He should've told the next client, because I wasn't buying it. Beginning with my parents, my background taught me what work really was.

I didn't need a story from an attorney to explain their importance, especially an attorney I didn't retain. I had friends who could make stuff up for a far cheaper price tag. The entire concept was ass-backwards. I mean, what do attorneys really do? They weren't actually at the scene. Therefore, opposing attorneys spew out secondhand information, at best. Both sides in a trial ask questions a certain way, avoid anything that doesn't help their cause, and spin a story to favor their client. You wind up with a version of the facts that best fits your cause and may the best storyteller win.

All the attorneys I attempted to retain declared I "needed" them to crack the case. Give me a break and save the legal jargon for someone else, guys. Using the internet and public law library I researched penal/civil codes, cited prior cases, and did other investigative stuff an attorney or PI might do. But because most people don't know protocol in court and don't know how to file motions, because most people didn't pass the bar or don't have time to decipher the ridiculously worded law (and I do mean ridiculously*), they are reliant on an attorney. No, I'm not naïve. I don't think a layman should represent him- or herself, at least not with the current systems in place. At the same time, if given the chance to speak, I could've easily proven my own innocence in my criminal case. I could do the same with my civil cases if it were as easy as just speaking with someone. Be honest, guys. I understand how the world works. I really do. You don't have con me.*

When you think about it, how many attorneys have you run into that don't charge hundreds of dollars per hour? It has become a necessary evil to retain very expensive counsel. Lawyers have in essence cornered the market with a legal monopoly. They know we need them, and they make us pay. Even as an educator I noticed the lawyers were running the show. I couldn't get anything done, not even a menial task, without checking with an attorney first for fear of a lawsuit. The court systems are flooded with nonsense.

Don't get me wrong. I know the majority of lawyers and court personnel are excellent people, but that's not my point here. The system is designed in a way so that attorneys can't care. That's why they don't and why they only have a vested interest until the money runs out. Those are cold, hard facts. It doesn't mean that attorneys are inherently heartless. It means the field is a business. It would be tough for an attorney to argue against my points since he or she would only know his or her point of view. I was in the courtroom, able to experience and witness many attorneys in action about once a mo from the other side of the law. It wasn't a room with a very good view.

I used to think the bureaucracy of the educational system was bad. The fact is, education runs like a Swiss watch in comparison to the criminal and civil systems. There are civil procedure laws and regulations that are supposed to be followed. They're never followed! That's why my cases were stalled for months, years. That's why cases go on forever—two, three, five, even ten years—without justification. And the little guy, me included, rots.

As a high school administrator I handled misconduct every day, including larceny, bullying, harassment, *assaults, drugs, weapons possession, automobile infractions, threats, etc. They would have been considered*

225

misdemeanors and sometimes even felonies if they were committed outside of school. I handled crimes way more serious then what I was accused of, and they never took years to settle. The most extreme incidents took maybe a day or two for me to resolve. I didn't ask for a student to file a complaint, wait a month to get the other student's side, wait another month to see if there were any other strategies, and on and on. I got the stories and all evidence as quickly as possible so they wouldn't taint over time, and I dealt with them right then and there. And here is a novel idea. Call me crazy, but I actually had a conversation with the accused party. How could I possibly punish a person without speaking to him or her directly? If that meant extra time during the day, then the case got extra time.

The longer these things are put off, the more the truth is tainted. A crime is a crime, whether it's in school or on the street. Cases don't need to take so long (civil or criminal) and shouldn't. Remember, though, the personnel in the system all have to make money. If cases settled too quickly, there would be a few unemployed people—like school principals, for example. During the many court motions and appearances, it became quite apparent that attorneys were not needed much of the time.

As an administrator I never turned off my cell phone. I arrived at work no later than 6:30 a.m. and stayed until the day dictated I was done. There was no official start or finish time. I was paid a yearly salary, so more time didn't mean more money. That didn't stop me, though, because I chose my job, and I knew that a thousand lives depended on my decisions every day. Many times I was needed at late hours, early in the morning, or on weekends. That was my job. The problem with my criminal case in the twisted system was that I could only access in the neighborhood of $100,000. Nick saw $30,000 of it. Therefore, he had to work on a slew of other cases. I don't blame him for that—he had to earn a living, and his law firm had to generate income. Thirty thousand dollars over a three-year period wasn't going to do it, so my case was not going to get the attention it deserved. In hindsight I would rather have just paid him and not wasted my money on another attorney who did absolutely nothing for me. Maybe he would've done more work sooner and the case would have unraveled faster. I wasn't looking for deals. I was looking for justice.

The scary thought is that if I didn't have the wherewithal and ability to access money to survive, I would've been convicted of crimes and served time in jail. The systems in place dole out justice to the highest bidder. They are driven by money, greed, and power instead of facts and efficiency. The *systems will never change unless we challenge those who are at its head. They will never change, because too many people are getting rich because of it.*

Am I scarred? Are my views tainted? Is my judgment based on an exception rather than the rule? Believe me when I tell you I often wondered all of these things. And believe me, I know there are mostly genuine, good people working in the system. Regardless, it's time to start looking at the system's efficiency. I don't have all the answers, but I have a few suggestions. A serious problem exists, and I truly hope this story sparks a movement to create change. When is tort reform going to finally occur?

March 2013

The New York State Unemployment Insurance Appeal Board told me they were going to take away my income tax returns every year until they recovered the $26,000 they claimed I owed them because of misconduct in Hampton Bays. I never committed misconduct, damn it, and I needed that money! I just couldn't figure out why I was not being given the same opportunity the commissioner of labor was afforded. I reached out to them again, and Janet Beaudoin, the supervisor for the appeal board, responded to me on March 4. I swear she didn't even address the issues. That was why I responded back to her on March 7 and respectfully illustrated her errant response. I did not hear back from her.

April 2013

Because I was persistent and knew I was right, since not one person had shown otherwise since February 2006, I sent another letter to Ms. Beaudoin on April 12. All I wanted was the same fair treatment that Hampton Bays and the commissioner of labor were given. Equal freaking treatment! Ms. Beaudoin didn't respond to my last letter either, and they did take my state and federal tax return money.

June 2013

Although three separate attorneys told me I would never be able to acquire Michelle Konik-Brosdal's personnel records from her school district, I did it. Their attorney was kicking and screaming in her argument to the court to not have them released. However, once again, Judge Rebolini read my argument and gave another quality, detailed decision, which cited my points and showed he put some thought into it. He thought I made good points, one of them being that Michelle had lied under oath at her deposition, and allowed me certain documents. That's twice he decided in my favor. Maybe he was a judge who was going to do the right thing? I thought it proved if my arguments were given fair time, a judge would agree with me. Honorable Judge Wall, and Honorable Judge Rebolini are proof of that.

I hate to be a broken record, but once again I was right, and Michelle's personnel records prove it. I won't go into the disturbing details, however, Michelle was issued a very harsh warning to never perform certain behavior again, or else. That didn't stop her though. Just a few months after that the school district had to deal with her again for other, let's just say, questionable behavior.

In my opinion she should have been the one not allowed to return to work, not Jim. Instead, just three years later, knowing Michelle was *extremely* inappropriate with students and staff, her school allowed her student Stephanie Veraldi to go to her home unsupervised! It was all hidden under the guise of community service. Working at your teacher's personal home for her personal business is not community service! Stephanie never filled out a permission slip or application, there was no documentation or log entries as to what Stephanie did or when she was there, and not once did a school supervisor ever visit the house. There was absolutely no oversight prior to, during, or after the "community service" concluded.

Not only did the school do nothing to Michelle in 2001, but they knowingly created an environment so that Michelle could once again form an inappropriate relationship with another student. And this came after the school district warned her of the consequences she could face if she did it again. Michelle, in my eyes, did worse things the second time around because she was given free rein to do as she pleased while alone in her home. These findings further proved that the issues regarding *potential* conduct unbecoming a teacher, endangering the welfare of a child, and other behavior have been brought to the attention of Middle Country Central School District and other officials numerous times from 2001 to the present day. Meetings were continually denied and cancelled, documentation was never reviewed, and witnesses were disregarded. As an administrator with knowledge and experience in disciplinary investigations, I could honestly say there's absolutely no excuse to justify such inaction. Educators have been fired for much less then what the evidence alleges.

Michelle Konik-Brosdal continued to flaunt her relationship with Stephanie. On her dog breeding website Doriann Bichons, she proudly displayed that Stephanie Veraldi was in her wedding party. How was it that this student and teacher, worlds apart in age, became so close that she was in her wedding party in 2007? Inexplicably, nobody wanted to ask the obvious questions. I'm not in any way trying to claim that she raped teenagers in showers. However, didn't we learn from the Penn State scandal that inappropriate behavior with a child at any level cannot be tolerated? Penn State University officials were fired and charged with perjury and failure to report the possible child abuse. They could have stopped the abuse dating back to 1998 but wrongfully decided not to perform a proper investigation. As a result of their inaction, there were more victims. (See page 249-250 which shows pictures displayed on the Doriann Bichons website)

Those who cover for the misconduct place the welfare of others in jeopardy. Just ask me and I can tell you firsthand! The evidence shows, with better than average certainty, that Middle Country Central School District, the Suffolk County Police Department and District Attorney's Office, and the New York State Education Department all turned a blind eye to strong evidence suggesting a teacher did inappropriate things with students. And because of those relationships, others suffered. No one is above the law. If Penn State and Joe Paterno could go down, then surely so could those entities.

What other lies were told? What other evidence was withheld? What else was conveniently forgotten? Were other students impacted? When would the lies stop? When would the cover-up end? Were they waiting for another tragic incident, a third man to be arrested and destroyed? Were they waiting for another student to be wrongfully manipulated before they addressed the root of the problem? The longer these things are avoided, the harder they are to prove. Evidence gets lost. Witnesses disappear. That was their goal. I was sure a lot was already lost.

It's one thing to not take action against her. This story is not about punishing her or anyone else. But what about Jim? What about me? Why did I have to suffer because of the actions of Michelle and others? How is that fair?

A Layman's Opinion

On April 22, 2006, Michelle's therapist called to warn me that Michelle's love was a dangerous love. She may well have been right about that. However, I wondered if she had any insight into Michelle's mind, if she knew what compelled Michelle to such hate, or if she knew anything about Michelle, period. I formed a personal opinion. It's a layman's diagnosis, but a layman with a very good foundation to form an opinion. And no professional could tell me different. I know what I lived through.

It was a cycle of highs and lows that Michelle went through. She quickly developed a hero worship in her relationships. She wanted to spend every moment of every day with the person she claimed to love. She was so nice on the surface but when her feelings were not reciprocated, her fear of being left alone made her act without caution. She turned against the individual with the same intensity of hate. She became a woman who needed to take action against what she considered mistreatment. Meanwhile it wasn't mistreatment, it was simply rejection that she could not cope with. It's no wonder she spent so much time with her dogs and student, both of which offered the unconditional love that she craved. Again this is just my opinion based on my own experience, but when it looks like it and smells like it, you call it what it is.

I was a great friend to Michelle, but because I didn't fall in love with her did not give her the right to shamelessly enlist the help of her vulnerable student to achieve her goal of destroying my life. As a school administrator I have experience in disciplinary proceedings. I could honestly say that her lies, masterful manipulation, and illegal activity does not meet the moral standards of a teacher. Who was harassing whom? How long was she using her body as a weapon and offering up easy sex while slowly working behind the scenes to take away my life?

I first made this statement years ago, and I felt even stronger about it after uncovering the truth: she needed help. I no longer thought this as a friend but as a human being who did not want another man or student to be mistreated.

The next thing on my agenda was to schedule the deposition of Wayne Heter, the arresting police officer himself. I had to find out, once and for all, what Nick Marino was supposed to find out. I had to find out if they had probable cause to arrest me.

July 2013

My latest appeal in the criminal matter was denied by the presiding justice of the Appellate Term of the Supreme Court of the State of New York for the Ninth and Tenth Judicial Districts. Wow, that was a mouthful. In fact, that was longer than the decision, because yet again absolutely no reason was given. I was denied even though the opposing party didn't bother to argue against me. They didn't even argue against me! Once again, with all due respect to the court, I felt that my papers, Mr. Jusino's papers, weren't given the time. I was told that the type of motion I was making was not the most popular to bring to court. I wasn't trying to win a popularity contest. I was trying to save my life. I would've bet my life that if the judge truly read my papers, he would have agreed with my points just like Magistrate Judge Wall and Supreme Court Judge Rebolinil showed they did on three occasions. Yep, I repeated my thoughts. That's because there were times I felt like I was the only one listening. There was no way I could let this case be over just like that. The New York State Court of Appeals was next on my radar.

I had a meeting at my attorney's office on July 31. We worked very hard on our motions and Mr. Jusino was very taken aback by how the case was being treated. He did not think it was fair at all and so he reached out to certain media representatives and politicians, including Governor Cuomo, Senator Kirsten Gillibrand, Senator Chuck Schumer, County Executive Steve Bellone, Assistant Attorney General Kimberly Kinirons, the Attorney General Eric T. Schneiderman, and even John B. King, the commissioner of education. That was the short list. There were many more.

My brother Sal continued to do what he had done from the start and also mailed letters, and made phone calls. My sister Maria followed suit. She had enough of what Long Island was doing to her younger brother. My younger brother Rocco, who followed in my footsteps to become a teacher/administrator, reached out to the same offices from the perspective of an educator. All three of them made different points regarding the huge mess that was created. It didn't matter. Between my attorney's, mine, and my siblings letters and phone calls, most of the recipients didn't even bother to respond, and those who did steered us back to New York Attorney General Eric T. Schneiderman. His office never responded either.

August 2013

On Thursday, August 8, at about 3:30 p.m., the now superintendent of Hampton Bays, Lars Clemenson, invited me to interview for a position. Honestly, I didn't want to, because I knew he wouldn't hire me and that it would be the same humiliating experience as when I interviewed in 2009. The position was for assistant principal in the building that I don't mind saying, I helped bring back from the dead from 2003-2006. There was simply no way they could find a more qualified candidate for the entry-level administrative position. I had already performed the job at an extremely high level—except I did it before they separated the building into a middle school and a high school. The job was much easier now.

I did appear for the interview. I figured since there was a new superintendent, maybe somebody had a heart. I even called their new attorney and asked if there was an opportunity for settlement discussions in the civil case. In spite of all the maliciousness that I truly believed took my life away, I was willing to take the lower-level position   so I could take the next step in completely getting my life back.

I interviewed in front of Lars Clemenson and some other guy I never met, Mr. Pagano. I have the résumés of both of those gentlemen, and I don't mind saying I've done so much more in education than both of them. I should have been interviewing them. Actually, I did screen Lars to be my assistant in 2006, and now he was the superintendent. I realize those words may make me sound arrogant and I'm sorry, but there was nobody more qualified for the job than I was. Trust that I was humble as ever and left any trace of arrogance out of the interview. As I figured, the questions they asked me were basic, entry level questions. Actually a couple of questions they asked could only be answered by a person who already performed that job and had experience. I wondered if they asked that question to the other candidates, and how the others could have possibly answered, if they did at all. Either way, not to knock the credentials of the other candidates, I am sure they all had fine qualifications. However I had the experience, the proven track record, and I was the best man for that job.

Their attorney never did get back to me and once again I didn't make it past the first round of interviews. It was just impossible. I thought about it—why would the school district's attorney want to settle the case when he could lose but then appeal and continue to bill his publicly funded client for years and years?

> *When I interned to be an administrator in Middle Country Central School District, I worked under the supervision of the Assistant Superintendent for Pupil Personnel, Nan O'Connor Roys. My first day meeting her, I showed up to her office early and overheard her giving some pretty bad news to an employee. When that employee left, Ms. O'Connor Roys came out of her office and introduced herself, and we started to chat. At some point, I asked, "How did you do that? How were you able to give such bad news to a person? I felt so bad, and I wasn't even the one breaking the news." She told me that it wasn't easy for her and that in all her years as an administrator things like that had never gotten any easier to do. She said, "Frank, the day that gets easy for you is the day you should stop being an administrator. Never lose your sense of humanity."*

Maybe I shouldn't have but I did lose respect for Lars. He did not have to call me in for the interview. I was minding my own business prior to his phone call to me. Why do that to a human being? Why humiliate me like that—for nothing? Why do that to a man? It's not like they wanted to learn more about my background and accomplishments. They were well aware of both and didn't have to waste my time. Regardless of what they claim, they knew damn straight I could do that job better than anyone. I honestly didn't expect anything so I wasn't disappointed, but I had a family that was hopeful, and what was done was wrong.

I already had my say about the media in general, but since February 2012 I had been in touch with an editor for a small newspaper that reported on my arrest in 2006. We communicated numerous times on the phone, and via e-mail. We even met at his office, and again at the Middle Country Public Library. He also spoke for about an hour with my attorney, Mr. Jusino. He seemed like a nice enough man. In fact I'm certain he is. I think he was sincere when he told me that he thought I got screwed. However, despite the fact that I gave him so much evidence, he was still reluctant to write a story based on those facts. I didn't understand why he or his paper wouldn't want to set the record straight. I would bet my life that in 2006 neither the police nor the district attorney's office personally met with anybody from the media or gave them any evidence. They just made a phone call, and that was all it took for everyone to publicly destroy me. Why waste my time if there was no intention of actually writing a follow-up?

You should never forget, as a school administrator, member of the media, police officer, attorney, judge, or anyone else for that matter, there are human beings involved. I want everyone reminded that there is a person here—a human being behind the résumé, behind the evil allegations, behind those juicy headlines, and behind the court papers. A human being that was brushed aside and left to rot. The events dating back to February 2006 did not just affect me. I am someone's son, a brother, a cousin, a nephew, an uncle of young children, and a friend. Every day numerous people have been distraught, up at night crying, and praying for my life. Don't ever lose your sense of humanity. What if it were your loved one?

On Tuesday, August 20, 2013, Mr. Jusino shipped off our latest application to the New York State Court of Appeals. It's an awesome document that he, along with his dad and myself, spent many hours and days putting together. It is quite inflammatory. If I had Mr. Jusino from the start I wouldn't be in this mess.

October 2013

My goodness, I turned forty-two this month. On October 7 the honorable judge of the New York State Court of Appeals dismissed our application, because what I was appealing "is not appealable under CPL 450.90 (1)." The decision was made without an opposition being filed. I was as confused as ever, and that says a lot. You mean to tell me that a judge from the appellate term could make a decision without giving any reason for that decision, and even though it may be completely wrong, there are no checks and balances? He could do whatever he wanted? That didn't even make sense.

This is the United States. I swear I never had intentions to disrespect anybody, including the judges, and I don't have those intentions now. Everyone, in every aspect of life, including judges, should have someone who could check his or her actions. Everyone should welcome any such check, including judges at any level.

In his application, Mr. Jusino emphatically referenced endangering the welfare of students, ID theft, all the police and prosecutorial misconduct, due process violations, and *elements* of the Duke Lacrosse and Penn State Scandals. He included a ton of evidence and great case law in support. We were not asking the judge to make a decision based on the criminal procedure law. We were asking the judge to use an existing alternative method by which the court could use its² discretion based on extenuating circumstances and in the interest of justice.

Honestly, I thought the judge misunderstood what our application was requesting and I found it hard to believe that she didn't care about the allegations we made. Maybe we should have done a better job of isolating the key issues? I didn't know but as harsh as I am on others I am just as harsh on myself and I never have a problem self-reflecting. That's why an application to reconsider was already in the works and would soon be mailed out. I thought she would see our points if we perhaps pointed them out a little clearer.

Given the serious issues involved what would it hurt to have the details of my case reviewed, from soup to nuts? All the witnesses were still local, and all of the evidence was intact. So what was the big deal? I couldn't figure out why someone wouldn't want this case reviewed given all that was uncovered.

After-all, there were other cases on Long Island that were reopened for investigation, some that happened well over a decade ago. If Kathleen Rice, the Nassau County Long Island District Attorney, had the sense of fairness to reopen and investigate such cases, then why couldn't the Suffolk County Long Island District Attorney, Thomas Spota do the same?

November 2013

On November 4 I received correspondence from Jayson S. Meyers, the Chief Administrative Law Judge for the New York State Unemployment Insurance Appeal Board. It was basically yet another denial of my request to reopen the Hampton Bays misconduct hearing based on my new findings.

It was also filled with the same nonsense as all the prior communications, none of which made sense. I immediately responded to him, to set the record straight. I didn't expect a response. At least not a response that would make sense or have any semblance to justice.

Detective Wayne Heter Deposition

Yep, he became a detective, and on November 19, 2013 I reacquainted myself with him. This was my ninth deposition already and I had a pretty good grasp on what I wanted to ask. Although I learned quite a few things, I limited my summary of this deposition to the issue of probable cause. For years, I was on a quest to find out the reason I was arrested, charged with crimes, cuffed in front of throngs of people, and plastered all over the media.

My understanding had always been that probable cause *must* exist for a police officer to make an arrest. From what I learned, probable cause is sufficient reason, based upon "known facts", to believe a crime was committed. The key words are "known facts". The police have to have something, anything, at least one "known fact" to act on. They can't just pick random people off the streets and arrest them. This is the United States of America.

Police officers have to make split second judgment calls so it's expected that a mistake may be made, *in some cases*. And probable cause can exist even if there's some doubt as to the person's guilt. However, although the police lied on the paperwork, my case did not involve a "crime in progress". Therefore a split second judgment call was not made. The police had plenty of time, many months of investigating, under their belts. To be sure, a "thorough investigation" was claimed to have been done. One could only conclude that the police uncovered "known facts", at least one, prior to arresting me. Right?

Once again, there were four complaints, four "victims", and a fifth statement filed against me, dating back to December 10, 2005. That's two months prior to my actual arrest. Not to mention dozens of other leads for the officers to pounce on, to add to the victim list. If I was such a predator, such a terrorist, why would the police let me continue to commit the crimes, let me continue my employment as a school principal, and let me continue to be around students? Especially since they claimed, albeit wrongfully, that one of the alleged victims was a former student? I pondered those thoughts for many years, and stayed up late at night asking myself those questions. In September 2011 I concluded that the police could not have had any evidence to verify the truth of those complaints.

As I had been throughout the course of my saga, my thoughts were correct. I asked Heter why I wasn't arrested prior to February 8, 2006. According to his sworn testimony, throughout his month's long, thorough investigation in 2005-2006, he never verified if I made the alleged calls, if those complainant's were telling the truth, or if they even wanted me arrested. He had nothing to act on, no "known facts". That's why he didn't arrest me at that point. Then what caused the arrest? What was the spark that caused me close to eight full years, and counting, of personal and financial hardship?

Detective Heter swore under oath that the decision to arrest me was based solely on Michelle Konik's February 7, 2006 claim that I threatened her over the phone on February 5, 2006. That was it, bottom line. That was why I was arrested on February 8, 2006. So, prior to arresting me, based on that single complaint, did Heter have probable cause? How did Heter verify that a call was made to Michelle Konik on the day she claimed? How did he verify that I was the one who made the alleged call? How did he verify the content of the threatening conversation that she described to him? How did he verify that it was a phone call at all? The bottom line, did Heter have sufficient reason, based upon "known facts", to believe I committed a crime? Here are the "known facts";

1. The recording Michelle gave the police was completely altered/doctored. The conversation I had with Michelle on February 5, 2006 was twenty seven minutes long, not ten, as Michelle claimed.
2. The conversation on the recording was not even the same as what Heter himself described, in his own handwriting, as the February 5, 2006 conversation.
3. Heter did not have my phone records from February 5, 2006. Even if he had Michelle's records, my number still would not have appeared on those, because it was blocked.
4. There wasn't one reference to the time, day, or year on that recording. It could have taken place in 2001 for all he knew. In fact, there's no indication that it's even a phone call. It could have been an in person conversation, or many different conversations spliced together.

5. Heter testified that he never even verified it was my voice on the recording prior to handcuffing me. The one and only way he concluded I threatened Michelle over the phone that day was because she told him I did when she handed over the recording.

6. Michelle's complaint came; after she gave Heter a sworn statement a month and a half prior which he already could not verify, and after she confessed to stealing my identity, accessing my personal information and cell phone without my knowledge, and contacting a woman I went on dates with. Heter had absolutely no reason to believe she was telling the truth. In fact, he should have arrested her!

Based on those "known facts", there could only be one conclusion. Heter never verified a damn thing! He didn't have any "known facts", not even one, to show probable cause. If Michelle said it was the Pope on that recording would he have been arrested instead of me? After I was already arrested, and in the precinct, the police took two more complaints from Stephanie Veraldi's parents. They too were never verified. Of course the authorities claimed to have all sorts of complaints, victims, and evidence in 2006 when they scorched me to the media. But what did they really have? Absolutely nothing! Nothing but smoke and mirrors. They arrested a man, with no proof against him, without ever letting him have his say.

That is not how I thought the United States of America operated. It's definitely not how the United States of America should operate. Unfortunately the only thing this deposition may ultimately have brought is more frustration because nobody was listening to me. I just wanted to be heard. Everyone wants to be heard. It's human nature. Never once in eight years was I able to tell my side of the story to a police officer, a district attorney, or a judge before my livelihood, my freedom, was taken from me.

Based on Heter's testimony, I decided if my recent application was denied by the Court of Appeals, I would somehow try again, maybe there was some other avenue. Courts are supposed to review the actions of police, and balance the interests of law enforcement against the interests of a civilian's personal liberty. I recently wrote a letter to the US attorney general but did not receive a response. Were these heads of office receiving these letters, or were the letters not making it past the mailroom? Was there anyone else to reach out to? Could anyone else put pressure on New York authorities to do the right thing? Congress? The Senate? The House of Representatives? Perhaps the President of the United States?

The mental pictures and diligent notes that I took since 2006 seemed to morph into a distress signal, a message in a bottle. I did it. I solved the case. Somebody, anybody—listen to me. I do not accept the fact that certain educators, police officers, and prosecutors have done the wrong thing for years yet I was the one who took the fall. It's one thing to turn a blind eye to their actions but why did I have to be their patsy? Why couldn't they just leave me alone?

I was minding my own business on February 8, 2006. I just wanted to take my mom to dinner on her birthday.

Epilogue

Some people advised me not to publish a book because I would label myself. Label myself as what? A guy who fought for his rights? Sometimes the powers that be do not want the truth to be heard. Those powers can't always get away with oppressing others. Our country was founded on the principles of fighting for what we believe in. I stand on principle, and as you've just read, that's not always an easy thing to do. This time those individuals, those bullies in the courtyard, picked a fight with the kid who was willing to stand and get his licks in win or lose.

Others sternly advised me not to mention names. Why not? I don't recall any negative words about any individual, save the small few who contributed to my misfortune. Even then, I simply summarized what happened, what was said to me, and what was said on documents given to me. My respect for education, police, prosecutors, and the legal system in general, has never wavered. There's a small percentage of every profession that makes the rest look bad. As luck would have it, I believe I stumbled upon that defective sample population.

I tried so hard not to write this story, not to publish this book. It was the last thing I wanted to do. For almost eight years I made phone calls, and wrote letters. I literally begged to be heard, to end it all quietly and respectfully. In spite of the public humiliation they brought me, I did not want to publicize the issues. I simply wanted the issues to be addressed. They decided to ignore me. Instead they wanted to finish me off and I don't understand why.

I do know that their actions were not a simple mistake. The chief complainants didn't just go down to the police station and file a report. They methodically and criminally schemed and planned my demise for months, maybe years. The officers involved didn't just slap the handcuffs on the wrong guy after a split-second decision. They thought about it for months and planned exactly how the malicious arrest would be carried

241

out. There was a witch hunt for months after—knocking on doors, making phone calls, and trying to drag witnesses out against me. Hampton Bays Schools didn't just make a split decision to end my career. It was a premeditated, drawn-out process. The prosecutors didn't automatically look at the statements and evidence, and admit that something was awry. They waited years and withheld evidence to force a plea. They tried for years to dig up evidence against me, and they failed. Here's what they did find:

If you look closely enough at the Zapruda film, you can actually see me in the grassy knoll holding something shiny and emitting smoke as I run away. Just on the other side of my shed was a previously unidentified body. Crime lab testing has shown that it's the remains of Jimmy Hoffa. Pin that one on me too. Here's a ticker for you 1980s fans. I shot J. R. Ewing! Of course, I can't confirm these things, but in today's society you don't have to confirm a damn thing before it gets plastered in the news. Sorry, I guess I got carried away. And while I'm apologizing, I will also apologize for anything else that I wrote which may have been offensive. Please understand that, for the most part, those words were raw emotions placed on paper as the frustrating events occurred.

Either way, if anyone in this story is offended, I'm not the guy to be angry with. The statements I made were based in large part on information given to me, on documents created by and/or handed over by the very subjects in this story. Maybe it's time for those people to self-reflect. A human life is much too short to be taking years away, and that's what they did to me. They had years to say or do something, so it couldn't have bothered them too much. They never seemed to care. This story was not written with intent of revenge. I never cared that much about their lives to want revenge, and I'm not that type of person anyway. This story is their doing, and it's more of a reckoning if it's anything at all.

Lord knows I no longer care what lies are said about me. I have nothing left to lose and I expect many more; that's for sure. I do hope I've exposed the necessary elements and those individuals have lost their credibility. If you could believe it, there's even more damaging information that I discovered but did not include. If anyone decides to lash back at me, to go the childish, mud-slinging route, I hope they have the guts to man up, and put their name to it. If so they should be ready to have their quiet lives made very public. Take it from me—it is not a very comfortable feeling. To say it disturbs and interrupts a life is an understatement. As I approached this struggle, I will take the same stand against them, day and night, at all hours. They will be taking on a battle that will impact years of their own lives. By the way, they will be taking on a melee they will lose. You can't win that type of fight. Believe me when I tell you first hand, *there are no winners* in that type of fight. Either way, I will gladly and respectfully discuss the issues, the relevant issues, preferably in a public forum, with anyone, any time, any place.

I received so many nice correspondences over these past eight years. I also received some very negative, low-level, ignorant cheap shots from individuals who didn't know me, and knew nothing except what they read and heard in the media and/or on the internet. Quite a few tried to deter me from writing a book and quite a few told me to give it up and admit guilt. Two examples include; an e-mail that said I was trash, I should be ashamed of myself, and that my time in jail should give me additional adventures in journalism. Another e-mail stated:

> As a 1985 grad of HB [Hampton Bays] and a student of psychology I find it ridiculous that you would write a book. It's about as narcissistic a thing I have seen in a while. First, to believe that it will sell, or there is any demand whatsoever outside of a few people close to the situation. Second, that you would choose this approach rather than just admitting that you have a problem and getting the help you need. I get it. You have to save your reputation right? Man up, admit it, and move on. Spare your family the embarrassment of further ridicule.

The two words I have for those people are; ignorance and indifference. And it's nothing new. The greatest injustices in history were because individuals, communities, cities, and even nations were ignorant and turned a blind eye. Nobody seems to care until it happens to them. Until people speak out as a collective unit, the injustices go on.

I apologize if anything here seemed narcissistic. I surely have my faults and, morally speaking, I certainly have done some very questionable things that I regret. However, those actions had no context here. Those actions did not make me the felon of the century in February 2006.

The world is filled with such immensely negative individuals, and they love to offer advice on what you should and shouldn't do. There's a running joke amongst those who are closest to me: "If you don't want Frankie to do something, don't tell him he can't do it." I want everyone who sent negativity my way to know, your correspondences, and advice, pushed me harder in my fight. Thank you, I sincerely forgive you, and if you ever need my help with something I promise to be there for you as best I can.

This story does not have a perfect ending, but not all stories do. Sometimes the bad guys get away. It honestly was never about the bad guys being punished, it was about an injustice and preventing others from suffering what I had to endure. I still have unanswered questions, but how many people have their identity stolen and find out the truth behind all that was said and done? Not many, if any. I still have pending civil cases, and I hope those judges will be fair with me. However, winning monetary sums in civil judgments, if I do, is not the point. If they cut me a check for one billion dollars, I still lost. Rest assured I will keep fighting for what I believe is right until there's nothing left inside of me.

Life isn't fair, especially when an individual is plastered in the headlines for the sake of selling a one-dollar newspaper. Individuals in those situations don't completely recover; lives are irreparably damaged. After the stories and the juice are over, those human beings somehow have to go through this thing we call life. Believe me, it's not easy, and *that is the point.* Perhaps my lasting victory is that this story will prevent others from suffering such a catastrophic event. Perhaps that is my greatest lesson as an educator.

If I could offer any parting advice, I would say please do not make rash judgments after reading or hearing about something. Sometimes that ruins lives. We live in a crazy era where it's increasingly thought that high-profile individuals should be judged with a higher standard because they are role models for the general public. As much as I try to understand that, for the life of me, I just can't. How could our role models be individuals we only know by way of media? People we actually know should be role models, not actors, politicians, or athletes who are strangers to us, or school administrators for that matter. They are humans with personal faults like all of us. Respect them for their professional achievements, not because you think they should be perfect people. We should all live by the same standard: the human standard. No individual, including the president of the United States, should be judged at a higher level than me, because they are not better than me. I hope everyone thinks as highly of him- or herself. Hold people accountable to the positions they occupy, don't take their life away.

Live your life as a microcosm of all the good things this world should be. We can't change the world. Evil existed long before we got here, and it will exist long after we leave. However, we can do our share of good to balance it out. That's all we can do. The first step is your own life. Don't wait for everyone else, because then it will never happen. We can all do something, one good thing for someone, every day.

I've achieved quite a few goals in my life, but I believe what I've endured here is by far my greatest accomplishment. Even during the coldest nights in my car, I took my licks, and I stood tall. My adversaries wanted me to do bad things. They wanted to justify their actions. They tried to completely wipe me out. They failed. Instead, I recreated my life as best I could to educate and help those who need it most. I've also furthered my own education with hopes of helping others even more. I would like to share my thoughts with the right people so that can happen. It's what I do. It's that pact I made with myself long ago.

I'm not quite sure where life will take me from here. I have a long way to go to fully recover, financially speaking, I may never recover. From a personal standpoint I have recovered, and then some. I lost track of my personal life while working day and night, seven days a week in Hampton Bays. If I had a better balance back then, this tragedy *may* have been prevented. I failed myself while helping others. I found a balance. A balance that has allowed me the ability to help others even more. A balance that will allow me to have a successful relationship, a lasting relationship, with a significant other, whenever that opportunity presents itself.

It's late in the afternoon on November 28, 2013, Thanksgiving Day. I'll soon be at my sister's, enjoying good food with the company of my family. If you could believe it there are things I am thankful for. I'm smiling and making a difference in the lives of human beings. It's nice to be appreciated. I will try to build on that. You've read enough about me to know that I am far from done. I have plans.

I recall a conversation I had with my former boss Nicholas Dyno. Our discussion left us pondering—was there something else besides being school administrators, something more we could do to make a difference in people's lives? I thought if I could somehow fight through the malicious allegations in 2006 I could get a positive message to people. I was determined to somehow turn the disastrous maelstrom of events in my life into a positive. I hope there was at least a little piece that you were able to take from my story and apply to your life for its betterment.

One final thought: it's been said that history is written by the winners. I lost a lot in this saga, so I can't claim to have won. However, I'm proud to say that I wrote this story and this is my history. Sleep well knowing that if you do right by people and truly care, then there will be someone, somewhere who will care and want to do right by you. If you can't find anyone, please look me up. I could always use a friend. Thank you for taking the time to be a part of my life.

Still standing eight years later. © *Photography by Gina Esposito*

The half picture that was turned over by the prosecution

247

The full unaltered picture of me and Michelle at Disney ©Photography by Gina Esposito

*Left to right: Top middle is Michelle Konik-Brosdal,
followed by her husband Gordon Brosdal, and Maid of
Honor Stephanie holding one of the dogs*

Left to right: Stephanie, Michelle's mom, Michelle Konik-Brosdal, and her husband Gordon Brosdal

Since November 2013

Frank J. Vetro v. Middle Country Central School District

Winter 2014: In spite of the claims in this book and ongoing litigation, against them, a Middle Country board of education member has been contacting me. He even asked me if I ever took part in group sex and intimated that I join him and his friend in such acts. The inappropriateness is off the charts. It trickles down from board of education to their teachers. Their shame has no bounds.

August 2014: Gordon Brosdal became Superintendent of Mount Sinai School District. As a first year teacher in the mid-nineties, a veteran explained to me, "The shit rises to the top". Now I get it.

October 8, 2014: This case was dismissed. Over five years and I never once saw the judge. Actually the judge who dismissed the case was not even the judge who presided over the case. I'll file a motion to reargue in the same court and a notice of appeal in the Appellate Division.

December 18, 2014: Motion to reargue was denied in less than a week. Appellate Division here I come.

February 2015: I was told Middle Country isn't happy because their public library stocked copies of this book. I hope the library doesn't cave to any pressure to have it removed.

June 26, 2015: I filed my appeal in the Appellate Division. Just to be clear. It's important to note, although the case was dismissed by the lower court, claims made in this book have never been denied or argued against, nor have they been ruled otherwise by the court.

Frank J. Vetro v. Hampton Bays Union Free School District

July 14, 2014: In spite of all the evidence, and witness testimony including the admissions of the board of education (p. 176-177, 201, 215-219), the case was dismissed. With all due respect, this judge made a huge error here. To conclude that there isn't one relevant fact, not one, that was misapprehended, defies logic. I detailed tons in my motion. Hampton Bays admitted to my claims. They admitted to them! Not to mention my motion wasn't even opposed by their attorney. I'll file a motion to reargue in the same court and a notice of appeal in the Appellate Division.

November 2014: Motion to reargue was fully submitted.

July 2015: My re-argument motion was denied with one sentence, "Plaintiff failed to demonstrate that the court overlooked or misapprehended the relevant facts or misapplied any controlling principle of law". That sentence is simply what the motion is, it's basically the statute. That's it. No facts or justification. That's because nobody can justify denying me. Over six years and I never once saw the judge. I apologize. I mean no disrespect but this is my life and I deserve better than a one sentence decision which merely regurgitates the statute. Next stop, Appellate Division.

August 2015: I filed my appeal in the Appellate Division.

Frank J. Vetro v. Suffolk County

April 2014: I've been waiting five months for Detective Wayne Heter to turn over evidence that he said was in his possession when I deposed him (p. 236-238). He'll never turn it over. It's too damaging.

May 2014: The NYS Attorney General held a conference on corruption. His assistant, who recognized my name and face before I could say hello, promised to review documents I sent to the office.

July 10, 2014: I was told there's nothing the Attorney General can do for me at this time. Apparently no other office can do anything either. Where's the checks and balances? I can't explain how disappointed I am. I hope they have a change of heart once they learn about the evidence that I know Heter possesses.

May 2015: I'm right again. Heter admitted the evidence he was in possession of was recently destroyed! My lawsuit against Suffolk County claims among other things; the authorities used Michelle Konik-Brosdal to illegally obtain evidence, used doctored evidence, did not use official identification procedures, violated my Miranda rights, falsified arrest records, had no probable cause to arrest me, and withheld evidence which would have proved my innocence and lead to the arrest of Michelle Konik-Brosdal.

Suffolk County is aware of these claims. The court is aware of these claims. Heter admitted to being in possession of the evidence. They all knew I asked for it. They all knew they had to turn it over. Yet after a year and a half of delaying, the evidence was destroyed! That has got to be spoliation of evidence, and the most egregious and contumacious act yet. If they're willing to risk the consequences of destroying evidence, surely the consequences would have been much more severe had they turned it over. Why else would they openly destroy relevant evidence right in the face of the court? Even more, how much misconduct was done when the court wasn't watching?

That evidence was precise proof of my claims against the authorities. Not only was it the final link to my set up, but the evidence was also damaging to their professional career, and perhaps personal life as it showed a personal relationship with Michelle Konik-Brodal, and how/why they destroyed my life to protect her, cover for her crimes, and save her career as well as their own.

These claims were submitted to the court and Suffolk County never argued against or denied them. They didn't even deny them! That's how obvious this scandal is. When am I going to get justice? Will I ever get justice? I hope the court does not stand for this type of disrespect for the process, for the law, and for the court. These people really think they are above the law.

From day one, February 8, 2006, I sincerely never wished harm on anyone. I just wanted my life back with the least amount of people, hopefully no one, negatively impacted. However, this latest event is just too much, too over the top. Someone needs to face consequences. I just can't wrap my head around why they would do this to my life.

June 22-26, 2015: I already deposed Michelle Konik-Brosdal (p. 219-220), and Stephanie Veraldi (p. 222-223). The judge in this case allowed me to depose the five others who filed complaints in 2006. Nancy Maletta (Stephanie's mom) and Michelle Rogak (married name Michelle Coyne) were served the subpoena but didn't bother to appear. My niece Sophia recalled that I properly obeyed a legal subpoena in 2008 and was wrongfully retaliated against (p. 156-157, 168, 176-177). These women ignored a judge's ordered subpoena and suffer no consequences. Anything wrong with this picture?

Allison Engstrom, Christina Impastato, and Stephanie's dad Rocco Veraldi did appear. They testified mostly as I expected. In summary: If they weren't lied to, if they knew all the nonsense and illegal activity regarding Michelle Konik-Brosdal, if they knew her history, and knew the extent of her inappropriate relationship with Stephanie Veraldi, they wouldn't have been so quick to file complaints. One individual completely changed their story, as in, testified to the exact opposite of their filed complaint in 2006.

The People v. Frank J. Vetro (The Criminal Matter)

September 2014: Phil Jusino and I submitted another motion to vacate my plea and bring back the criminal matter. It's based on even more evidence, officially acquired in January/February 2014.

December 2014: Our motion was denied. No reason given, just some boiler plate rhetoric that it lacks merit. I would love for someone, anyone, to prove how the points made in this book lack merit.

January 2015: We submitted a motion to re-argue as well as a notice of appeal in the appellate term.

February 2015: New judge, same result. Our motion was denied using the boiler plate, "without merit".

You have got to be kidding me. Without merit! The district attorney's arguments against us don't even make sense. They didn't even argue against most of our points! Why is it that I never, I mean never, get a legitimate explanation as to why I'm being denied, in any of my cases?

Indomitable

From the backseat of my car in 2010, I visualized a plan to get my life back, and more importantly, help others. It began with authoring a book. When word got out about Vetro, the author, I received some negative comments. So I did what many people who know me expected. I decided to also edit, design, self-publish, and market the damn thing. Four months later I was off and running.

March-April 2014: Before the book even hit the streets certain educators offered unfavorable reviews to deter others from reading it. Those educators didn't even read the book. They couldn't have. I don't even have a finished copy yet. I guess nobody explained to these "educated" people that sometimes terrible reviews make people even more curious.

August 21, 2014: I should've hired those genius educators as marketing agents. Book sales are just fine and I'm receiving many requests for interviews. I held a book signing at the Book Revue, in Huntington Long Island. It was a huge crowd of family, friends, and new found acquaintances. I was asked a great question by an audience member, "How do we know you tell the truth in your book"? I answered as I always do, with my public challenge. Let's have all seven complainants, all four arresting police officers, all three prosecutors (and whoever was/is behind the scenes), and every single defendant and defense attorney in the Hampton Bays, Middle Country, AT&T Wireless, and Suffolk County cases on stage for a public debate.

That's over forty chairs. On the other side will be just one lone chair. My chair. That challenge will never be accepted.

October 2014: The Dr. Phil Show wants me as a guest. However, only if Michelle and Stephanie appear. Never in a million years. There's just no way they will confront me, period, never mind in a public forum.

November 2014: I was asked to be a board member for a not for profit organization in New Jersey and Manhattan. Their mission is to promote racial harmony and acceptance, build ethnic pride, and assist youths in the growth of positive values. It's hours from my home but I agreed to do what I could. After all, that was the point of my struggle, to ultimately help others. Meanwhile my book has garnered national attention. From New York to California, Texas to Canada, and many states in between. Oh how I love the negative comments from the doubters. Can someone tell me what else I can't do?

January 2015: I received a call from David Levenstein, a producer at 103.9 FM LI News Radio. He read my book and asked if I wanted my own radio show titled… "Standing on Principal". His only request is that I have an attorney as a co-host to add credibility with legal discussions. I already have the perfect person. My friend Phil Jusino. A man with views similar to mine yet different enough to create an excellent dynamic. A man I trust and respect. A man who, dare I say, is now my partner in crime. If done right this show will springboard me to the next phase of what I visualized years ago.

February 11, 2015: "Standing on Principal", the radio show, premiered at 8pm EST. It's a live broadcast. A blend of law, politics, and commentary on local and national news. As expected there were some kinks tonight but I'm not concerned. Phil and I will quickly improve and we'll be a big hit.

June 2015: So many people are contacting me through the radio show because of injustices occurring in their own life. It keeps me up at night because I can't help all of them, at least not yet. I want those people to know that I'm not ignoring them. Please stay strong. I'm trying to find a way to help.

July 2015: Now that we know the authorities destroyed evidence, and three witnesses submitted new testimony, it's time to reach out to the Attorney General, and other offices, again. And of course there will be more court motions. As I already made clear, "I never quit. I don't stop, ever." (p. 199). I'm trying to salvage a morsel of hope that this is still the great country, the great United States of America that I grew up in. I was told to lay down the sword because I'm moving forward and doing great things. Why? My fight is not just for me. It's for a greater cause. At some point all this stuff cannot be brushed aside. At some point the levy has to break. When I was a young science teacher I visualized a five year plan to move up the educational ranks (p. 30). It went exactly as planned and I became a young principal in Hampton Bays, NY. I had everything I visualized and wanted in life. Then the bottom completely dropped out in February 2006.

Fast forward years later to another multi-year plan, another visualization. It's been just over a year since the book was fully released. Within that year I interviewed nationwide, held book signings and public speaking engagements, contributed to monthly newsletters, joined a board to help the underprivileged, and began hosting a radio show that is attracting politicians and high profile guests. In addition to our original show, Phil and I are partnering up with Eric and Linda Koppelman to start an internet radio station, WLINY.com. And soon I will be hosting a solo show, "The Frank Vetro Show" on WLINY.com. My hope is to increase my reach from Long Island to worldwide and give others an avenue to have their voices heard. It's time the common man had a forum to truly be heard. It's time to stand up, as a collective unit, against the corruption and injustices.

My personal freefall has stopped. My heels are firmly dug into the ground, and I'm slowly plowing ahead. Everything that has unfolded is most of the plan I visualized when I hit rock bottom. Will the bottom drop out? Will I be cut at the knees again? Regardless of what happens to me, if the bottom drops out on you, if all is lost, if it seems hopeless, don't quit. At the very least you can always vent to a person who will never judge, and who truly understands. I still, to this day, can always use another friend. If I don't hear from you I'm confident you will hear more about me. You didn't think I was done, did you? I said, "Everything that has unfolded is *most* of the plan." Stay tuned friends.

Contact: frankvetro.com

Me and my friend Phil Jusino

CPSIA information can be obtained
at www.ICGtesting.com
Printed in the USA
FFOW01n1109150416
23144FF